Cram Me With Eels!

Steven Appleby

J.B. MORTON

Cram Me With Eels!

The best of Beachcomber's unpublished humour

Edited and introduced by Mike Barfield
with a preface by Richard Ingrams
and drawings by Steven Appleby

Methuen

First published in Great Britain 1994
by Methuen London
an imprint of Reed Consumer Books Ltd
Michelin House, 81 Fulham Road, London SW3 6RB
and Auckland, Melbourne, Singapore and Toronto

Text copyright © 1994 by the Estate of J. B. Morton
Introduction and selection copyright © 1994 by Mike Barfield
Illustrations copyright © 1994 by Steven Appleby
Illustrations on pp. 233–7 copyright © 1994
by the Estate of J. B. Morton
Preface copyright © 1994 by Richard Ingrams

The authors and illustrator have asserted their moral rights

A CIP catalogue record for this book
is available at the British Library
ISBN 0 413 69030 X

Typeset by Falcon Graphic Art Ltd
Wallington, Surrey
Printed in Great Britain
by Clays Ltd, St Ives plc

Acknowledgements

This book appears after much kind and generous assistance from Amanda Jane Doran and Richard Ingrams. My thanks also to Tim Barfield, Keith Beard, Michael Bott, Michael Cummings, Lord Deedes, John Duncan, Robert Edwards, Katie Green, Alannah Hensler, Patrick Howarth, Ian Jack, Sir Edward Pickering, Chapman Pincher, Michael Pointon, Snibbo Ltd, Reg Spelling, Anthony and Raglan Squire, Miranda Taylor, Harry 'Three Times' Thompson, Colin Valdar, John Young, and all those whom I have either overlooked or who prefer anonymity. Any mistakes are my own.

For patience beyond even imperial measure, credit must go to Steven Appleby, Jessica Duncan, and the majestic Geoffrey Strachan.

Contents

Preface

'A gloomy little man' was how his illustrator Nicolas Bentley described J.B. Morton to me, when I asked about him. It was a fair description. I only met Morton twice, the second time in the company of Malcolm Muggeridge, and on both occasions found him very heavy-going and uncommunicative. It was not so surprising. He was an old man of eighty and his beloved wife, Mary, had recently died, leaving him in a state of dreadful depression. All the same, one gathered from talking to his old friends how, having been a wild man in his youth, he had become something of a recluse.

It is always tempting to search for clues about the author in his published work – however far removed it may seem from his personality. In this context it may seem unkind to make a parallel between Morton and Mrs Wretch, the retired belle of Wugwell's Circus (but I think it is a fair one). Like Mrs Wretch, Morton had been, in his youth, the member of a kind of circus, a group of heavy-drinking journalists and poets, many of whom had fought in the First World War. Later, like Mrs Wretch he gave it all up and got married, resisting the calls of his old drinking friends to join them on the occasional spree. It must have seemed sad to some of them that this romantic swashbuckler who had written endlessly in praise of wine, women and song and the Pyrenees (following the example of Hilaire Belloc) should end up in a nondescript suburban house in, of all places, Worthing.

In a sense, of course, it was. Yet if things had turned out otherwise we would probably not have had the vast corpus of comic literature labelled 'Beachcomber', from which Mike Barfield has compiled this new and vastly entertaining collection. Like his great and equally prolific contemporary, P.G. Wodehouse, Morton was indifferent to his surroundings. Like all great artists, he made his own world more real to him than the humdrum reality around him. It was a world of pure nonsense inhabited by his strange creations – Dr Strabismus, Charlie Suet, Lady Cabstanleigh and Dr Smart-Allick.

It seems to be true of all nonsense writers that they have dual personalities. You can see it in Edward Lear who produced hundreds of topographical watercolours in the Victorian mode that seem to bear no relation to his limericks and comic drawings. In our own day Spike Milligan (incidentally, a great admirer of Beachcomber) has combined the role of Goon with writing serious poetry and campaigning on behalf of the whale.

Morton's other self was a sort of 'Son of Belloc' who wrote books of French history, all of which are now forgotten and unread. Nevertheless these books meant more to him than his journalism, which he regarded as a sideline.

Perhaps it was because his nonsense came so easily to him and demanded so little effort that he looked down on it in comparison with his historical works. Whatever the reason, he remained a devout and humble man, referring to his Beachcomber material as 'my stuff'. In old age he started to write his autobiography but tore it up because he decided it was all too boring, and when he died he left no family, no papers – nothing. His 'stuff' remains his only memorial.

Richard Ingrams, July 1994

Introduction

J.B. Morton, alias 'Beachcomber' of the *Daily Express*, is one of
the great English humorists of the twentieth century. His work
and his wit easily survive – indeed, deserve – comparison with the
best of Evelyn Waugh and P.G. Wodehouse. Both men were ardent
Beachcomber fans. Waugh said Morton showed 'the greatest comic
fertility of any Englishman'. Dr Wodehouse confessed: 'Every time
I hear the name Beachcomber mentioned I fling my hat in the air
and give three rousing cheers ... for one, if not more than one,
of England's greatest men.' Similar high praise for Morton's work
has come from the likes of Clive James, Spike Milligan, Osbert
Lancaster, Bernard Levin, Arnold Bennett, A.P. Herbert, and J.B.
Priestley. More importantly, millions of ordinary *Express* readers
loved him. Not that Morton ever professed to care. He wrote his
column, he said, for two reasons alone – to entertain himself, and
for the money. We can be sure he was amply rewarded on the first
count.

The material in this selection comes from 'By The Way' columns
published over the period from 1958 – about the time of Morton's
last published original Beachcomber collection – to 1975, when
Morton was forced to retire. The majority of it pre-dates November
1965, when the column went from daily to weekly. To the best of
my knowledge, none of it has ever before appeared in book form.
That it deserves reprinting after more than thirty years and that
it is of the same dizzyingly high standard as previous collections
will be borne out by any random dip into the pages that follow this
introduction. The words are the work of a pensioner – Morton was
born in 1893 – but you will find no grey whiskers on the jokes. All
his paragraphs walk unaided. Most break into a gallop, unable to
contain the enthusiasm of their author's unbridled imagination.

Morton was furious when, though he was still going strong at a mere eighty-two, the *Express* decided he was too old for the job.

To be overly precise, Morton was born at Park Lodge, Mitcham Road, Tooting, south London, on 7 June 1893. An only child, he was given enough forenames to furnish a small family. Christened John Cameron Andrieu Bingham Michael Morton, he was known to friends as Johnny. His father, Edward, was a journalist and drama critic with a desire to write for the stage. His greatest success was with the book for *San Toy*, a Mikado-esque musical comedy which premiered at Daly's Theatre in 1899 and ran for several years. Morton described his father as exuberant with 'the loudest voice in Europe'. His beautiful mother, Rosamond Bingham, died when he was twelve.

Edward Morton was a great Francophile. From his father, Morton inherited a love of France and French history that was to last all his life. He was also introduced to wine at an early age, ostensibly to put him off later becoming a whisky drinker. As Richard Ingrams has explained in his account of Morton's life in *The Bumper Beachcomber* (published by Bloomsbury), Morton senior began by giving his son watered-down wine, then gradually reduced the dilution. The method was entirely successful. The story is told of how at lunch on his first day at Harrow school, new boy Morton was offered the water-jug by a friendly fellow pupil. Morton declined politely, saying that he preferred to wait until they brought round the wine.

Morton hated Harrow, and was an indifferent student; a surprise, given the erudition and breadth of knowledge shown later in his Beachcomber column. He loved Oxford, but had to leave in his first year to help support his father who was both broke and seriously ill after a stroke. (Edward Morton died in 1922.) Ambitions of becoming a poet were shelved, and at the start of the 1914–18 War he was writing revues for a showman in the Charing Cross Road. Morton enlisted as a private in a battalion of the Royal Fusiliers, and in 1915 was sent to the Front. Every one of his friends was killed. Given a commission in the Suffolk Regiment, he was at the Somme in 1916. Badly shell-shocked, Morton was sent back to England and spent the rest of the war working for the improbably-named intelligence department M.I.7b, and for the Ministry of Labour. A first novel, *The Barber of Putney*, came out of his war experiences, published in 1919. Morton believed it to be the first story told from the angle of the ordinary soldier. That same year, he was given a staff job on the *Sunday Express*.

Morton was taken on as 'a tame poet and book reviewer.' He also contributed fairy tales and walking stories. Walking was Morton's one great hobby. Hard, rough country walking, done both in England and abroad. To call it rambling would be an insult. He walked long distances, often at a frantic pace, composing songs aloud as he went. (Singing was another special pleasure.) Alone, or in the company of friends, later with his wife, Morton walked across much of Europe, often carrying little more than his staff, Durendal, named in honour of Roland's sword. The Pyrenees captivated Morton. Here the story of Charlemagne and *The Song of Roland* came to life in his imagination. Once he neatly combined three of his enthusiasms by walking through France up the Burgundy wine-list. Memories of all these adventures were to filter into his 'Beachcomber' column.

In 1922 he was transferred to the *Daily Express* as a reporter, a job for which he was ill-suited temperamentally. As he told *The Times* in 1975:

> I remember being asked to interview the mother of a boy who'd killed someone. As I went along in the cab, I thought: 'Do you realise what you're doing?' Then I decided I couldn't go on.

Morton used to boast that he had never contributed one piece of real news to the *Express*. By a fortunate coincidence Morton shared an office with the paper's then literary editor, Dominic Bevan Wyndham Lewis. The two struck up an immediate friendship. They had much in common. Both were recent Catholic converts, with a shared love of wine, walking, and what Lewis called 'dago culture'. Both were scholarly men absorbed by French history. Both exhibited a wild, lunatic sense of humour tempered with great learning. Hilaire Belloc called Lewis the wittiest man he had ever known. Since 1919 Lewis had been exercising that wit daily as 'Beachcomber', pseudonymous author of the 'By The Way' column.

Lewis – as even Morton mistakenly believed – was not the original 'Beachcomber'. The 'By The Way' column first appeared on the *Express* leader page of 27 July 1917. It was a daily nine hundred or so words of military and society tittle-tattle and fey topical comment. Indeed it was merely a renaming of an existing column leadenly titled 'Gossip of the Day'. The 'Beachcomber' signature made its debut a week later. Behind it was one Major John Bernard Arbuthnot MVO – a former Scots Guardsman. Arbuthnot became Assistant Editor of the *Express* in 1919, the year Lewis took over the column.

Lewis essentially set the style for every Beachcomber column from then until its demise in 1975. A grab-bag of individually headed paragraphs, including verse, literary parodies, travel notes, historical anecdotes, aired prejudices, puns, tap-room stories, and topical satirical comment. Morton's genius was in reinventing the column within this format by bringing to it his unique and eccentric cast of recurring characters, moving it far away from the standard newspaper diary. Of the two, Lewis's imagination flew rather closer to the ground. A collection of his pieces – the first 'Beachcomber' book – appeared in 1922 under the title *A London Farrago*. In the foreword Lewis revealed his Beachcomber to have the forenames Henry John Aloysius.

Morton took over the column some time in April 1924, when Lewis resigned on what the editor, Beverley Baxter, called 'a point of order'. He made Morton the new 'Beachcomber' on Lewis's recommendation.

Morton wrought no dramatic overnight changes in the column, but the tone lightened – Morton was a more accessible and knockabout humorist than Lewis – and soon-to-be regular characters began to appear. The eccentric scientist and inventor Dr Strabismus (Whom God Preserve) of Utrecht had already shown up in Morton's preface to a 1923 poetry collection. The column's pet poet, Roland Milk, was another early cast member, with Milk's rival, the fellow avant-gardist Dr Sicherheit, destined for obscurity. Lady Cabstanleigh, Mrs Wretch, and Prodnose – Morton's pedestrian *alter ego* – all followed soon after. However, Oswald Thake, a gullible clubland bachelor, was the first character to leap from the column to collection between hard covers. *Mr Thake*, Morton's first 'Beachcomber' book, was published in 1929. Other favourite characters such as Mr Justice Cocklecarrot and the Twelve Red-Bearded Dwarfs, and gallant rogue Captain de Courcy Foulenough, were to come in the Thirties.

The copy for the column – some five to six hundred words under the Strube cartoon, every Monday to Saturday – was handwritten. This may have been commonplace on a national daily newspaper in the 1920s, but it was pretty much unique by the 1970s. Morton never learned to use a typewriter, confessing 'a fountain pen is the nearest I can get to managing anything mechanical.' He wrote his paragraphs on half-slips or on blue Basildon Bond notepaper, judging the word-count by eye. The subs then dropped paragraphs or added ones held over to make the column fit the page. No one ever rewrote his copy, though it was always checked by the lawyers. Luckily for Morton, the savage mocking and abuse of a public figure is quite distinct from libel. Oswald Mosley was lampooned as 'Tich' Hitler. Morton called repeatedly for one politician to be boiled down for glue.

His handwriting presented more difficulties. It was a small, fidgety script and, though not illegible, it was certainly open to interpretation. Colin Valdar, *Express* features editor in the late Forties, remembers a woman by the name of Hilda Coe who used to be kept on as nobody else could follow Morton's writing; she typed out the copy for the compositors. This would have included Morton's many bizarre made-up names as well as frequent French, Latin, and German passages (usually cut to avoid baffling most readers). Miss Coe held an awesome responsibility and the odd mistake was inevitable. On top of this, Morton often returned to a continuing story without quite recalling all its details. At the risk of angering purists, I have standardised names and places to ensure that only Morton's intended confusions remain.

In the early years he wrote in the *Express* offices in Shoe Lane. Later his copy would arrive through the post from wherever he happened to be living. Typically he wrote a week or so in advance, which at times put an odd echo into the column when it touched upon current events. The words always came quickly to him and a day's worth never took more than a couple of hours. It was out of the way by lunchtime, leaving him free to pursue other interests. Morton's total literary output was prodigious and included travel books, magazine articles, short stories, novels, biography, and many serious historical studies. 'By The Way' was the perfect, well-paid, part-time job. He certainly enjoyed writing it. At Shoe Lane he was reputed to dance after completing each paragraph, and would laugh out loud at his own inventiveness. This, he said, was not through conceit but simply an honest reaction to a good joke. As he explained in 1945:

> If I don't think what I'm writing is funny, how the devil can I expect someone else to?

Sometimes the column was written in as little as half an hour.

When I'm in form the ideas come in right away, and the characters almost write the stuff for themselves ... But it's not always as easy as that. If I get tired of a character I drop him in mid-air and hope that another will turn up.

This meant that often a long-running story would simply come to a halt, never to be resolved. Even in those sagas that did reach a genuine conclusion there might be many days, weeks sometimes, between consecutive instalments. These benefited from being brought together when reprinted in 'Beachcomber' collections. Aborted stories were generally left out. I left most of them out of this book.

'Beachcomber's' identity remained unknown to *Express* readers right into the Thirties. Morton enjoyed this anonymity. Occasional drawings in the column (not by Morton, unlike the doodles in the Gallery at the end of this collection) showed Beachcomber as a Flapper-ish young woman. Arnold Bennett assumed 'By The Way' to be the work of several different hands. Fans variously pictured its author as a bald cripple, an unshaven hobo, 'tall and pale', and 'a middle-aged woman who has seen life and suffered'. Morton was actually a bullet-headed five foot four, somewhat tubby, with close-cropped balding hair and a florid expression. He smoked a pipe and favoured tweed suits. His personality was a bewildering mixture of contradictions.

Morton was a shy extrovert who abhorred 'progress' and sensationalism, yet worked for the country's then most go-ahead and sensationalist newspaper. Irascible, opinionated, invariably indignant about something, he marched about Fleet Street thumping pub counters with his staff and roaring for beer, yet was otherwise courteous and polite, with the manners of an earlier age. He was more Catholic than those born Catholic, more Irish than true Irishmen, but after moving to Dublin he found he missed the countryside of England too much and soon moved back. He professed to hate everything that had been invented since he was born, yet – ironically – in his column he was a prophet of technology. His electric toothbrush and TV-cum-telephone (the Vizziphone) were years ahead of reality. A right-of-centre satirist, he disliked businessmen and financiers as much as Socialists, and on many matters he was a visionary: real ale, real food, the promotion of wine-drinking, England in Europe, protection of the countryside, banning bloodsports, the growing tyranny of the motorcar.

Often gloomy in outlook, Morton was given to wild and surreal antics. The classic tale is of his talking into a pillar-box in the pretence that there was a small child trapped inside, and vanishing once a large crowd had formed. Fabled *Express* editor Arthur Christiansen was greeted on his first day by Morton entering his office on all fours, barking like a dog. Chapman Pincher – the spy writer – recalls Morton riding another journalist into an editorial conference with loud cries of 'Yoicks!' Too many similar stories have been lost to time. The best remaining portrait of the madcap Morton is to be found in A.G. Macdonell's novel, *England, Their England*. He is thinly veiled as the *faux* Frenchman, Mr Huggins, whose exuberance of spirit verges on mania. Morton calmed down markedly after his marriage in 1927 to an Irish doctor, Mary O'Leary. They had no children.

That Morton went on to write his column for over fifty years is particularly remarkable in the light of proprietor Lord Beaverbrook's at best ambivalent attitude towards it. The memoirs of many ex-*Express* men contain stories of The Beaver pointedly soliciting their opinion. Luckily Morton's wit appealed to most editors, though it certainly divided the readers. In the early Thirties the paper highlighted 'The Beachcomber Feud' between 'By The Way' devotees and those with violent antipathies. George Orwell hated it, considering Morton's constant jibes at tea and cricket almost treasonable. Edith Sitwell, sick of Morton's debunking of avant-garde arts, wrote accusing him of being 'funny on purpose about once a year'. Any reaction – good or bad – tends to appeal to editors.

During the Second World War, the paper shortage reduced the *Express* to only four pages, but the column remained, although as just a few paragraphs. Morton mocked the Nazis and British wartime red-tape in equal measure. Recognised as having done much to raise morale, he was made a CBE in 1952. His column, however, stayed small, owing to the ongoing battle between news and features for space on the Opinion page. In 1965 it went weekly and was enlarged, but this put an end to all the long-running sagas. Then in the Seventies they began cutting his copy again. Morton was furious. Having hoped to die in harness, he was fired during the editorship of Alistair Burnet (knighted in 1984). The last column appeared on 29 November 1975. It contained the startling headline 'Lawnmower Used on Vet's Whiskers' and the final paragraph concerned a Dublin statue of William Conyngham with 'Dame

Vera Lynn' written on its base. Morton retired to his home near Worthing, declaring that he was going to move to Ireland and write French history. His wife Mary had died in 1974. Lost without her, J.B. Morton died on 10 May 1979 – aged eighty-five – in Worthing. He was buried next to her in Windlesham cemetery near Bagshot.

There were eighteen collections of material drawn from the 'By The Way' column during Morton's lifetime. Michael Frayn, in his introduction to *The Best of Beachcomber* (Heinemann) calls them 'the eighteen holy books of Beachcomber'. Three contained only Thake stories. The first mixed selection, 'By The Way', appeared in 1931. Its opening words form the title of this collection. The last, *Merry-Go-Round*, was published in 1959. The books contain the merest fragment of what I estimate to be a total of in excess of five million words. You may find them in secondhand bookshops, though I am still shy of a few and would rather you didn't try. A BBC television series loosely based on the column was made in the late Sixties, and Richard Ingrams and I have compiled three Beachcomber radio series. A Will Hay film, *Boys Will Be Boys*, was set at Narkover school.

Finally, in editing this posthumous collection I have avoided once topical material in favour of the timeless. The book would be full of footnotes otherwise. For example, the Beatles became the Six Singing Cockroaches. The Concorde was The Discorde. VAT was Value Subtracted Tax. One can't have everything, as I suspect Prodnose would point out.

Mike Barfield, May 1994

How to Blow Glass

But, hush! Who is this stealing upon the scene as softly as the morning dew which falls on the upland pastures of Navarre, as gently as the whisper of the young leaves in the forest of Iraty?

PRODNOSE: You again, presumably.

MYSELF: I and none other, and in no mood to brook your infernal meddling, abominable pest.

PRODNOSE: Welcome home, whispering dewdrop.

Few people can answer, instantaneously, a question which is being asked more and more frequently as the century matures: If you stand on your head, does a knock-kneed man look bandy-legged, and vice versa? Of course, a moment's thought gives the answer, but one surprised—

PRODNOSE: Excuse me, what is the point of all this?

MYSELF: That will be made clear as time goes on. Such matters cannot be elucidated at breakneck speed. At least, not without offence to vested interests. Please go quietly, leaving your hat with the attendant.

Glassblowing hints

A correspondent asks me how one becomes a glassblower. My experience of this is confined to a puzzled hour at a Murano glassblowing works. I have no hesitation in saying that glass-blowing is largely a matter of breath-control, like singing. Blow too hard and you get an impossibly gigantic tumbler or wine-glass, or even a miniature conservatory. The men who blow frosted glass chew ice, and the coloured glasses out of which some people drink hock are the result of inhaling coloured matter into the breath. Sometimes twins are employed to blow a pair of spectacles, but not often.

Get on with your breakfast

A device which claims to prevent boiling eggs from cracking will not prevent cracked eggs from boiling. But there is a new egg-cup with a false bottom, which contains a tiny set of tools for mending cracks in boiled eggs which have cracked after being placed in the egg-cup. The tools include a thermometer to register the temperature of the egg, a miniature camera to photograph the crack, a tube of glue, an adze for chipping off fragments, a lever for raising the egg higher in the cup, a clamp for holding it steady, and a gimlet for boring a hole in the top of the egg, to let in the air, or something.

Leave it to me

'Mrs Lyons complained that the neighbours' spaniel broke into her sitting room.'   (*News item*)

'Spaniel in the Lyons' den,' vouchsafed a passer-by.

Record smashed by big girl

A big Wapping girl, known locally as the Wapper, has been elected Boiler Queen. She balanced a domestic boiler on her head for nine hours and forty-one minutes, Greenwich time. Asked what her thoughts had been during the ordeal, she said, 'I was thinking of the boiler all the time.' Asked if she intended to go on doing this sort of thing, she said, 'I've been offered a job with a firm of boilermakers, but I don't suppose they'll expect me to balance boilers on my head. At least, not always.'

(*Beachcomber News Agency*)

Dr Rhubarb's corner

E.N. ASKS: Can you tell me a cure for mice in the larder?
DR RHUBARB SAYS: What are they suffering from? Over-eating?

If they merely have a nervous complaint, leave them alone.

For older readers

It always seems to me absurd
    That cheese is nothing but a curd.
To scientists its chief attraction
    Is what is called bacterial action.
Enzymes prepare the cheese for us
    By catalytic stimulus.
But if your cheese seems putrefied
    The wrong bacteria are inside.

'Vital and human'

Mr E.F. Whelke, reviewing the new and revised edition of the *List of Huntingdonshire Cabmen* (Groyle & Wherret; 42s. 6d. net), says: 'The compilers of this *vade mecum*, eschewing rhetoric, have given us the plain facts in alphabetical order. These cabmen live. One seems to know them. It is a book to be opened at random, dipped into under the bedside lamp. The reader in search of sensation will, no doubt, be disappointed, but he who craves food for the mind will find a mine of information. Which of us, for instance, could have guessed that there were three Pofflehursts, E.L., J.N., and W.P.? And there is surely all the poetry of far-away lands in the simple name, "Votpoog, N.T.O." The compilers are to be felicitated on their integrity, awareness, and sense of values.'

More praise

The new edition of the *List of Huntingdonshire Cabmen* can safely be left about in homes where there are children ... The *List* is a welcome change from the filth and violence of so many books today ... Excellent for use in schools as a memory test ... There is no monotony where names and initials vary so frequently ... A factual account of what can only be called nomenclature ... There are ample initials to vary what might have been a mere catalogue of names.

Labour-saving device

Dr Strabismus (Whom God Preserve) of Utrecht has invented an electric spoon which raises mouthfuls of pudding to the mouth. When the spoon is plugged in, a tiny switch propels it, like a bulldozer, into the mass of pudding. A lever on the back of the spoon controls its movements, and a button on the plate releases it with its precious cargo. At the touch of a second lever the spoon disengages, and is raised, by a miniature crane on the plate, to the expectant mouth.

He only wanted to help

A correspondent has expressed his dislike of the amateurs who used to sing or play the piano at parties. A story is told of a wealthy dowager who engaged a celebrated violinist to play for the guests. He failed to turn up, and she was in despair. A breezy friend of hers offered to take the celebrity's place. 'Why, Charles,' she said, 'I never knew you could play the violin.'

'I can't,' he said, 'but I could try.'

Good question

What is a family to do when grandmother runs away to sea, as the phrase goes? Only Mrs Dietrich could carry off such a capricious action. 'Before or behind the mast is all the same to me,' one can imagine grandmama saying, 'so long as I get away from the racket at home.'

PRODNOSE: Who is this grandmother?

MYSELF: I am merely considering an imaginary incident, with a view to reporting it to the authorities.

In passing

'The VC is not easily earned.' This remarkable understatement

4

recalled a story of one of Napoleon's Marshals, Lefebvre. A young man expressed envy of the Marshal's medals and decorations. 'You can have them all at cost price,' said Lefebvre. 'Come into the garden and I'll shoot at you sixty times. If you are alive at the end of it, the medals and decorations are yours.'

Nothing to do with me

Would you like to win an airliner, three weeks on Lake Como, a Ming vase, 20 tons of lard, two dog kennels, a snakeskin hat, a ticket for the Derby, a pet lion-cub, a saw-mill, a soup tureen, and a skating-rink? If you would, don't pester me about it.

Cold ham for auctioneers

Dear Sir,

Your story of the grandmother who ran away to sea reminded me that my husband's grandmother tried to go up the chimney to get away from the family. She got stuck and dislodged a lot of soot. When the fire brigade extracted her she was black in the face and had lost a shoe.

(Mrs) M.H. Clumbering

Twenty years of uproar

Complaints about acoustics in a concert hall mention 'an echo'. The classical case is, of course, the row that ensued when a love-duet in an opera was completely ruined by echoes. Rustiguzzi, in Vesuvian eruption, had declared her love to Broccoli, and her tenderest phrase was repeated and flung back to her from the walls of the theatre. Broccoli, who had not been warned about the acoustics, was heard to mutter, 'I heard you the first time.' The diva gave him a look which made nonsense of the sentiments she was expressing.

Porter's radishes win prize

Dear Sir,

When reading Mrs Clumbering's letter about the grandmother up the chimney, none of our family could understand the headline: COLD HAM FOR AUCTIONEERS.

Regular Reader

I must confess that it puzzled me too.

5

Printer's frolics

Angry words from a general who claimed that his speech had been bowdlerised recalled the incident of another general who was referred to in a morning paper as a 'bottle-scarred veteran'. By a printer's frolic, the correction appeared next day as 'battle-scared veteran'.

Granny knew her onions

Dear Sir,

When family life became too much for my husband's grandmother she used to pretend to faint and would cry 'Brandy! Brandy!' She would then retire to her room with the bottle. Later she would come down beaming and saying, 'There is nothing like brandy when you're upset. I feel better already.'

S.E. Felspar

Pea-pushing news

An invitation to Evans the Hearse to push a pea with his nose from San Francisco to New York has been refused. The wizard of Aberbananer said in an interview: 'Such stunts can only get nasal pea-pushing a bad name. Moreover, pea-pushing is such a leisurely sport that the time wasted in the suggested undertaking might well be employed to more useful purpose. I am not out to break records with my heavily insured nostrils. There would be something ludicrous in the spectacle of a grown-up man crawling across the American continent behind a pea.'

Nosebags for ladies

An article says that you can persuade rich ladies to go in for any foolery, so long as you say it makes them look smart. I have never abandoned my campaign to make them use nosebags – dainty ones, of course, in ravishing materials. To see them holding out the nosebags to waiters, and having them fastened, by lovely ribbons, around their necks, would put a keen edge on any man's appetite. And it would muffle those piercing voices which turn any conversation into a screaming match.

Chaos in Cheltenham

The shortage of spoons in Cheltenham has led the council to

issue a statement. 'Three or more people with small mouths can easily share one big spoon. Those with large mouths should form a queue for the ordinary spoons, using them one at a time per person.' In a struggle for the handle of a jam spoon, Ernest Nuffe, 29, a platelayer, dislocated his thumb. A laundress who witnessed the incident said: 'It was his own fault for being greedy.'

(*Beachcomber News Agency*)

Granny won

Dear Sir,

It was not we who got on Granny's nerves. She got on ours. She used to bang an African drum given her by a nephew and shout 'Walla-walla-woo!' One of my brothers joined the Army, another the Navy. Father lived in a potting shed, and mother went out to work. I married to get away from it all and Granny was left victorious.

Mrs Myrtle Faffnage

The rue Pirouette

A street with only six houses in it claims to be the shortest street in Europe. Twenty years ago in Paris the rue Pirouette had only one house in it, which was numbered '3'. Perhaps it is still there. In the old days there was a pillory there, and the street got this curious name because the victim had to move his head about at stated intervals, to show that he was awake.

Lines to a film star

Idol of millions, every cretin's dream,
  The more you smile, the sillier you seem.
And, what is worse, since you became a star,
  The more you talk, the sillier you are.

The proposal

A savant with an originality which should win him the freedom of Cleethorpes for his services to social research says that 'in marriage husband and wife are partners. Neither should dominate the other.' I pointed out long ago in my *Aspects of Tendencies* that the man who says, during courtship: 'Will you be *mine*?' is a potential tyrant. If, however, he says: 'May I be yours?' he is inviting the girl to be a tyrant. The ideal proposal is: 'Let us be ours.'

Here, there, and everywhere

THE Great Yarmouth ironmonger who found a female locust in a potato has won £16 4s. 9½d., in a local badminton rally.

GIVING the name of Shrivel, a retired engineer walked on his hands round the roof of a Surbiton furniture depository. He was questioned by the police.

CALLING at a lonely farmhouse near Taunton, a Greek sailor said: 'I am Professor Kindleman's grandfather, and I am saturated with marmalade.'

Solicited testimonial

... My cheeks used to wobble like a blancmange in a typhoon whenever I laughed. At parties it was always, 'Here comes Fat-Face,' never 'Hello, Stanley.' Silly women would pinch my cheeks, crying, 'Are they real?' Wits would ask, surveying my face, 'How much an acre?' Then one day a friend persuaded me to rub my face with Snibbo. And now, at parties, it is nothing but 'Good old Stanley!'

O passi graviora

From that admirable little paper, the *Pedestrian*, I take this story. A man was standing on the pavement of a busy road. Growing tired of waiting for a chance to cross the road, he shouted to a man on the other side, 'How did you get across?' Back came the answer, 'I was born on this side.'

How do you spell it?

A reference by the Hon. Secretary of the Cambridge Tiddlywinks Club to the forthcoming World Tiddlywinks Congress in the Palais de Tiddeliwingues in Brussels raises the question of spelling. Some interpolate an 'e': tiddlEywinks. Some use a hyphen: tiddly-winks. Lance Gosper, the captain of Walthamstow United, says that as ping-pong is called 'table-tennis', tiddlywinks should be called 'floor-football'. The Argentine team, which plays on horseback, prefers 'hand-polo'.

Trivial jest

'... She complained that the joint had stood in the window for at least a week, and had gone bad.'   (*News item*)

Obviously a matter for the standing joint committee.

The inconstant lover

(i)

Who, on a golden summer's day,
   When even a constant heart may stray,
With one soft glance, stole mine away?
   Mrs Whackstraw.
Who, when I mentioned Mrs Hoofe,
   Administered a stern reproof,
And was impossibly aloof?
   Mrs Whackstraw.

(ii)

Must I now break my lover's oath,
   False to a double-plighted troth,
Because I'm sick and tired of both
   Mrs Hoofe and Mrs Whackstraw?
Yes! I am under the strong spell
   Of Agnes Bottlehurst, the belle
Of Palace Mansions; so farewell
   Mrs Hoofe and Mrs Whackstraw.

(iii)

It's scarce a week since first I met
   Miss Bottlehurst. Now I regret
I was so anxious to forget
   Mrs Hoofe and Mrs Whackstraw.
Is there no cure for my despair?
   I wonder if . . . Why, I declare
I've found the answer to my prayer –
   It's Mrs Gurge.

(iv)

Who would have thought that life could be
   So disillusioning for me?
I shudder every time I see
   Mrs Gurge.
I never, never met before
   Such an unmitigated bore.
Ah! Could I only see once more
   Mrs Hoofe, Mrs Whackstraw, or even Miss Bottlehurst.

(v)

So, once again, my life's gone phut,
  Now I have run the whole gamut,
And yesterday I even cut
  Mrs Gawkynge.
The hour of love's brief dream is past,
  I'm a misogynist at last –
Except for Mrs Prendergast
  And Sarah Faffnage.

Before Mr Justice Cocklecarrot

The Return of the Red-Bearded Dwarfs

In the Court of Uncommon Pleas, Mr Justice Cocklecarrot yesterday quoted a statute of Edward III, to the effect that dwarfs
are subject to the laws governing habergeon (i.e., the wearing of
sleeveless coats) even if the wearer has a red beard.

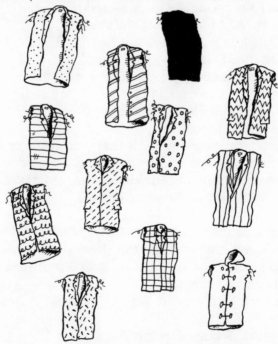

Twelve red-bearded dwarfs are taking an action against Gunderbridge Drikleeneries. They allege that the coats were returned
without the concomitant sleeves; that the backs of the coats
bore signs of having been walked on by muddy boots. The case
continues.

Gunderbridge Drikleeneries claim that the dwarfs' coats were returned in error to a Mrs Webcraft who appeared to have used them as a bathmat before sending them back without the sleeves. Cross-examined by Mr Honeyweather Gooseboote for the defence, Mrs Webcraft said, 'I do not use coats, with or without sleeves, as a bathmat, nor do I walk over them in muddy boots.' This caused so much mirth that Cocklecarrot said, 'This court is not a music-hall, despite appearances.'

Asked by Mr Tinklebury Snapdriver (for the prosecution) where she was at 3.12 p.m. on January 9, Mrs Webcraft replied: 'At Grover & Mimpson's, buying treacle.'
SNAPDRIVER: How can you be sure of the exact time?
MRS WEBCRAFT: What exact time?
SNAPDRIVER: The time you say you were where you were.
MRS WEBCRAFT: It was you who said 3.12 p.m., wasn't it?
SNAPDRIVER: I am asking the questions.
MRS WEBCRAFT: And I am asking the answers.

A red-bearded dwarf was then questioned.
SNAPDRIVER: Your name is Scorpion de Rooftrouser?
ROOFTROUSER: What else could that be but my name?
SNAPDRIVER: You will please answer yes or no.
ROOFTROUSER: Yes or no.
COCKLECARROT: Mr Rooftrouser, is that your name or is it not?
ROOFTROUSER: If you don't know my name, how did you guess it?
COCKLECARROT: I think, Mr Snapdriver, we may assume that is
    his name, without further waste of time.

Cross-questioning the dwarf Churm Rincewind, Mr Honeyweather Gooseboote asked him whether the sleeves of his coat had been torn off or cut off. 'For all I know,' said Rincewind, 'they may have been eaten by a horse.'
    From the back of the court Farjole Merrybody shouted, 'Mice, maybe.'
    'Sharks,' yelled Sophus Barkayo-Tong.
    'Badgers,' bawled Cleveland Zackhouse.
    'Dromedaries,' shrieked Molonay Tubilderborst.
    'Bacilluses,' screamed Listeris Youghaupt.
    A director of Gunderbridge Drikleeneries affirmed (on oath) that no such creatures were kept on the premises.

Questioned by Mr Gooseboote, Frums Gillygottle described how he tried to make sleeves for his coat out of a heap of cardboard. 'It was a Tuesday,' he said, 'by the calendar, 9.18 by Greenwich time, 4.21 in Australia. And as the day wore on—'

Mr Gooseboote interrupted him. 'Were the entire sleeves missing?'

'Was my beard red,' replied the dwarf, 'when I put my arms into a heap of vacuum that was not there! It was like blowing your nose and finding you hadn't got one.'

'That will be enough,' said Cocklecarrot.

'Carried unanimously,' said Gillygottle, 'by both of us.'

The missing sleeves.

The case of the dwarfs' coats is to be settled out of court, greatly to the relief of Cocklecarrot, who said, 'The perpetual uproar and the shouting of totally irrelevant remarks might lead one to believe this was the House of Commons.'

Mr Gooseboote announced that the Drikleeneries was ready to come to an arrangement.

'We too also,' cried Edeledel Edel. 'We want no legal trickery. We shall leave this court without a strain on our second best coats, and our photographs will not be needed by Scotland Yard.'

Gunderbridge Drikleeneries agreed to supply the red-bearded throng with new coats, a publicity-seeking gesture which does them credit. When this was announced, the twelve red-bearded dwarfs shouted in chorus, 'Long live us!' and Amaninter Axling, not to be outdone, offered the firm a waistcoat given to him by his aunt, as a memento, he explained, 'of their delicious action.' As Cocklecarrot left the court, they all offered him their autographs.

The Fishizene Case

In the Court of Common Warranty and Retainder, Mr Justice Cocklecarrot is hearing a curious case: Edgar Bottlesham (known as 'Bitter Jack') and the Ruffington Brass Foundries versus Myrtle Gringram, Mrs Howland Flockett, Piers Detmold and the Elmwood Fish Distillery. An injunction is being sought to restrain the defendants from using a room in a lodging house to carry on a fish-distillery business for the purposes of preparing the drink known as Fishizene.

There was a dramatic moment when Cocklecarrot asked what fish were being distilled. 'Porpoise, m'lud,' said Mr Gooseboote.

A voice at the back of the court shouted, 'What about a writ of Habeas Porpoise?' When the laughter had died down, Mrs Flockett, cross-examined, said that she understood that the fish were caught in the Bosphorus, brought to Hurstpierpoint, where Mr Detmold lived, and from there taken by road to the Hamsden Bakery, the present lodgings of Miss Myrtle Gringram, 'the nom-der-ploom of a famous dancer'.

'I find you difficult to follow,' said Cocklecarrot.

'That's what Sid Faffnage said,' replied Mrs Flockett, 'when he followed me down Oxford Street, into Holborn, and lost me somewhere off Farringdon Street.'

It transpired yesterday that the Ruffington Brass Foundries, represented by the chairman, Mr Edward Oshe, had been dragged into the wrong case. Mr Oshe said he knew nothing of fish-distilleries in lodging houses, and reference to various documents soon cleared up the mystery. The Brass Foundries case against Lady Goober for breach of contract in reference to a big brass bowl, sealed at the top, should have been heard in a different court. Cocklecarrot said: 'It is ludicrous to attempt to try two cases simultaneously which have become inextricably mixed up. Nobody knows what anybody is talking about.'

Giving what is humorously called evidence, a Mrs Multiple said that when she called on Miss Gringram she found the room stacked with porpoises. Asked whether they were being distilled, she said: 'Not that I know of.' Asked where she was on the morning of October 3, she said: 'Bishop's Stortford.'

Said Cocklecarrot: 'This gets us nowhere.'

'It gets us to Bishop's Stortford,' riposted Mrs Multiple sulkily.

Colonel Ferreter was then called. He deposed that while buying bread in the bakery, he smelled burning rubber.

'Why burning rubber?' asked Mr Snapdriver.

'Why not?' replied the warrior.

'Do you often smell burning rubber?' asked Mr Snapdriver.

'Whenever there's any to smell,' was the inconclusive answer.

Asked by Cocklecarrot whether she did indeed use her room at the Hamsden Bakery as a fish distillery, Miss Gringram said she did not understand the question.

'Let me put it more simply,' said Cocklecarrot. 'Do you distill porpoises for Fishizene Ltd?'

'Of course I don't,' replied the lady angrily, 'I have no porpoises, no machinery for distilling, and have never heard of the firm you mention. Where would I get porpoises?'

With a very cunning look Mr Gooseboote said, 'Perhaps from Mr Detmold of Hurstmonceux, who imports them from the Beikos Porpoise Fisheries Ltd, on the Bosphorus.'

'I think you are all mad,' replied Miss Gringram. 'I've never heard of any of this nonsense.'

A perplexed silence fell on the court.

After reading a note handed to him, Mr Tinklebury Snapdriver addressed the judge. 'M'lud,' he said, 'it appears that there has been a mistake. Miss Gringram should be in another court, answering a charge of pushing a milkman onto a heap of rotting leaves.'

'What has that got to do with a fish distillery in a lodging house?' asked Cocklecarrot.

'Absolutely nothing, m'lud,' was the dejected reply.

'Then,' said Cocklecarrot, 'it appears that we are back where we started, wherever that was.'

(*Case suspended.*)

Cocklecarrot on Advertising

Many people must have read with surprise that it is illegal to run within three miles of Charing Cross for purposes of advertisement. Any man who runs down the Strand in a shorts and a bowler with 'Snibbo' printed on his hat-band is breaking the law. But what if he walks, and then breaks into a run to avoid a car backing onto the pavement? And if he runs within 754 yards of the British Museum crying 'Buy Topplehurst's Tinned Potatoes!' he is still within three miles of Charing Cross. If he pushes an empty wheelbarrow over Blackfriars Bridge is he not advertising wheelbarrows? Suppose a steel firm organises a three-legged race round Trafalgar Square, does that count as advertising steel within three miles of Charing Cross, and within the meaning of the Act?

Mr Justice Cocklecarrot, interviewed on the subject, said, 'The line between advertising and running is very finely drawn. It is conceivable that a man might run along an imaginary line exactly three miles from Charing Cross, with one leg on each side of the line. If he bore on the left trouser-leg inside the line a chalked invitation to buy some commodity, and no such invitation on the right trouser-leg outside the line, it is clear that while both legs would be running, only the left leg would be guilty of advertisement. Yet one could not arrest one leg without the other. Again, if the man placed one leg before the other, and ran along the three-mile limit as on a tightrope, would he be within or without the limit? It is a delicate legal problem.'

'Furthermore,' continued Cocklecarrot, 'if a man on the exact three-mile limit from Charing Cross – and what part of Charing Cross is scheduled as the central point from which the distance is calculated? – if that man runs along with a pill advertised on his hat-band, and if that man's hat is blown off and lands *outside* the limit, and if that man continues his progress minus his hat, can that man be said, after the loss of his hat, to be advertising the pill? *De minimis curat lex.* I leave it at that.'

*   *   *

An article on bores says that it is impossible to stop them talking. There is one way. Outbore them. Thus:

'Excuse my interrupting you, old man, but my aunt, the one who lives in Appleby, at least she did until they moved to Chichester – but was it Chichester? No matter. She had cousins there, the Relfs, who had come to Battersea about three – no, it was four years before. I remember because it was the year the Armitages' boiler burst. Well – where was I? Oh, yes. Their boy had measles at the time – not the elder boy, the second, the one who's with Whippon & Telscote – you know, the big carpet firm. Well, this aunt of mine – she was my mother's only sister and married a man called Spott, and my mother always said that she . . .' And so on. Game and set.

Old song resung

Some time ago a vegetarian group protested against a new version of 'Mary had a little lamb,' in which her father killed, cooked and ate the lamb. A still newer version runs:

> Mary had a little sprout,
> Its fleece was green as grass.

17

She hitched it to a bit of string,
 The silly little ass.
From week to week, from month to month,
 She kept the sprout in tow,
And everywhere that Mary went
 The sprout was sure to go.

Super-fortissimo

An account of a concert in which the pianist 'played so furiously' that he nearly hit the piano for six indicates that the school of such *virtuosi* as Peildreiver, Otto Thumping and Sledjhammer is influencing young pianists. On an occasion when the latter was accompanying Rustiguzzi in the lullaby, *'Dors-tu, Ninon!'* a loud voice in the stalls cried, 'If that's the way to get a baby to sleep, what do you two do to wake the poor little thing?'

Short story

The cocktail party was in full swing. Garth Wensleydale, smartest member of the Earls Court Road set, dipped his little sausage into his rum-and-vodka cocktail. There was a nervous silence. Nobody was quite sure that this might not be the very latest craze. Not wishing to appear unsophisticated, several guests copied him in a rather embarrassed fashion. It was only when he added an anchovy on a biscuit, a bit of cheese, and a dainty of uncertain denomination, and stirred the mess with his cigarette into a kind of porridge, that they realised he was fooling. Only that outsider, Polham-Frant, of the Bayswater set, attempted to eat the soggy contents of his glass. Jeered to the echo, he left in comparatively high dudgeon.

Dr Rhubarb's corner

MR J. WRITES: My little boy asked me yesterday, 'What is the use of giraffes?' What can I tell him?

DR RHUBARB SAYS: Tell him they are used to help tightrope walkers to get into position when there is no ladder available. Drapers use them to model the enormous collars displayed for advertisement in their shop windows.

Narkover's finances

A paragraph in a paper about high fees at public schools has prompted a Narkover parent to reply. It is often said that Narkover never increases its fees. This parent points out that this is owing to the high cost of places in the cricket, football, fives, and rackets teams, and the tariff for promotion to a higher form. He adds, 'I myself was persuaded by threats of certain disclosures relating to my private life to contribute to a fund for a new school library. The library turned out to be a kind of casino, and my son's gambling debts amounted to considerably more than the term's fees.'

Dr Smart-Allick replies

To the parent who objected to the new Narkover casino, which was described as a library, the headmaster has pointed out that a room in the casino contained a carefully chosen selection of books on games of chance. The word library was used to appease the Governors. As for the purchase of promotion to higher forms and of places in cricket and football teams, the headmaster says, 'These subscriptions are voluntary. Any parent who is swine enough to deprive his son of scholastic or athletic distinctions and honours is free to do so.'

Grand National on ice?

Thirty-four Patagonian milkmen were chosen yesterday to attend the annual meeting of the Lapp branch of the P.E.N. Club. 'This is only a beginning,' said a passer-by.

Patagonian milkmen honoured

Every spectacle, says a connoisseur, is more exciting when it is on ice. This, no doubt, would apply to the Grand National. But there is the difficulty of teaching jockeys to control horses on skates.

PRODNOSE: Is that not the wrong heading?

MYSELF: No. It's the wrong paragraph.

Strabismus has been busy

Gadgeteers who read of the battery-powered electric spaghetti-fork, America's latest contribution to gracious technological living, may have thought that this country is lagging behind. Not at all. There is the Strabismus five-pronged hydraulic shoe-horn, which can also be used to make toast, and the electric hat, which is plugged in and worn in draughty rooms.

The Sage of Waggling Parva has also invented a tiny roller for flattening jelly, a four-legged petrol-driven towel horse, for riding in windy weather, to dry towels, an automated egg-cup with zinc handles, a mechanical shredder for mulberries, stained-glass spectacles for protecting the eyes from grapefruit juice, a self-revolving corkscrew, a sieve with a nozzle at the edge for damping lard, waterproof braces and shoelaces, and a mini-diesel-bulldozer for extracting pips from apples. Oh, and an electric safety-pin.

Another complaint

Dear Sir,

My son won a prize for Latin translation at Narkover last term. He came home with a handsome edition of Byron's poems. Two days later I received a bill for this book. When I wrote an indignant letter, his form master replied, 'Surely you didn't expect your son to pay for the book?' Comment would be superfluous.

Angry Parent

Striking testimony

Mrs Woolgrass writes: 'Before taking the new Snibbo weight-reducing tablets I had to go into my house sideways, edging my way in inch by inch, and pushed and pulled by kindly neighbours. Today I can even squeeze through our tiny larder window, and when I trip about the house the plaster no longer falls from the ceilings, and when I tread on our cat, Mustard, it purrs with delight.'

Carpenter's Song
(For a politician)

A face of wood to match a wooden gesture
And wooden words; a thing without a vesture

Of reason or intelligence displayed.
From such material cabinets are made.

Footnote

For gracious living there is nothing like a fog-horn container upholstered in pink Javanese horsehair – unless it be the new kneecaps for rocking-horses in plastic foam.

3

Life Aboard the Houseboat

Mrs Withersedge Remembers

One who lives in a houseboat has said that it is more house than boat. Emma Withersedge, caretaker on the *Ocean Nymph*, put it more forcibly. Said she: 'It's not a reel nautical life, no roundin' the 'Orn or bound for the Rio Grande stuff. We 'ad a cove aboard for a week-end, and 'e got plastered, and roared "Land ho on the port beam!" It was land ho all right, two foot away, and us fastened to the shore snug as a fieldmouse in a 'aystack. Talk about the tang o' the salt! Smell o' the mud's more like it, and no ruddy 'ornpipe to liven things up.'

Continuing her remarks about life on a houseboat the caretaker Emma Withersedge said: 'To see the boss on deck scannin' the 'orizon you'd think we was weighed down with a cargo o' py-annas and barb wire for Port o' Spain. And to 'ear 'is guests bawlin' about Shenadoor's daughter and the Missisoori we might be tattooed all over and livin' on dog-biscuits in the Artic Ocean.

'One day the boss roared to one o' the guests, "Make three bells, Charlie!"

'An' Charlie, 'e replied, "Make your own ruddy bells. I ain't no foundry-worker." '

Said Mrs Withersedge: 'One week-end we 'ad a guest wot asked the boss where the sails was, an' the boss says wot would we need sails for, an' this guest 'e says, sarcastic like, well, sails 'ave their uses on a boat. For instance, says 'e, you might want to sail somewhere for a change. This, says the boss, isn't that sort of boat. Then, says the guest, you might as well be on land, an' the boss says a boat on land would look as barmy as an 'ouse in the water, an' the guest says well this is a bit of both, an' the boss sulked till tea-time.'

'One time,' said Mrs Withersedge, 'we 'ad a clergyman friend of the boss aboard for the day. 'E brought 'is singin' mouse with 'im, and our cat Tibbles soon put an end to that. Four years' trainin' wasted, said the reverent, and to cheer 'im up for the loss the boss showed 'im 'ow to wet 'is finger an' read the wind. There wasn't none, but to 'ear the boss you'd a thought we was in for a mongsoon or a sheerocker or somethin'. When 'e left, the reverent give Tibbles a dirty look with no reeligion in it, and we 'aven't seen 'im since, but Tibbles lives in 'ope.'

'We 'ad a guest once,' said Mrs Withersedge, 'an' 'e 'ad bin all over the world in ships. You could see that all the others felt pretty silly when 'e talked of faraway ports. "We just sit 'ere and go nowhere," said the boss's son.

' " 'Ow do you expeck me to take you to Peru in a 'ouseboat?" says the boss.

' "Wouldn't she even float down to Cookham?" says Master George.

' "She might," says the boss, "an' again she might not, an' Cookham isn't essacly Peru, not that I've ever 'eard. Take a turn on deck and clear your 'ead, Georgie boy."

'An' George, 'e cussed and swore and went ashore to the Mermaid pub.'

'One Saturday,' said Mrs Withersedge, 'they was playin' bridge in the droring-room, when a passin' speed-boat set up a 'ell of a wash. We started to rock, and one woman yelled, "The anchor's bin tore out, Sir Geoffrey, an' we're adrift!" You'd a thought there was icebergs bearin' down on us, and mountingous seas, and trade winds.

'The boss was quite calm. "She'll stand up to worse than this," 'e said, an' I muttered "A.I. at Lloyd's."

' "It's comfortin'," says a guest, "to see the shore so close," as though we was back from Spitbergen after tossin' 'elplessly for days and nights, at the mercy o' wind and wave, as they say.'

'A cheeky lad wot the boss called a longshoreman stood on the bank one day,' said Mrs Withersedge, 'and arst 'ad we brort 'im back a parrot from Bunose Airs. 'E wuz ignored by all on deck, an' 'e went on larfin'. You've lorst yer crow's nest, 'e says, an' O lor', wot a stormy passage! Yer main-top-gallant was washed overboard, I dessay, in Biskey Bay, an' you ain't got a bit o' riggin' left. Clap me in irons, 'e says, if ever I saw such a lousy outfit. Nex' day the boss 'ung up a notice sayin' trespassers would be persecuted. But 'e took it down when a guest said it weren't nautical. An' the lad come back and shouted up anchor and away for the Spanish Main!'

'One day,' said Mrs Withersedge, 'the boss arst me if couldn't look more nautical-like. I says to 'im it's far from 'ouseboats I was reared and if 'e wanted me to look like Capting Foulenough on the Riveerer 'e could buy me a peaked yacht 'at and call me Mrs Commodore Withersedge, me late 'usband 'avin' bin an aquarium-keeper, which was as near as 'e ever got to Cape 'Orn. Nex' day when 'e 'owled for a sangwidge I shouted Aye aye, Cap'n, and 'e seemed pleased. So I said all shipshape abaft the binnacle, an' 'e scowled and said not to overdo it.'

'While they was all playin' bridge one day,' said Mrs Withersedge, 'our cat Tibbles, the one what et the parson's singin' mouse, fell overboard with a splosh. Miss Huxtable was sittin' on deck, an' she threw a lifebelt to poor Tibbles, nearly stunnin' the poor creature. There was a butcher's boy watchin' on the bank, an' 'e says if you 'ad two o' them lifebelts you could use 'em as tyres, an' this old battle-cruiser could go on land. So I threw the other lifebelt at 'im, saying', in the words of George Robey, take this ring, it was my mother's. Then I 'auled Tibbles aboard, an' life resoomed its normal course, not arf it didn't.'

'One night,' says Mrs Withersedge, 'Mr Clark come aboard well plastered arter a session at the Mermaid. 'Ardly 'ad 'e got 'is foot on deck when Romper, the bulldog what the boss bought to guard this liner, rushed 'im and tore 'is trousers from stem to stern. When Mr Clark complained, the boss says well, you might 'ave bin a burglar. They 'ad a row, and Romper, 'earin' the racket, came up behind the boss and ripped 'is coat up the back. Ha-ha-*ha!* says Mr Clark, you might 'ave bin a burglar. Good doggie! Ha-ha-ha-*ha!*'

'When the boss 'ad "Ocean Nymph" painted on the stern of this old skow,' said Mrs Withersedge, 'young Mr Crouch, 'e said 'e never saw nothin' less like a nymph, ocean or otherwise.

'So the boss says, 'e says, "Does that cross-Channel boat *Maid of Orleans* look like Joan of Hark?" That floored 'im proper, it did.

'Then, stung by taunts, the boss 'ad a whackin' great binnacle and compass fixed up. "Now," says Mr Crouch, sardonic like, "we'll always know where we aren't goin'. Lay a course, purser." '

' "Mrs Withersedge," says the boss, "we've sprung a leak. There is water on the floor of my cabin."

' "We better lower the boats," says I, "an' I'll dust the lifebelt. Lucky we aren't roundin' the Cape. 'As a iceberg 'oled us, or 'ave we collided with a liner?" '

'Well, I went and 'ad a look. Our cat Tibbles 'ad knocked over a jug o' water. "That cat," 'e says, "is allus up to mischief."

' "It keeps 'im from goin' barmy with boredom," I says. "No self-respectin' mouse ever boards this craft. I don't blame 'em." '

Said Mrs Withersedge: 'An offshore breeze blew the boss's yachtin' 'at into the water. I yelled, " 'At overboard," and we raked it out o' the water with 'is brolly 'andle.

'A boy on the bank laughed 'is 'ead off, and the boss said, "I suppose 'e thinks I oughter wear a bowler aboard."

' "Tut, tut," I says, "we 'ave to keep up appearances. Wot about oilskins for me?" 'E looks daggers at me. "I'll settle for bell-bottom trousers," I says, "as the old song 'as it. 'Bell-bottom trousers an' a suit of navy-blue, an' I'll climb the riggin' as me father used to do.' "

' "Nonsense," says 'e, and turns away.'

'Last year,' said Mrs Withersedge, 'the boss, thinkin' 'is guests might like a nautical touch, 'ooked a little dinghy onto the *Ocean Nymph*. One arternoon 'e says, "This orfshore breeze will give us a nice run to Cookham." So seven of 'em clambered aboard, up went the sail, and Mr Crouch sang out they was bound for the Rio Grande. They all got in each other's way, and about eight foot from the 'ouseboat the dinghy capsized. No need to call out the Bourne End lifeboat. They swam 'ome.'

'Never,' said Mrs Withersedge, 'will I forget the day the rope what 'itched us to the land bust, and we was adrift, "at the mercy of trade winds, gulf streams and typhoons," as one guest put it. We drifted backwards a bit and run into a sort of jetty. We got a horse from a farm to tow us back, and we was as proud as any barge-load between Uxbridge and Watford. She was tied up again to the shore, and the horse was given a feed, and to 'ear them all talk that evening you'd think we'd crossed the Indian Ocean and back by the skin of our teeth.'

Suspicious of the absence ashore of a rather rowdy guest, Mrs Withersedge was heard singing softly to herself, to the tune of 'My Bonnie is Over the Ocean':

> My bonnie's fed up with this cruisin',
> E's gorn into Egham for tea.
> I bet 'e'll come back fairly plastered,
> Don't bring back my bonnie to me.

Said Mrs Withersedge: 'One time we 'ad a mist come down as thick as your 'at, an' the boss 'e started the fog-'orn. After an hour o' this a feller on the bank yelled, "For the love of 'eaven put that poor ruddy cow out of 'er misery."

26

'Nex' week an RSPCA official visits us. "If this is a cargo-'ouseboat," 'e says, " 'ow many 'ead o' cattle 'ave you aboard?"

'The boss shows 'im the fog-'orn, grinnin' all over 'is mug.

' "Oh," says the official, "that's different," 'e says, an' 'e left us looking angry like.'

'The boss,' said Mrs Withersedge, 'wonders whether we could 'ave a very small swimmin'-pool somewhere on deck. Oh, lor! Fill it up with 'ot champagne like in 'Ollywood, I suppose. Mind you, I don't blame nobody for 'esitatin' to bathe in our backwater. It's a sort o' private beach for orange-peel, bottles, fag-packets, and wot 'ave you. I pointed out to the boss that we was rather too near the shore to 'ave naked actresses lyin' about the place on deck and roastin' their skins in the rain. 'E drew 'isself up and said, "That was not my idea at all, Mrs Withersedge." '

Said Mrs Withersedge: 'My friend Mrs Sprott says to me, she says, the way you go on about that craft o' yours, anyone'd think you spent your youth roundin' the Cape afore the mast instead of servin' taties in that grocer's shop in Maidenhead. I says, look, I says, a boat what don't move an inch is a conteradiction in terms. If she can float, she can move, even if it took a 'orse to tow 'er. All I want is a change of scenery, and I'll settle for Marlow, I says. Go on! she says, you fidgit! A born rover – that's what you are. Like 'ell, I am, says I.'

'The boss,' said Mrs Withersedge, 'was gettin' what 'e calls 'is sea-legs the other day, when 'e fell over the cat. A cat on board ship, 'e says, is a damned nuisance. The way 'e said on board ship you'd think we was ploughin' our way through a typhoon in the Injun Ocean. I says, it keeps the mice down, I says, an' we 'aven't no traps. I should 'ope not 'e says. Mousetraps on board, 'e says, why, we might as well live in a warehouse. A boat's a boat, even if she don't cruise about the place. I 'alf thought 'e'd say put that cat in irons, bosun. Lor! What a life!'

Song of the Houseboat

Oh, we don't muck about with the yard-arm,
  Or 'eave on the anchor chain,
We're better orf 'ere in the backwater

Than out on the ragin' main.
We man no bloomin' crow's nest
In search of a bit o' land,
So rant it and roar it, my bully-boys,
We're not bound for the Rio Grande!

*　　　*　　　*

The Fishcake Controversy

Dear Sir,

I resent the accusation that a fishcake-maker is sophisticated.
My niece has been making fishcakes for nine years, and a simpler
girl it would be difficult to find. Possibly the fishcake-makers
in smart hotels or restaurants lose their simplicity, but they
are not typical. The humbler practitioner has no time for the
la-di-da attitudes of intellectuals, but merely gets on with the
job. Legitimate pride in the finished product need not lead to
sophistication.

(Mrs) Edna Trowser

Dear Sir,

Mrs Trowser's sneering reference to sophisticated fishcake-
makers just shows. My uncle knows a girl who makes fishcakes
in a very high-class restaurant in Kilburn. She reads Henry James
and can dance the wa-pa-ca-pa, yet at heart she remains simple
and unspoiled. A low-brow fishcake-maker is not necessarily
unsophisticated, but may be merely stupid.

(Mrs) Eva Noshley

Dear Sir,

Both Mrs Trowser and Mrs Noshley seem to think that sophistication as applied to fishcake-makers is a derogatory term. Far from
it. I myself, while filling this position at the Osokosi Oriental
Tea-Rooms at Wibbering-on-Sea, was attending the night-classes
of the Wibbering and Mufflestone Study Circle. I was the first local
fishcake-maker to read a paper to the circle. I remember it was on
'Improved Relations between the Public and Litter-Wardens'.

(Mrs) Penelope Sniddle

Dear Sir,

Give me the good old roustabout, huggermugger atmosphere for fishcake-making and Mrs Sniddle can keep her sophistication! I work in 'Dad's Den' at Kippermere and believe me it's all slapdash, noise, and go-as-you-please. The customers throw the fishcakes about in sheer high spirits. It is all very low-brow, I suppose, but I was never one to take fishcakes seriously, and doubtless the la-di-da West End diners-out would find our place rough going.

Ethel Gulping

Dear Sir,

I have been making fishcakes at a superior restaurant in Swindon for forty-two years, and I say without fear of contradiction or hope of reward, that there's a happy medium between sophistication and sheer savagery (see Mrs Gulping's revelations of fishcake throwing at 'Dad's Den'). I have never found it necessary to read Henry James. But that does not mean I am illiterate. Only a low music-hall mind, on the other hand, finds anything funny in fishcake-making.

(Mrs) Olga Wagtale

Crisis

What! Blame the politicians? Not at all!
They are consistent; it's the same old try-on.
We pay the piper for the tune they call.
They made the bed which we must once more lie on.

The Strabismus Boomerang

Back and There and Back Again

Now that it is so important to be able to travel to New York and back between breakfast and dinner, the Strabismus Boomerang Stratocruiser should be hurried into the air. This amazing plane works on the boomerang principle. On reaching New York it will automatically turn round and come back to London without landing, or even pausing. Dr Strabismus (Whom God Preserve) of Utrecht claims that a large number of man-hours will be saved by this process, and sees a prospect of a busy man being able to go there and back twice or three times in a single day.

Interviewed yesterday, Dr Strabismus (Whom God Preserve) of Utrecht said, 'The whole point of the Boomerang Stratocruiser is that it will save so much time. At present, when people fly to places, they land before coming back. The Boomerang will give them no chance to waste time in this way, with the result that they will be back home and ready for another return journey long before those who have landed and waited for the next plane back.

As the Boomerang will never land in foreign countries, there will be no delay in the Customs, and nobody will need any luggage.'

Perhaps some simple explanation of the principle on which the Strabismus Boomerang works is necessary for those who are not trained technicians. The whole secret is residual combustion. When the volatile constituents of a secondary oxidation become explosive, the catalytic thermal pressure causes ignition, which in turn causes the adiabatic compression which produces detonation by contact with the sulphurous accretions of gaseous air. Thus the Boomerang, by an accumulation of Stinnes vibrations, is retarded, on reaching its goal, to such an extent that it is forced, by a process known as groll-ventilation, to return to its base. The whole thing is a triumph of endemic and diametrically inflammatory trinbrolics.

Yesterday the Boomerang made what could have been called a trial flight, if there had been any flight. But the beautiful, gleaming plane after taxiing down the tarmac, turned gracefully and taxied back to the starting post. 'Never for a moment was it airborne,' said a high official. It was found, after a prolonged examination, that the chock-strut which controls the Benskin hammer-catch had got jammed in the Niemeyer joint-casing, and vice versa. The fault was put right, but at a second attempt the plane would not move, even on the ground. So it was pushed and pulled by unwilling hands into its shed for further overhaul.

Yesterday the Strabismus Boomerang made a second attempt at a trial run. After taxiing superbly down the runway it suddenly began to move sideways and then fell over, injuring the starboard wing. Experts at once swarmed over it, and it was found that a horse-coil* had fouled the lower friction-bolt on the Parminter plunger, thus disturbing the balance of the delicate monster, causing it to veer and finally lose its equilibrium. 'She is buoyant, but not quite airborne,' said a high official.

In the presence of Commodore Caparison, Mrs Gulpepper, and the Horsecroft twins, the Strabismus Boomerang Stratocruiser underwent a third test yesterday. And this time it took to the air like a teetotaller to water, and disappeared in less time than it takes to

* The technical name for the gorm-end ratchet.

skin an armadillo. It was soon back and off again and back again. A regular one-plane shuttle service. The heads of the watchers on the ground swung to and fro as at Wimbledon, until the pilot brought the great beast to rest on the runway. The boomerang principle has been vindicated triumphantly. 'Now for New York and back,' said the sillier of the Horsecroft twins.

All was ready for the first return flight of the Strabismus Boomerang to New York. The passengers were in their seats, and hostess Rosalie Pipp was ready to serve oysters, caviar, Burmese ortolans and champagne. But the gigantic gadget refused to move. Mechanics pushed and pulled in vain. Officials shouted contradictory orders and advice. The pilot dismounted in a rage. The passengers waited impatiently. And then a cadaverous mechanic said excitedly, 'Oh, I know what it is. We forgot to fuel her. How stupid of us!' A sentiment endorsed by the entire gathering.

Fuelled (this time) and ready for anything, the gleaming Boomerang nosed its way into the wind like a huge hostess turning a street corner. A cheer from the spectators sent it on its way to New York and back. Presently it disappeared in the empyrean, and the man in the control tower, who had been nervous, lit a pencil and inhaled. 'Wind variable on high ground,' said a meteorologist's tout, consulting a phrenometer. The remark was ignored. Then came a radio message from the Boomerang. 'Off course. Over Newcastle, over Newcastle, over.' 'It must be going sideways,' said an official.

(The Strabismus Boomerang is being overhauled.)

* * *

Is a man who has played the hind legs of a rhinoceros in a pantomime entitled to call himself an actor? What eminent actors forget is that it is by no means easy to create the illusion of actually being the hind legs. What leading actor would care to undertake the part? They are all fond of talking about 'getting inside the skin of your part'. Well, here is their chance to get right inside the skin. My own belief is that no well-known actor would take such a part, because he would not be recognised, and would miss the burst of applause which usually greets his entrance.

How to do it

Some say that there is no scope for acting in such a part. That
is nonsense. The man who plays the hind legs can twitch his tail
saucily or flamboyantly or shyly, and he can convey a hundred
nuances by the way he moves the legs. He can make the man who
plays the front part look very foolish by refusing to synchronise his
movements with those of his comrade. He can give an individuality
to the hind legs by using his imagination – which is called stealing
the limelight. Or he can work in such harmony with his coadjutor
and other half that an intelligent audience can hardly believe that
it is not watching a real rhinoceros, one and indivisible.

For young actors

A little booklet issued by the Royal Academy of Dramatic Art
has this to say of playing a rhinoceros: 'In all except the sheerly
farcical scenes, the rhinoceros is an entity, and the two component
parts must "think rhinoceros", until their combined movements
are realistically rhinocerian. "United we stand, divided we fall"
should be their guiding principle. The attempt of each half to
act independently may win laughs from the groundlings, but as
a contribution to dramatic art such fairground antics are deplor-
able. Tom Bundle, the greatest hind legs of all time, used to say,
"Two minds with but a single thought, four legs that beat as one
rhinoceros." '

I will pass this on

Dear Sir,

Lady Bieswacks asks me to say that she might be prepared to
engage the three Persian seesaw men to appear at a large evening
party she is giving in July. Would you kindly put me in touch
with them so that I can settle the fee and other details? Lady
Bieswacks would also like to know whether the Persians require
a musical accompaniment, and whether their plank will fit into
her drawing-room.

Yours faithfully,
Edna Drosse (Secretary)

The Persians reply

I have sent to Lady Bieswacks the following reply of the Persians:

Ho yes but wot munny doth er laddyship pay for seesaw in the bewdwars of the Hupper Ten? We ask no musicul hiccumpennyment, as we three humm Persian hares as we go hupdown, hup-down, offten braking into some old foke song of the Thurralibad maoutings. We will not be in eavening dress too. Such garminks is folly on a seesaw. Arsk er to kepe er ighborn jests in order, not to rush the seesaw for hortygraffs wich we give at hextrar price after our exeebishun. We persoom free fude and luvly wines is hinclooded in our contrack, and we do not mean a stail sandwidge and a glarss of milk with er sarvints in a low-born kittchin.

For waddlers

Do you waddle? Buy one of the new gadgets which fit inside the hat and go 'quack, quack' as you walk along.   (*Advt.*)

Thank you, Miss Batterthwaite

Dear Sir,

It is far easier to act a speaking part than a mute one. My father toured as the hind legs of a pantomime horse, and he always

said that keeping silent was his greatest difficulty, especially as his colleague in the front part of the animal was allowed to get a laugh by saying 'Gee, folks!' I had no idea that the Royal Academy of Dramatic Art trained actors to play rhinoceroses. My father was self-taught.

Enid Batterthwaite

Could it be Foulenough?

The cocktail party was at its height when word came that a maid had discovered an enormous hamper on the doorstep. On it was a label which read, 'To the finder. I am an abandoned orphan.' The hostess herself went to investigate, but the poor little thing was so warmly wrapped up that the lady could see nothing but the tip of one ear. 'It will suffocate,' she said. 'Fetch Harris and Mason, and bring the hamper in.' The hamper was carried in, the guests crowded round with exclamations of sympathy. Gentle hands, moist with drink, removed the coverings, and out stepped de Courcy Foulenough, very red in the face.

'Who on earth are you?' cried the hostess.

'General Sir Hampton Court-Court,' came the reply. 'My parents being dead, I am an orphan, and,' added the intruder, ogling a pretty girl, 'I am often called abandoned. I fear exposure has weakened me. I am going to faint. Brandy! Brandy!'

'You will kindly leave at once,' said the hostess.

'As there seems to be no brandy on tap,' replied the warrior, 'it will be a pleasure to go elsewhere. This is not the first time a Court-Court has been caught. I salute the company.' And off he went with his hamper in search of a more hospitable house.

The Suet touch

A recent publication of the Stationery Office, *The Design for Forms in Government Departments*, should, I think, have made due acknowledgement to C. Suet, Esq. It is Suet's tireless efforts which have raised the Official Form from a frequent exasperation to a daily torture. Suet was the designer of C. 2618 1.b./29 f.H./16(b)/p.r. 72½/834 b.f., dealing with the Care and Maintenance of Ferrets. It includes the controversial questions for applicants: Great-grandmother's religion (block letters), and Size in Collars.

Again, it was Suet who insisted on returns in quintuplicate of the form of application for an application form for a licence to keep peacocks and/or peahens in tanyards. His fuller and more comprehensive revised version of the 94-question form on the subject of Prevention of Rust on Railings (Government Property) Less than 4ft. 2ins. in Overall Height is still in use.

Prelude to rehearsal

When the three Persians arrived at the Bieswacks house for a rehearsal, Kazbulah embarrassed her ladyship by kissing her hand very loudly and crying: 'Yum-yum!' As she withdrew her hand, he snatched the other and repeated the ritual.

Ashura cried: 'This poolayshul rosidency were made for seesaw!'

Rizamughan asked Lady Bieswacks if she would like to take his place at the end of the seesaw. 'All Briton ladies ride horsebacks,' he said, 'and so seesaw will come to them has easily has tumberling off of a fire-log.' The offer was refused with contumely.

'Hump size, 66¾'

'The Edwardian straw hat is laughed at today,' says a sartorial spokesman. I know an old explorer who still wears one. Last time he was in the desert his camel took one look at it, and being a young animal, and apt to deride old fogeys, lay down and died of laughter. Above his tomb a camel-driver placed this inscription:

Here lies a camel whose untimely death
　Was caused by laughter and a loss of breath.
A most unfashionable hat, alack!
　Was the last straw that broke this camel's back.

Printer's frolic

'The offender was given a severe dressing-gown by the magistrate.'
(News item)

No embroidered pockets, no fancy lapels, no fur collar. A plain, workmanlike garment, as a token of esteem.

It was cheating

A criticism of the 'mechanical playing' of a pianist will recall to many concert-goers the occasion when the Norwegian virtuoso Slejhammer played Gottschalk's *Tangerine Suite*. It was discovered that he was using a pianola, through sheer laziness. He admitted that he had cheated, and was demoted to the triangle in the Bergen Philharmonic.

Dom Pérignon

If the still Champagne of Bouzy had ever become better known, what music-hall jests would have flown about. Its name in an article about wine took me back to that hotel at Châlons-sur-Marne with the magnificent name – the Haute-Mère-Dieu. Not far away is Hautvilliers, where, at the end of the seventeenth century, Dom Pérignon, the cellarer of the Benedictine Abbey, discovered how to give you bubbling champagne. To keep the sparkle which comes at the second fermentation, he substituted corks for the customary bits of hemp soaked in oil. These corks were found to be more airtight than the hemp.

Doing his bit

He reeled and stumbled down the street
  And got in everybody's way
And told the policeman on his beat:
  'This is my staggered holiday.'

Seesaw rehearsal

If the seesaw interlude at Lady Bieswacks's party is a success, no doubt other hostesses will engage the three Persians from Thurralibad. At a rehearsal yesterday in the spacious drawing-room it was decided that the performers should not blow kisses to the audience or shout at them. Said Kazbulah: 'A Sundyskool hatmispere doth not soot seesaw. A kiss blowed to a pretty gazelle is a komplimink. Let not er liddyship be fearing we will hilope with er jests. We are having wifes off our own.'

Strange hobbies

Discussing strange hobbies, a chronicler told of an actress who collects balls of twine. But great minds often have an unexpected side to them. Aristotle, as we know from his *Poetics*, was a verdigris-grater, Sappho made mud-pies, Bismarck rode a rocking-horse, Jenny Lind chewed stubble, Cromwell made large hoops from macaroni, Rimbaud slept with a heron's egg under his pillow, Gustavus Adolphus smeared his knees with honey, Mithridates wore boots made of sorrel, Catherine the Great read poetry to a goat, and Tacitus combed his hair with a hay-fork.

At the breakfast table

Snibbo is this week launching instant bacon. You drop a beauti-
fully packaged powder into hot milk. The whole thing coagulates
in the form of rashers. 'It tastes like spinach,' said an executive,
'but it's bacon all right. Look. You can see the word "Bacon" on
the packet.'

Was it a horsefinch?

The bird which, according to a report from Sidmouth, was seen
by several people to be flying upside down was probably the
horsefinch. This migrant flies the wrong way up so that it will
land on its back if it falls. An old Arab in Ramanieh who loved
riddles once asked an English lady, 'Why is a swift like the chimney
in my son's house?'

'I'm afraid I don't know,' replied the haughty dame.

'Because it hath a crooked flew,' said the Arab with screams
of desert laughter.

Dr Rhubarb's corner

F.C.L. WRITES: Every time my uncle visits us, he seizes a saucepan
and clamps it on his head, and says, 'William the Conqueror at
Hastings' to amuse the children. It gets tedious.

DR RHUBARB SAYS: Fill your saucepans with bits
of fish.

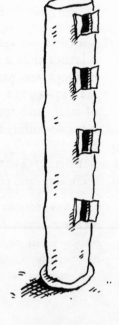

Fashion note

The new four-storey hats have tiny windows
in the sides to keep the head cool. To match
them there are backless gloves in flame-
coloured *plomberie*, with webbed ducks-foot
fingers ending in camel-skin *poufferies*.
Imitation lobster-claw buckles in shantung
are popular for the serge cocktail bootees.

Rustiguzzi's acute sensitivity

A letter-writer who wonders whether opera-singers really feel the emotions they portray should watch Rustiguzzi. Once, in the Second Act of *Cocómero* she cried so piteously that Broccoli, the tenor, broke down and blubbered. The chorus of fishermen was soon infected with the general misery of the proceedings, and tears bedewed their cheeks. All over the stage this boo-hooing went on, until Rustiguzzi recovered sufficiently to go into hysterical laughter, and then everybody else began to howl with laughter, including the orchestra and the conductor (Richter). The audience joined in but the critics sulked.

Sensation at Narkover

Feeling that the most famous disapproved school in England has a certain standard to keep up, the headmaster of Narkover has sacked two masters who, having lost all their money, were going about in rags. One of them even begged in the High Street. When reproved by Dr Smart-Allick for getting the school a bad name, he pleaded that he had been cheated by a whist-syndicate, and had been robbed of the money he stole back from them. 'You knew what to expect when you came here as a master,' said Smart-Allick. 'If I allowed my staff to go about in tattered clothing and to beg in the streets, people would think that there was no way of making money at Narkover.'

Here, there and everywhere

A DOPED HORSE in the 2.30 at Nobblesham broke out into such a lather that a barber who had drunk too deeply rushed into the paddock and started to shave it.

MRS WHANTER, 33, of 2 The Crescent, Udgeforth, bought a sack of coal, and found in it four stones, two slates, a dead sparrow, a horse-collar, the skull of a goat, a rat-trap, and a small lump of coal.

A BOILERMAKER who can wag his ears is the new caretaker in a condemned cottage at Stoke Nymcoe.

Mrs Rumpus dances

'Couples whose style of dancing does not harmonise should agree
to sit it out.'   (*Expert*)

When Mrs Rumpus dances
She meets disdainful glances,
So powerful, so aggressive is her style.
Manoeuvring for position,
She brooks no opposition,
And steers her struggling partner with a smile.
But those who do not love her
Are not slow to discover,
As she pushes them ferociously about,
That one might be less harassed,
Less publicly embarrassed,
If she would but consent to sit it out.

5

Captain Foulenough, Suitor

Accused by a friend of loving Vita Brevis only for her money, Captain Foulenough made himself clear. 'I love everything about her,' he said, 'and her money is one of the things about her. She and her money are inseparable. If the only way I can get her is to get her money too, why should I let her wealth stand in my way? I love Vita too dearly not to rejoice in her good fortune in being rich.'

Foulenough to Vita Brevis:

My ring-dove, it is spring. You always say I love you for your money. What man who loves as I do could be happy to see his sweetheart poverty-stricken? I should love you just the same if you were twice as rich as you are. Someone repeated to you the story that, having lost at cards, I gave a UOMe to a man. That was only a sportive translation of IOU. Your aunt says I am an adventurer. Does she imagine that you are the kind of girl to marry a teetotal undertaker in Bootle?

Be mine, Vita.

Yours for the asking,
de Courcy

Vita Brevis to Foulenough:

No, de Courcy. We have nothing in common but the IOUs you have showered on me as though they were presents. As my father once said, 'My dear, you can't possibly marry a man who would come home at 4 a.m. with his hat on back to front, singing, and falling over everything.' Your undeniable skill at cards would hardly recommend you to my bridge club. You once, it is true, offered

to give up drinking for my sake, adding, 'Anyhow, vodka.' And
I happen to know you dislike vodka. Do not spoil our not very
beautiful friendship.

Vita

Foulenough to Vita Brevis:

Cruel goddess!

If I come home at 4 a.m. singing, it is only to keep my heart
up because there is no Vita to welcome me on the mat. As to
my skill at cards, gladly would I teach your friends nearly all I
know. You refer to my drinking habits. Well, I drink to forget
your cruelty, and then, when I have forgotten it, I drink again for
fear of remembering it. The IOUs which I gave you would be but
chaff in the wind if you married me.

Still hoping.
Your devoted de Courcy

Vita Brevis was pacing her garden and talking to her uncle the
Dean, when Foulenough appeared. 'Fly with me!' he cried. 'My
swift Arab car is pawing the ground at the gates of your tent.'

'Who is this lunatic, my dear?' asked the Dean.

'Reverend sir,' said Foulenough, 'you are in the presence of
the Sheik Spittin el Khuspidor of Rub-ud-Dubdub three men in
a tub.' He then kissed Vita's hand with a sound like a mackerel
being replaced clumsily on a fishmonger's slab, and withdrew.

Vita Brevis to Foulenough:

De Courcy,

Your escapade yesterday was beyond a joke. How could I explain
your foolery to my uncle? You wonder why I continually refuse to
marry you. When I told my uncle you were not a lunatic, but
merely unconventional, he said you must have been drinking. As
you never do much else, it was not a very shrewd guess. Please
consider my feelings before you think up more crazy nonsense.

Miss Constance Brevis, Vita's aunt, to her brother, Raoul Brevis:

. . . This man Foulenough is still hanging round Vita. I found him with her in Clarges Street the other day. He is really impossible, and jokes all the time about bookies and bailiffs, and drink, and card tricks. What on earth she sees in him I can't imagine. He said to me, 'I hope your niece's intentions are honourable,' and winked. Vita says that he amuses her. Of course, she will never marry him, but she ought not to be seen with him in bars and restaurants. I reminded her of the day he arrived at her house when I was there, and was announced by the maid as Monsieur Hotspot of the Madagascan Embassy, and she roared with laughter at the memory. There's an odd vulgar streak in our Vita . . .

Raoul Brevis to Constance Brevis:

. . . Of course the man's a thorough rogue, but Vita is old enough to know her own mind. The only time I met him was in a Mayfair bar. He had taken the place of a barman who was ill, and when a pompous fellow ordered a drink Foulenough poured it out and drank it himself. Everybody laughed, and he said, 'Anybody else like to stand me a drink?' Now, Connie dear, I know that's not your idea of the way to behave, but somehow the rascal carried it off, and women seem to realise that nothing is ever dull when he's present. Possibly that's what attracts Vita. I heard that when somebody asked him point-blank if he cheated at cards he said, 'I only swindle people who try to swindle me.' Don't be too hard on him, Connie . . .

Mrs Thirdleigh to Constance Brevis:

. . . And so, dear, I thought you ought to know that Mrs Pelmett told Rita Loughbury that Lorna had seen them together at Vecchiati's, and that this man Foulenough offered to sign the bill with his thumb-mark. They sent for the manager and Foulenough said that he couldn't read or write, that he was Baron Silberplatz, and a lot more nonsense. Vita was apparently highly amused, and he finally haggled about the bill, saying: 'It's my Eastern blood. Will you take such-and-such a sum? I'll give you such-and-such, and that's my last offer. If you don't want my money, I didn't want your food.' The manager thought he was drunk, and Vita finally got him away. I thought you ought to know all this . . .

Mrs McAwphall, Vita's married aunt, to Raoul Brevis:

. . . As the man of the family, you really must put your foot down. My husband and I are really disturbed. We went to see Vita yesterday and that dreadful man was there. Ronald asked him where he went for his shooting, and he said, 'Soho.' Ronald foolishly laughed at this, which encouraged Foulenough to make the lowest kind of jokes about cards and racing. His attitude to Vita was quite openly that of a suitor, and when he called her his 'gorgeous icicle' I thought the floor would open and swallow us. Now, Raoul, can't you open Vita's eyes to his vulgarity and shocking lack of restraint? When we left he ostentatiously kissed my hand and murmured, 'Adios, Carissima,' and Ronald, like a fool, laughed again . . .

Betty Brevis, Raoul's wife, to Vita Brevis:

. . . Sylvia Cragge thinks that you are sacrificing yourself to try to reform this frightful man Foulenough. That's all very noble, but have you thought what it would mean? The constant vigilance against drink and gambling and low company would wear you to a shadow, my dear. Raoul pretends to find Foulenough amusing, but that is the rake in every man coming out. And then, my dear, suppose he got you involved in some scandal on a racecourse. You owe something to your family, you know. I hope what Raoul says is not true – that you have always found conventional men dull. Forgive me for lecturing, but we are all so upset at this report that Foulenough runs a bogus antique shop . . .

Foulenough to Vita's Aunt Lydia:

Dear lady,
   My fondest wish, after leading your niece to the halter (joke), is to call you aunt. Your disapproval cuts me like a blunt razor. Do give me a break. May I call to see you one day, so that the mephitic clouds of distrust and disapproval may be dissolved in one of your enchanting smiles?

Your humble petitioner,
de Courcy Foulenough (Captain, retd.)

'Vita', said Aunt Lydia, 'I have received a preposterous letter from your vulgar friend. Read it.'

Vita read it. 'It seems to me,' she said, 'that he has his eye on you in case I disappoint him. Why don't you let him call on you? He's really very amusing, after some of our staid friends.'

'A circus clown is amusing,' replied her aunt, 'but that is no reason why I should ask him to tea. As for our friends being staid, I presume you mean that they don't cheat at cards.'

'I sometimes wish they did,' said Vita. 'Life would be less dull.'

Aunt Lydia ignored the remark.

Foulenough to Vita Brevis:

Dear refrigerator,

Since your aunt ignores my letter, I have a good mind to call one day in a dog-collar and tell her I'm newly ordained, and that, as a curate, I have come for a subscription for a new pew or two. I'd sing her a psalm if it would put me right with her. 'Dear lady,' I would say, 'a pew from you would send the vicar off his rocker with delight.' The snag is that I don't suppose I look the part. A girl once said to me, 'What bloodshot eyes you have!' I answered, 'It's the reflection of the sunset.'

Yours till Quinquagesima, as it were.

To Captain Foulenough from 'A Friend':

Dear Fouly,

Some of us think that your letter published in the *Daily Express* was a dangerous joke. Simple people will really believe that you have been ordained, and are a parson. What is Beachcomber's hold over you? How can he get all your private correspondence? 'Tufty' Snadger was asked in a bar the other day whether you had really gone pious on us. He said: 'His sermons would make you cry.' Then they both had a good laugh. All the same, go easy on this sort of stuff.

Your old pal,
'Guts' Hearne

'Isn't it better,' said Foulenough, 'that I should love you for your money than that I shouldn't love you at all?'

Vita Brevis laughed sardonically. 'Plenty of men do that,' she said.

'Which proves,' retorted the Captain, 'that there is something irresistible in large fortunes. I could go far with you.'

'Try going far without me,' said Vita, 'the farther the better.'

'Come,' said Foulenough. 'Confess that your pulse beats faster when I am near you.'

'Oh, yes,' said she, 'with exasperation.'

'That's a little advance on indifference,' said Foulenough. 'Sometimes exasperation is the dawn of love.'

'Pay the bill – if you have any money – and let's go,' said Vita.

'There you are,' grumbled Foulenough, 'you're always thinking of money.'

Captain Foulenough has sent this notice to Vita Brevis. If she approves, it will be inserted in the papers:

> The engagement is not yet announced between Captain de Courcy Foulenough, only son of General Sir Claude and Lady Foulenough, and Vita, youngest daughter of Sir Edgar and Lady Brevis.

*   *   *

I am afraid that that story about the mice who gnawed their way through the organ pipes in a Norfolk church will encourage people who are troubled by mice to buy or build organs with traps attached to the pipes. It would be cheaper, and no sillier, to leave about the place dummy organ pipes made of cheese. While the feast was on, the householder would spring out of hiding and capture the hearty little eaters. It is not generally known that mice always eat in a north-easterly direction. Hence the sailors' phrase gnaw-gnaw-east. And mice-versa.

Establishing a precedent

'It was announced,' said the man, 'as a three-legged race, but my father used both his legs.'

'Well, so did you,' said the magistrate.

'No,' said the man. 'I couldn't use my right leg because it was tied to his left one.'

'Naturally,' said the magistrate, 'and the same applied to him. You both used one leg freely, but the remaining two legs were used as one, making three in all.'

'No,' said the man, 'two legs tied together are still two legs, and two and two make four.'

'Mathematics apart,' said the magistrate, 'even if, strictly speaking, there were four legs, two of them acted as one.'

'You might as well say,' replied the man, 'that if two men wear one large hat they've only got one head between them.'

'Rubbish!' shouted the magistrate, 'the two men wouldn't each have a spare head with no hat on it.'

'If,' said the man, 'all four legs had been tied together, would you say we had only one leg?'

'Try that on a horse!' roared the exhausted magistrate.

Perfectionist

A schoolmaster says that it is a mistake to over-praise a pupil. A boy was once asked, 'Now Galbraith, what does 9 + 2 come to?'

'Eleven, sir.'
'Very good, Galbraith.'
'Very good be damned, sir! It's perfect.'

Sly little thing

I read that 'there is nothing like champagne to loosen the tongue of a shy girl.' As the song says:

> Her lack of conversation
>   Might well be called unique.
> Her escort cried, 'Damnation!
>   Will nothing make her speak?'
> 'Perhaps some wine . . .' he muttered,
>   And suddenly he heard
> The first sound she had uttered:
>   She whispered, 'Mumm's the word.'

Interlude

Dr Strabismus (Whom God Preserve) of Utrecht has invented an illuminated dial to be attached to weathercocks on steeples. A mobile pointer on the dial registers the direction of the wind.

PRODNOSE: Then what is the use of the weathercock?

MYSELF: The dial would not register without it. It is controlled by the movements of the weathercock.

PRODNOSE: Then who will bother to climb the steeple to look at the dial?

MYSELF: Time alone can answer that.

PRODNOSE: And why should the dial be illuminated?

MYSELF: For the convenience of those who go up there by night.

Who would have thought it?

A Moravian artist named Polonek Swetter has created a sensation with a still-life picture called 'Watercress'. The bunches of watercress are so lifelike that an art critic approached the canvas and tweaked them. To his surprise he found that they were bunches of real watercress stuck to the canvas. Swetter explained that this method was a realist protest against abstract art. 'It is a new angle,' he said.

Dr Rhubarb's corner

T.N. WRITES: My brother-in-law's name is Thomas Stummick and wits call him Tommy Tummy. My husband pretends to be an Indian, and bangs my brother-in-law on the back, shouting, 'Hark to the tom-tum in the reserve.' I don't know why I tell you all this.

DR RHUBARB SAYS: Nor do I.

A notable absence

Conspicuously absent from the Boat Show is the famous skow, classed at Lloyd's as a houseboat. Says Mrs Withersedge: 'The boss thought it would be undignified to 'ave our craft transported by road. Water is 'er element, 'e says, an' she can never 'ave enough of it. By water 'e means our slimy, muddy ocean 'ome, where we lie like a lump o' litter. When the wind 'ums in our cat's whiskers you can almost smell the tang o' the open sea, not arf you can't.'

Walsall

This is Millet-Cake Day in Walsall. Soon after dawn, the millet-men, dressed in yellow smocks and green trousers, parade through the town singing 'A millet! A millet! And who shall say us nay?', a song that is said to date back four hundred years at least. Then, a baker, chosen by a vote of the council, drives his cart through the streets, throwing the cakes through any window left open for the purpose. The chief millet-man, carrying a long pole with a garland of flowers on it, hands the mayor a special cake of enormous size, and all sing the millet song before dispersing.

Enough to go on with

'Calmness in emergencies is a matter of will-power.'

(*Morning paper*)

A man thundered on the door of a burning house, and when it was opened he shouted, 'Your house is on fire, lady.'

'Is that all?' replied the householder.

'Well,' said the man, 'it's all I can think of for the moment.'

Among the artists

Polonek Swetter, the Moravian artist whose 'Watercress' I wrote about the other day, is the acknowledged leader of a group of young artists who favour what they call Transexperimentalism. They do not all stick concrete objects to their canvases. Bulto, for instance, shoots jam out of a water-pistol onto a sheet of corrugated iron, to get a stormy sunset effect. Mosprey suspends the canvas from the ceiling, lies on his back with greased roller skates on, and kicks out. Most daring of all is Ernest Gawdril, who pours fish-scales through a sieve onto an old map of Bulgaria.

False alarm

'Her son, she said, eats till he almost bursts.'   (*News item*)

> 'Has he burst yet?' the neighbours cried,
>   And, frigidly polite,
> The mother of the lad replied,
>   'Not quite.'

6

Rissole Mio

The New Chronicles of Marine House

Today Marine House becomes Rissole Mio. Mrs McGurgle warned her boarders that they must not expect her establishment to become Italianised, and that the change of name will be no excuse for goings-on. From her place at the head of the table, Mrs McGurgle rebuked with a disapproving frown the lodger who cried facetiously: 'Rosti beefi and due veggi con poudini de Yorkshirone.'

'Bongjaw, Merdam,' ventured Mr Crisset, as he sat down to the groaning board, intending a jovial reference to the new foreign name of the establishment. Miss Umbles tittered, and was understood to murmur something about men who see nothing in Paris but the Folly Burjerrs and Moolong Rooge. Mrs McGurgle, dispensing gravy with a Lucullan aplomb, paused. 'Mr Crisset,' she said, 'I am sure your parents told you as a lad that to talk a foreign tongue in the presence of those who may not understand it is a mark of ill-breeding. French may be the language of diplomacy, but we here find the language of Chaucer and Milton adequate for conversational exchanges.'

'Miss Twang,' said Mrs McGurgle, 'Mr Twelvetrees reports that you are keeping a hen in the linen cupboard on your landing. Whether so gross a breach of the rules of this establishment be attributed to love of animals or distaste for the eggs served at breakfast, I leave to you and your conscience. Were I to close my eyes to such goings-on, doubtless some thoughtless guest would end by keeping a cow in the bathroom.'

Miss Twang replied in a low voice, 'It doesn't lay.'

'Then what is it there for?' asked the chatelaine.

'It got in, and I had not the heart to evict it,' replied the culprit.

'Miss Twang,' said Mrs McGurgle, 'sentimentality is a luxury I cannot afford. Mr Twelvetrees will help you to drive this interloping foundling from the dubious comfort of the linen cupboard to some locale, such as a poultry-run, more congenial to its habits.'

A pea, flicked with unerring aim across the lunch table, glanced off Miss Twang's cheek and fell onto her neighbour's plate. The marksman was a new arrival, Mr Hopton, who had evidently been exploring the inns of the neighbourhood. When rebuked, and requested to desist, he said, in what Mrs Henchman described as 'a public house voice', 'Free and easy does it. We're all friends here.'

'Friendship,' said the chatelaine, 'does not necessarily imply the deliberate throwing about of food. My own nephew, who, in a mood of exuberance, flung a bit of gristle up to the ceiling, where it stuck, was expelled from this establishment in 1958. Be warned, Mr Hopton.'

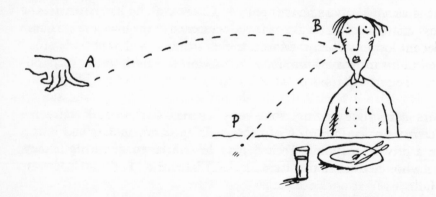

Miss Twang was so dejected after the loss of the hen in the linen cupboard that the McGurgle's heart softened. The morose boarder was given a double portion of spinach. A disgruntled young man muttered: 'It seems that one must keep hens in linen cupboards if one wants special treatment in the way of spinach.'

Mrs McGurgle's green eyes flashed with fire. 'Mr Wivenhoe,' she said, 'I and I alone am the arbiter of helpings in this place. Only yesterday I waived the rules and allocated you a second banana because you do not like blood-oranges.' The young man looked foolish, and a low murmur of approval from the boarders moved the chatelaine to announce that there would be cress sandwiches for tea.

When nine empty whisky bottles labelled 'Grampound's Lightning Hair Restorer' were found in the cupboard of the completely bald Mr Hopton, Mrs McGurgle, contemplating his head, said, 'Lightning appears to be working very slowly this year, Mr Hopton. I would recommend the purchase of a wig.'

Looking at Miss Twang, Mr Hopton replied, 'This place is a hotbed of informers. Do you imagine I drink hair restorer?'

'No more than I imagine you rub whisky on your head,' riposted the chatelaine, with a malicious smile of triumph.

Mrs McGurgle's satirical tongue became a scimitar yesterday. Somebody had put up a large placard on the front door with 'Hangover Hall' scrawled on it. Said the chatelaine, 'Three empty port bottles on the landing speak louder than words. If the perpetrator of this public-house vulgarity has any manhood left in his sodden frame he will confess his shame. If, however, as I suspect, he is as cowardly as he is depraved, I do not envy him the remorseless gnawing of an awakening conscience and the loathing of every decent lodger. When the fumes clear his brain, and he regards himself in his mirror, he will shrink back, appalled, and with a muffled cry of horror that a human being could sink so low in the mire.'

Mrs McGurgle's winged words evidently alighted on the conscience of a certain Mr Champling, and aroused his better feelings. In a private session with the chatelaine he confessed that it was he who, in a delirious moment, designated the house as Hangover Hall.

'It was a case of one over the eight, you know,' he said.

She, with a dignity tinged with charity, replied, 'Whatever the eight may be, there was certainly at least one over them. I trust that the coming year will see exuberance yield to restraint, and in that hope I am willing to let disgusting bygones be disgusting bygones.' With a wintry smile, she dismissed him from the room known as her boodwar.

Miss Wodger suggested to Mrs McGurgle that any guest suspected of alcoholic excess should be requested to say, with a clear enunciation, 'ironmongery, claustrophobia, psychiatry'.

Mrs McGurgle replied: 'Miss Wodger, such verbal ordeals, when imposed on the besotted, are more likely to arouse laughter and low jests in the onlookers than to shame the culprit into a less barbaric use of perilous stimulants. Nor do I anticipate any recurrence of such incidents as three empty port bottles on the landing. By the tradition of ample supplies of water at meals, I hope to implant in even the most abandoned a more dignified, nay, a more salubrious way of life.'

Mr Champling, the culprit in the 'Hangover Hall' incident, was once more in favour, which means 'three potatoes to everyone else's two, and a second whack of gravy if requested,' according to a jaundiced fellow-lodger. By this subtle cosseting, Mrs McGurgle hoped to convert him to good behaviour. Unfortunately he could not resist sipping his water, sniffing it, holding it up to the light, and pronouncing it a very pleasant vintage, but rather light. Mrs McGurgle said nothing, but she gave him the look which is called her deep-freeze.

'This fish,' grumbled Mr West, 'is very salty.'

'Fish,' said Mrs McGurgle, 'live in the sea, as you may have heard.'

'Sheep,' interposed Miss Garstang, 'live in the fields, but lamb need not taste of grass.'

'If sheep lived in the sea,' said the chatelaine, 'lamb would be more salty.'

'This conversation,' said Mr West, 'is getting us nowhere. You might as well say that if onions grew on plum trees they would taste of plums.'

'Or,' said Miss Garstang, with a giggle, 'if apples grew in office blocks they would taste like concrete.'

'The meal is over,' said Mrs McGurgle sternly. 'Pray disperse.'

'One more word,' said the irrepressible Mr West. 'What would rhubarb taste of if it grew on volcanoes?' There was no reply.

A vegetarian guest at Rissole Mio, who is laughingly called the her-baceous boarder, returned from a celebration in the Gaveldiggers' Arms somewhat the better for drink. Upon the groaning board was a joint of roast mutton. 'I'm gonna bust the joint wide open,' he shouted, and hit it a whack with his fist. With exquisite tact,

Mrs McGurgle drew his attention to a succulent nut cutlet on his plate and calmed him down with a promise of beetroot fritters to follow.

The talk was of rowing, for the sporting Julia Nowther had once rowed bow in a ladies' eight. 'Did you ever stroke a crew?' asked the herbaceous boarder, who intended to follow up with a discourse on keeping fit.

'I bet she did, every one of them,' muttered Mr Plasgrove.

Silence fell like a bomb. Mrs McGurgle was, for once, tongue-tied. The gentlemen sniggered uneasily.

Recovering quickly, as Julia left the table in tears, Mrs McGurgle said loudly, and with freezing dignity: 'There would appear to be some gentlemen here who confuse sport with debauchery. I trust that a lady's tears will haunt them and give them agony of remorse which raises even vulgarians above the beasts of the field.'

The herbaceous boarder has received a note from Mrs McGurgle: 'The consensus is that the voice heard singing, last Sunday, a low song about a kiss behind a larder door was yours. If such songs are the outcome of a vegetarian diet, I tremble to think to what feats of vulgarity you might be inspired, even on the Sabbath, if ever you became carnivorous. A repetition of this offence, I must warn you, will lead to a request to sever your connection with this establishment. It is my duty to maintain the good name of my house, as well as the moral well-being of its patrons.'

The herbaceous boarder has replied to Mrs McGurgle's ultimatum: 'Whatever the boarders read into my song about the kiss behind the larder door is their own affair. If the atmosphere of this establishment is conducive to lively songs, it is not my fault. Would you rather see me sunk in gloom, and singing only dirges? However, under your threat of expulsion, I will henceforth remain as mute as the proverbial oyster, rather than seek asylum elsewhere with the stigma of your disapproval dogging my footsteps like an avenging fury. To say nothing of being deprived of your largesse in the matter of beetroot.'

The herbaceous boarder has spiked Mrs McGurgle's six-inch howitzers. He now sings hymns, every Sunday, in a provocatively doleful voice, accompanied on the piano by Miss Tussock. Said Mrs

McGurgle: 'There is a happy medium between coarse music-hall ditties and hymns. This establishment is neither a church nor a night-club. It has been represented to me that your hymns are sung with satirical intent, not from any religious fervour. Otherwise, why does Miss Tussock giggle so much? I am afraid I must ask you to find other accommodation.'

'Adieu, carrot patties,' mumbled the herbaceous boarder.

The quality of Mrs McGurgle's mercy, having been considerably strained, dropped like gentle dew on the head of the herbaceous boarder. Magnanimously the chatelaine forgave the vulgar songs, and received the straying sheep back into the seaside fold. To see him pass the salt before being asked, or to spring to open the door for old Miss Ravensblood, is to realise the effect of charitable treatment on an essentially decent character. If, as a commercial gentleman alleges, Mr Hibbens (the herbaceous boarder) exerted a gentle but tell-tale pressure upon Mrs McGurgle's hand when he opened the dining-salon door for her, I attribute the gesture to gratitude rather than to any designs upon the lady's heart.

Over the fig-flan, Mr Hibbens shot a glance at Mrs McGurgle, a glance eloquent of admiration for her person rather than for her cuisine. This telltale look so unnerved the chatelaine that she lost her customary aplomb and *savoir-faire*, and added mustard to her ice-cream. Some even detected in her voice, when she spoke of the weather to Mrs Crabbe, a slight tremor. This led Mr Gluer to confide to Mr Pulpe that 'he could see Cupid's dart sticking out of her heart a mile'. That afternoon, like a rumour through an Oriental bazaar, ran the whisper that Mr Hibbens had been to Mrs McGurgle's sitting-room to apply for an extra coat-hanger, and had been closeted with her for five minutes.

The insinuations of Mrs Crabbe led Mrs McGurgle to confide in her. Her discomfort in the presence of Mr Hibbens is due not to the dawn of love but to an ever present fear of his vulgar habits. 'Every time he stares at me,' she said, 'I anticipate some coarse remark or depraved ditty. Miss Gelboe says that he leers at her, but I calmed her by saying it was his squint. I think he will have to go to some establishment which dispenses with a traditional decorum. He is but a poor advertisement for the vegetarian way of life.'

(Mr Hibbens has now found other accommodation.)

*   *   *

The Snorting Rally

The non-stop snorting rally at the Cheaveley Assembly Rooms has apparently brought many complaints. People living near said that they could not sleep and asked, not unreasonably, why the contestants could not snort singly instead of all together. The organisers pointed out that there were so many powerful snorters that even a solo would disturb the sensitive. Councillor Tufte added that solitary snorting becomes boring, and that by making the contest a mass exhibition, a kind of team spirit was fostered, which greatly encouraged the less confident snorters.

The pace-makers are an interesting feature of the snorting rally. They are trained snorters who set the pace, keeping a regular interval between snorts. A foreign tourist who had come to Cheaveley to see the old castle, hearing the noise in the Assembly Rooms, thought it was a meet of the local hunt, and bought some sugar from a grocer. An official explained what was going on, and accepted the sugar for the contestants to eat in the tea interval. A pace-maker who dropped out with vertigo emphasised to the visitor the importance of rhythm in snorting, to conserve energy. The foreigner shrugged. 'The English are raving mad,' he muttered.

On the second day of the snorting rally at Cheaveley, a tremendous snort shattered a window and blew a small competitor off his feet. An immediate investigation led to the discovery of a big farm-horse. The nag was taken away by two overseers, both of whom were kicked as they edged the intruder into the street. Several contestants laughed so heartily that, in four cases, a guffaw was marked up to them as a snort. A re-count has been demanded.

Among the letters:
... One wonders what useful purpose is served by encouraging these snorting contests. Such antics can hardly be deemed to prepare a young person of either sex for a career.
... If snorting rallies keep the young out of the coffee-bars it is a good thing. Snorting harms nobody, and keeps the addicts out of mischief. Is nothing sacred?
... Considering the grave times in which we live, the spectacle of people making an exhibition of themselves in this fashion is revolting. The parents are to blame.

During an interval for a snack (a glass of Poopsiboola and some shredded radish extract) nineteen-year-old Daisy Miffet, who had snorted 7,326 times in three hours and four minutes said to a Press conference, 'Oh, dear me!'
'Is it worth it?' asked a reporter.
Daisy gave a snort of contempt, which was not counted, of course, in her score.
'That was off the record,' vouchsafed a laughing referee, Bill Vetley, whose aunt keeps a tobacconist's shop in Basingstoke.

In an interview yesterday, Professor Piffl said: 'These snorting rallies are not, in themselves, to be deprecated. They are an outlet for puzzled and frustrated youth. They have their social value, as young people with a common interest tend to strike up friendships. It is too early to say whether marriages between snorters will turn out happily. It will depend largely on whether a girl can find contentment in the management of her home after the more exciting atmosphere of the snorting rally. It is too easy for the elderly to condemn snorting contests. They should try to enter into the snorter's mind and understand his intellectual make-up.'

Daisy Miffet was last night declared the winner, with 372,134 consecutive snorts. There was an argument among the judges as to whether, towards the end, when she was tired out, she was snorting or snoring. She was given the benefit of the doubt. She was presented with the Poopsiboola Gold Medal, inscribed SICUT EQUUS FREMIT (She snorts like a horse). Her success has already brought her offers to star in four films, to go to America as a model, to launch a liner, to write her autobiography, and to lecture on 'Trends in Modern Life' to the Selsey Drama League. Her father, a St Helens wig-maker, balding, fiftyish, and a keen numismatist, said, handing her a drink, 'You need a snorter.' Daisy fainted at the sound of that word.

The Landlady's Song

Somewhere by warm lagoons
    There are Hawaiian dances . . .
But I must count my spoons,
    One can't take any chances!

I hear the soft refrains,
    The music that bewitches,
While rubbing gravy-stains
    From careless lodgers' breeches.

O well-a-day! The dream
    Fades once again too quickly . . .
'The cat's got at the cream.'
    'Miss Whackstraw's feeling sickly.'

7

Drama at Egg Hall

C. Suet, Esq., Opines

While assembling a batch of eggs to be photographed by an Inspector of Grading at Lyme Regis, Mr Harvey Kippinge, a packaging overseer, thrust his face forward into the front row of eggs. *(Left to right: egg, Mr Kippinge, egg, egg, egg.)* Mr Kippinge has been reported to the Egg board. There will be an inquiry.

The inquiry into the appearance of Mr Kippinge's face in a row of eggs began yesterday at Egg Hall, the Egg Board's magnificent new annexe. Admiral Sir Horace Teakle was in the chair and his dog Snapdragon under it. Mrs Relf, representing the South-West Grading Authority, asked how it was possible for a photographer to mistake a human face for an egg. Mr George Vumper, a psychiatrist, said that at first glance an oval or ovoid face could look like an egg – especially to a man surrounded every day by eggs, as was the photographer. Mr Eric Boole, a Professor of Ovology at Runcorn University, thought that sheer vanity might lead a man to thrust himself forward while eggs were being photographed. He added that Mr Kippinge was reported to have said that he had worked so long among eggs that he felt almost one of them. The inquiry continues.

Mr Hugh Daddy, the photographer, told the Court of Inquiry yesterday that he was not struck by the incongruity of what he took to be an outsize egg in the front row. Had Mr Kippinge not been completely bald, the mistake would doubtless have been avoided. He was so accustomed to photographing eggs for the board that it never occurred to him to ask the supervisor if there was anything human among the group he had to photograph. Asked if he had not noticed eyes, mouth, eyebrows, ears, etc., he said that one does not look for such features in an egg, and therefore the incongruity escaped him. Mrs Remnant, a forewoman marker at the Ipswich Eggeries, said that boys sometimes drew human features on eggs for fun. Perhaps the photographer had been the victim of this illusion, without knowing it. This preposterous suggestion was ignored.

Mr Kippinge said that, in placing his face in the row of eggs, he had acted instinctively and without forethought.

Admiral Sir Horace Teakle said: 'I suppose you realise that by choosing the front row you completely blocked three eggs in the second row, which are missing from the photographic record.'

Miss Froppstead, representing the Graders' Union asked: 'Where on earth was Mr Kippinge's body? Did not the photographer notice a human being standing erect among recumbent eggs?'

Mr Kippinge and the photographer, Mr Daddy, agreed that Mr Kippinge had himself been recumbent. To avoid being out of focus, he had lain full-length on the floor, so that his face was level with the eggs.

'A most extraordinary proceeding,' commented the admiral.

Mr Nensworth, whose task it is to arrange eggs and pose them, in collaboration with the photographer, was asked if he had not noticed anything unusual. He said that he always tapped each egg with a tiny gavel, as a mere formality, and that he could not understand why Mr Kippinge's head, when tapped, had not given forth an un-egg-like sound. Mr Charles Faith, of the Spalding Sorters' Association, asked the present whereabouts of the egg displaced in the front row by Mr Kippinge's face. A Lyme Regis night-watchman said that Mr Kippinge had pushed it aside, and that it had got mixed up with a consignment for the Hammersmith Packing Centre. The Chairman then asked Mr Kippinge, 'Do you recall being tapped by Mr Nensworth?' Mr Kippinge said that he was so completely immersed in his surroundings that it seemed natural for his head to be tapped.

Charlie Suet gave it as his opinion that only gross negligence and absent-mindedness could account for Mr Daddy's failure to notice a human face among so many eggs. Suet quoted a leaflet issued from Shaftesbury Avenue (G.N. 4/264. d./19. cs. H. 42/e. M. 7-pg. 1278 R./326 1. K. 17/21/464 U.V.) on group photography of eggs. He was about to read extracts from a pamphlet on the regional machinery for assembling graded eggs with a view to providing photographic records, which could be examined for flaws, blemishes, chips, uneven surfaces, discoloration, bruises, shell fractures, asymmetry, partial amorphism, shrinkage, lopsidedness, topheaviness, and other peculiarities, when Admiral Sir Horace Teakle yawned loudly and adjourned the session.

There was prolonged laughter when Mr E.L. Givens, a Portsmouth egg-sorter, said: 'Bald egg-operatives like Mr Kippinge should wear wigs. A bald man among eggs is asking for trouble.'
    The Chairman then told a story of a weary bishop who, at a confirmation service, said to the elderly man with the large bald head who was kneeling before him, 'I declare this stone – this – er – ostrich's egg to be well and truly laid.'
    C. Suet, Esq., recalled the meeting to the points at issue by reading passages from a chapter of Professor Gong's *Some Aspects of Egg Codification*.

Mr Leonard Wrotte suggested that in future a supervisor should carefully check any group of eggs about to be photographed to make sure that there were no human intruders. The Chairman retorted that this suggestion implied that people were always getting mixed up with eggs during photography.
    Supervisor Montague Manley said: 'I hardly think that it would add to the dignity of my position if I were to be seen at that sort of work. Any egg suspected of being a human face could be detected by the veriest tyro among our operatives.'
    Miss Benskin, a receptionist at Egg Hall, asked if Mr Kippinge's face had been stamped. She was told it had not. The stamping had been done before Mr Kippinge pushed his way into the group.

The Chairman yesterday addressed the Court of Inquiry. He said:

'We have here the case of a trained egg-operative who identified himself with his charges to such an extent that he took his place among them for a group photograph. I suggest that this action argues either a remarkable degree of loyalty and conscientiousness, or an equally remarkable lack of common sense and balance. There are limits to the expression of legitimate pride in one's work. One can grow too egg-minded. It must not be forgotten that every human face in a group of eggs displaces an egg in the photographic records, and thus disorganises the entire machinery of egg distribution. Mr Kippinge must be singularly unsophisticated not to have considered this point. I trust that in future he will try to mix with his fellow beings, rather than with eggs.'

An egg purchased from a Hammersmith grocer had a heart pierced with an egg-spoon drawn on the shell in indelible pencil. Underneath was written 'Beatrice'. It is believed that this may be the egg for which Mr Kippinge, as it were, deputised in the official photograph. This theory is supported by a grader who says that Mr Kippinge is a kindly man and may have substituted his face for an egg which would have looked absurd in a photograph.

Commenting on the outcome of the Kippinge case, C. Suet, Esq., said yesterday: 'To read some of the newspaper reports, one would imagine that the inclusion of a human face in a row of eggs was an everyday occurrence. This is far from being the case. The only occurrence of a similar nature of which Egg Hall has any record was when a cleaner, a Mrs Futtermere, fell while dusting a batch of eggs which were being photographed. She appeared in the photograph, but not as an egg.'

*   *   *

There is an unsavoury rumour that the Press Council is to inquire into the activities of the Beachcomber News Agency. There have been complaints that some of the items of news supplied exclusively to this column are not genuine news. 'A deliberate intention of deceiving the public,' said a spokesman, 'lowers the tone of journalism, misleads the sophisticated, and engenders mistrust in the less credulous readers.'

If the Press Council decides to investigate the Beachcomber News

Agency it will no doubt discover that reports and items of news quoted here from other papers are often falsely attributed to the Agency by readers. The point is that the Agency supplies me exclusively, and owing to its high standard, it takes care not to send me the far more fantastic utterances and occurrences which I read elsewhere.

Bathmat drama

Accused of stealing a bathmat from a public library, Arnold Dishcart, 29, of Uplin Road, Lidgett, said, 'When I saw all those books, something came over me.' His father, a professional contortionist, lives in Eltham, and was bitten by a spaniel last July, having returned from a visit to relatives in Penrith, one of whom is a chartered accountant, whose aunt was locked into a Bingo hall in Preston by mistake last year. She got out through an open window.

(Beachcomber News Agency)

On the road

Some time ago I predicted that there would be cars with tiny built-in swimming pools. Today I read of a car with a bar, a dressing-table, a small garden, and a bird-cage. Probably the tank for tropical fish, the gold mousetraps, the miniature laundry, the mink-lined, panelled dustbin, and the hat-stand were crowded out. To the less sophisticated I recommend the new thatched car, with casement windows framed in honeysuckle, and wicket-gates instead of doors. An electric gramophone in a diminutive byre plays rustic noises. Cows low and cocks crow. An Elizabethan chimney on the bonnet emits real smoke, and tin corn sprouts from the boot.

Unge Udmer explains

The revival of a play by Guillaume Apollinaire in which the audience is shouted at through a megaphone and pelted with ping-pong balls can hardly be called a major breakthrough. It is an example of his influence on Udmer, who, in *Fill the Balloon with Treacle, Mr Ninger*, had a man parading through the stalls during the second act. He was dressed as a Greek Customs officer, and led a pigeon on a string, pausing here and there to say, 'They will not be at home yesterday.'

Asked in an interview what he was trying to do in his plays, Udmer said, 'You could say that I see mankind as a composite entity, negatived by its own reactions to circumstance, yet inspired to a corroboration of all its terminal attitudes by the imponderable necessity for an almost passive kind of action. That is really what is meant by opposing a symbolic tangle of forces to the no longer tenable estimate of a man as a congeries of self-willed faculties.'

Sauce for the gander

Dear Sir,

I was disgusted and revolted by Mrs Tidmarsh's account of the footballer who played in a match on the very day his cat had died. How would he like it if, so soon after his own death, his cat took part in a cat show?

Amelia Porchcroft

Tiddililywinks?

A demand for a ruling on the correct spelling of tiddlywinks points out that tiddly, tiddley, tiddli, and even tiddledy are all used. The English Association booklet which I have been sent gives tiddly-winks as the official spelling, but omits Professor Keigwm's derivation of the word from the Low Saxon, *htidhul hwoenk*, a round bit of tin. In the Landes the French play a game called *tiddliwingues*. The Germans call it *Tiddlischen-Ausgewinkschengesellschaft*. In Calabria it is popularly known as *tidalivinci*, and in Norway *tydølvinkstrøm* is played on ice.

Functional socks

A plea for ventilated socks, to keep the feet cool in summer, is reasonable enough. Smart men have always favoured a bowler with a ventilation grille in the crown, to keep the head cool, and to serve as an egress for steam in a heat-wave. Before the invention of the hat-ventilator it was a common sight, when a man took off his bowler, to see a kind of light mist rising, as though dawn had come to the Essex marshes.

Tra-la-la

'Her little boy jumped about in the neighbour's concrete before it was set, and was reprimanded by the neighbour.'

(*News item*)

'I thought you were fond of children,' said the mother.

'In the abstract,' answered the neighbour, 'not in the concrete.'

Enter Sir Charles

One day, looking for new worlds to conquer, Captain Foulenough persuaded a friend of his who ran a West End restaurant to employ him. His job was to lunch or dine frequently at the restaurant, and to praise the food and wine loudly to the waiters. For this purpose he was to call himself Sir Charles Hawke-Rattingstone. Now and then he was to entertain friends with mythical titles, to impress the clientele. For a time all went well. The patrons noticed the deference of the waiters to Sir Charles, and heard his praise and the compliments conveyed by the head waiter to the chef. The restaurant became popular. Then, as we shall see, the trouble started.

Spoonerisms

An article about Spoonerisms says that nobody now knows which were the genuine utterances of Spooner and which were falsely attributed to him. My favourite is his alleged remark to a lady at a cricket match: 'I bet you a pair of draws it's a glove.'

Talk about suspense!

He was unable to move a muscle, for they had bound him to the railway line with ropes. The express train whistled in the distance. A tiger was approaching from one side, a cobra from the other. He could almost feel their breath in his face. A shot from the stationmaster's office whizzed over him. The girl with the knife, hatred in her face, was stealing softly up. How did Miles Carradine escape at least five terrible deaths by the skin of his three remaining teeth? He didn't. End thriller.

Not in the contract

Sir Charles Hawke-Rattingstone (Foulenough to us) soon grew weary of praising everything. One day he had a row with his friend the proprietor of the restaurant over the reimbursement of a large tip. In spiteful mood he far exceeded his allowance of wine and liqueurs. The head waiter, summoned to his table, approached smilingly, expecting the usual compliments. By now Sir Charles was accustomed to talking very loudly, so that neighbouring patrons could hear what he said. On this occasion he shouted, 'This place smells of mice.' The consternation of the staff and of the customers can be imagined. 'Send for the proprietor,' bawled Sir Charles, who was finally pacified with some very old brandy.

Interlude

The man who is reported to be keeping a lion in his front garden is said to have his own reasons for doing so. Perhaps it is an advertisement for the new unbreakable biscuit, which can be jumped on by anyone who is inclined to jump on biscuits.

PRODNOSE: I don't see the connection.

MYSELF: That is what the man said when he changed trains at Crewe Junction and was stranded for eight hours. A fig of Smyrna for you and your precise mind! The new biscuit is called Leo.

Need I say more?

I see that Udmer is being compared with Frampi. The resemblances are superficial. Whereas Udmer's concept of reality makes no compromise with that dream-world of the subconscious which Gaestang has called the semi-conscious, Frampi integrates actual happenings and occurrences with the texture of an imagined opposition of the subconscious to the fully conscious, thus producing an interplay of action and inaction on a new plane. Udmer sees motive or impulse as a reasoned acceptance-reaction, Frampi as an involuntary contest in the mind. If Udmer derives from anyone, it is from Baschke. Frampi is a literary descendant of Horbolik.

Sir Charles entertains

Sir Charles had suggested that it would be a smart thing to include in the menu a few very rare dishes, such as *salpicon* of red mullet and partridge, or whitebait fritters. The suggestion was adopted, and Sir Charles gave a party to titled friends. Baron Olio-Sasso (Joe Scarper, the bookie) was there, and the Comtesse Eloise de Cherchemidi de Balzaguette (Connie Upchurch), and Lady Milldew from Motheton Hall (Aggie Royce). Unfortunately the meal was preceded by a too prolonged stay in the Assyrian cocktail bar, and Sir Charles ordered, in his parade-ground voice, sheeps' eyes with Arab sauce and *cornichons* (pickled gherkins). The guests, hearing that this delicacy was not on the menu, settled for hash Tolstoy with parsnip sauce.

Now I understand

I have been shown a copy of a letter sent to the Press Council by Prodnose. It says, 'I wish to draw attention to certain news items in the column to which I occasionally contribute criticisms. These items, purporting to emanate from a so-called Beachcomber News Agency, I believe to be fabrications. The standards of journalism are lowered by such impositions on the public. My own frequent protests are inevitably met with mockery and contumely.'

Sir Charles is sacked

Having heard Sir Charles order the Arab delicacy sheeps' eyes, several other people ordered this dish. The proprietor did his best, and next day sheeps' eyes were on the menu. But Sir Charles was again in a rowdy mood, and complained that he had been served with Mongolian oysters. The head waiter tried to hush him, and assured him that they were Mongolian sheeps' eyes, their resemblance to oysters being well known. After the meal the proprietor sent for Sir Charles and told him that, in spite of their friendship, he could not afford to employ him any longer.

'You're losing your nerve, Sam,' said Sir Charles. 'Anyhow,' he added, 'it was fun while it lasted.'

'For you, no doubt,' said the proprietor bitterly.

There's a gadget for everything

Melisande writes:

> You can have fun fixing your own holes in cheese. Little plastic holes, in two sizes, and in sets of twelve, can now be bought. And at a recent Exhibition I noticed a spoon with a handle consisting of three prongs. Held in the middle it can be used either to lift gravy or to pick up, as on a fork, any foreign bodies which have fallen into the gravy. It can also be bent double so that both spoon and prongs can be used simultaneously – e.g., for stirring things.

In passing

An article on cookery says rightly that too much fuss can be made about sauces. Nearly four hundred years ago Cervantes said: 'Hunger is the best sauce in the world.'

Unpardonable error

Lo! On my lady's shaven pate
  A mother-bird did once intrude,
In sweet expectancy to wait,
  Full fain to hatch her fledgling brood.
And many a tear my lady shed,
  Before the bird hopped off her head.

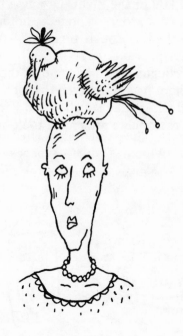

8

The Narkover Coughing Epidemic

Wild bursts of uncouth song aroused one of the housemasters at Narkover in the middle of the night. Dressing hastily, he went to investigate, and found a group of prefects holding revelry amid a litter of bottles labelled as cough mixture. Subsequent inquiries revealed that on the previous day all the prefects had suddenly developed hacking coughs, and had gone to the house matron for medicine. One of them had discovered that she was an agent for a wine merchant, and when they coughed and winked she dispensed the 'medicine' at a reasonable price, and took orders for more.

It was ascertained yesterday that the Narkover house matron who dispenses red and white wine in lieu of cough mixture at a reasonable price is the aunt of a new boy whose father is the wine merchant supplying the wines. There's such a din of coughing all over the school that you can hardly hear yourself speak. To give an air of genuineness to the racket, the masters who call for a bottle every morning wear mufflers and have their temperatures taken. One anxious mother wrote to the headmaster complaining that her son had, according to his letters home, been suffering from a cough ever since the term began, and that the bill for medicine seemed excessively high. Dr Smart-Allick replied: 'The finest medicine from the vineyards of France is an education in itself. We have to keep up this cough stunt because three of the school governors are teetotal.'

The Governors of Narkover have been informed of the conduct of the matron, 'who would seem to be more of a wine waiter than a matron.' Their informant was a new master planted by them for this purpose. Dr Smart-Allick at once offered him more than the governors were paying him, and he reported that he had been misinformed. Any small quantity of wine distributed was due to a chemist's error. But a *bon viveur* among the Governors remained suspicious. He visited the school, full of hope, and, coughing ostentatiously, asked the matron for a dose of the best, accompanying his demand with a roguish wink. The wily matron handed him a glass of nauseating cough mixture.

A prefect has complained to the headmaster that, when he went sick, he was charged 18s. 6d. for a bottle of *vin ordinaire* labelled 'Château Latour'.

'Hardly worth having a cough, was it?' said Smart-Allick, sarcastically.

When he asked the matron whether she was juggling with the labels, she said, 'My dear headmaster, officially I am supposed to be doling out medicine. Parents are already making a row about the bills. This boy ought to thank me for saving his father's money. The Latour goes at two quid. If I'd given him eighteen and sixpence-worth of cough mixture, he'd have some reason to make a fuss.'

'I know, I know,' said Smart-Allick, 'but he's the nephew of my turf accountant.'

'OK,' replied the matron, 'he'll get Latour next time.'

Thanks to a microphone concealed behind a large signed photograph of a bookie in the matron's room, the following conversation between her and a history master is now in possession of the Governors:

'Still coughing, Tom? What about a rather subtle Pichon-Longueville? Or a pretty Cos d'Estournel?'

'No, Bess, I rather think a Burgundy. Any of that Richebourg left?'

'Here you are. A quid to you – or a tip for the 2.15. What do you fancy?'

'Copper's Nark for the 2.15. Dead cert.'

'Right. If I win, you get your bottle for ten bob.'

'Fair enough.'

Dear Dr Smart-Allick,

Hearing that there is an epidemic of hacking coughs at Narkover, it occurred to me that you could use, say, three hundred bottles of *cough mixture* which I happen to be in a position to sell rather cheap. The lot consists of various reputable brands, and I don't think the house matron Bess (whom I knew as Irma some years ago) would object to my butting in on the firm which supplies her, if you tell her that the Golightly affair will remain a secret between us.

Yours sincerely,
de Courcy Foulenough

Dear Captain Foulenough,

The matron need know nothing of our deal, as I am laying down for my own use a fair amount of *cough-mixture*, in case I catch this cold that's going round; and also to supply some of the senior masters, who complain that Bess charges too much. Take care to label the cases correctly, as the last lot, by some absurd error, was labelled as wine, and the pipsqueak son of the proprietor of a temperance hotel blabbed to the Governors.

Yours sincerely,
Alexander Smart-Allick

The Governors of Narkover, stern-faced men who look as though concrete wouldn't melt in their mouths, descended on Narkover yesterday without warning. But 'Where there is wine, there is a grape-vine,' said Smart-Allick. The visit had been anticipated. On examination, the house matron's cupboard was found to contain nothing but repulsive medicines. From a nearby study came the strains of 'Lonesome for the Moon'.

'We encourage the house choir to practise frequently,' said the housemaster, Mr Brossells.

'Very commendable,' said the chairman. 'What are they singing?'

'An old English cantata,' replied Mr Brossells, red in the face with suppressed mirth. The crash of breaking glass was heard.

'That wretched cat on the prowl again,' said the matron.

The Old Narkoverian dinner

Disgraceful scenes marred the Old Narkoverian dinner at a West End restaurant last night. Dr Smart-Allick was in the chair, and, after the third course, an unknown sleeper was under it. The request that there should be no card-playing before the speeches was ignored, and only those with cheap and shoddy cuff-links emerged unscathed from the snatching started by a company director. Any old boy who laid down his cigar for a moment did so at his own risk. One late arrival brought an actress with him, saying she was his old girl. The plain-clothes detectives were helpless as their drink had been mixed by a very old boy. Five of them were relieved of their wallets. So great was the confusion that three of the speeches were made simultaneously, but the few who noticed this merely continued to sing songs in doubtful taste.

The culpable conduct of those plain-clothes men at the Old Narko-verian dinner who were not incapacitated by doctored drink has been explained. They were old boys masquerading as detectives. It was one of them who acquired the restaurant manager's note-case, that ingenuous fool having looked in to see that all was going satisfactorily. It was the brother of this 'detective' who started a fight at the top table when someone made an insulting remark about an old boy who had been in prison with him. An amusing incident occurred when the photographers came into the banqueting room. Several old boys ducked down under the table or covered their faces with napkins. The general opinion was that the photographs would be too useful to Scotland Yard.

Missing from the restaurant where the disgraceful Old Narkoverian dinner was held are 126 glasses. 1½ cwt. of cutlery, the toast-master's watch, and 42 overcoats belonging to guests who had dined in another room. An old boy who had broken out of prison to attend the reunion was arrested on the quay at Dover. The headmaster left during the fighting by a back door, chose a car, and drove to Hammersmith, possibly with a vague idea of an alibi in his mind. His aunt hid him in an outhouse for the rest of the day, and lost heavily at cribbage.

The Narkover way of life

Asked if corporal punishment is administered at Narkover, Dr Smart-Allick said: 'Corporal punishment goes on the whole time here, but it is unofficial. Any boy or master who wants to hit or beat somebody does it at his own risk.' Asked if there was no official caning for a boy who breaks a rule, the headmaster said: 'Rules are broken on such a scale that we should need hundreds of masters to enforce them, and even then the smaller masters would be quickly overpowered. It is best to let things take their course.'

A new boy at Narkover seemed to be singularly lazy during the writing of an essay. In fact he made no attempt to write a single word, but sat reading the racing news. The master questioned him. 'My dear sir,' replied the boy, 'my father told me never to put down anything in writing.' The master, hardly able to conceal his admiration for this excellent upbringing, eventually persuaded the boy that his essay would not be produced and used against him in a court of law. The boy then, with surly suspicion in his eyes, consented to write down a few innocuous sentences, but refused to put his name to them.

When the Filcham team visited Narkover for the annual soccer match it was arranged between the headmasters that the visiting team, before changing, should hand over all valuables to a reliable Narkover master, who would return them after the match. This was to prevent a repetition of last year's scandal, when the visiting eleven lost everything, including the match, and had to buy some suits of clothes from compassionate Narkover boys. This year Filcham were more alert. Though the articles they handed over could not be found after the match, two of their masters had made a clean sweep of several Narkover boys' studies.

Asked to comment on the finger-printing of boys at a school by detectives, Dr Smart-Allick said: 'Most of our boys come from homes where gloves are worn for certain jobs, so that when they arrive here the habit has been formed. After one rather scandalous incident (the theft of a roulette table from the music master's study) detectives came to finger-print all the masters and boys. A science master saved the honour of the school by saying this had already been done, and handing them a number of finger-prints of aborigines collected in Australia.'

One of the masters at Narkover reported to the headmaster that the only word a new boy seemed to be able to spell was IOU. 'There are few more useful words to know,' replied Smart-Allick. 'Armed with that word, most boys can go out into the world and hold their own.'

'Such an accomplishment hardly comes under the heading of education,' said the master.

Smart-Allick frowned and sneered. 'It will get most people further than Greek verbs,' he said.

The following notice has been posted up prominently at Narkover:

> Boys whose fathers have recently changed their names, for undisclosed reasons, are advised to take the new name of the parent to avoid complications. A boy who changes his name, owing to some temporary embarrassment, is advised to inform his parents, who might otherwise wonder what has become of their son. Masters who change their names should immediately inform the headmaster, in order to make it more difficult for the police to trace them.

A new boy at Narkover caused considerable speculation by flourishing wads of five-pound notes on all occasions. Asked by a master if they were genuine or counterfeit, he said: 'Well, what do *you* think? My father gave them to me. He said that anyone who used genuine notes at this sort of school was a simpleton.'

'That's all right,' said the master, 'it's just that we like to be sure.'

'Fair enough,' replied the boy.

Letter to Narkover boy

Dear Tom,

Your mother and I are worried about the story that a matron keeps red wine in her medicine bottles. Red wine is the best of all medicines, but, taken in excess by boys, it affects their card-sense. We gather from your last letter that your losses lately have been rather heavy. Either you are drinking too much medicine or you have forgotten the tips I gave you in the matter of poker. You ask what you can do to settle your card-debts, and your offer to honour your IOUs does you credit. Why not sell the motor-bicycle you say you found behind the cricket pavilion?

Your loving father

A regular rumpus has broken out at Narkover. A notice has appeared in the school magazine, the *Narkoverian*:

So long as the circulation of counterfeit money is confined to the school and its staff and scholars, no great harm is done. It is when local tradesmen begin to complain that there is a risk of a scandal. Parents who visit their sons are requested to make it clear that tips given to the boys in forged notes are intended for school purposes, such as card-debts, not for the purchase of articles from local shops.

The situation at Narkover has been called 'utterly preposterous' by a well-known (to the police) financier. The glut of forged notes has reached such proportions that there are not more than six poor boys in the school. The private bank, owned by a history master, apparently makes no distinction between genuine and forged notes, and the forgers rarely bother to make their productions resemble the real thing. As one master said: 'What began as an attempt to develop an unconventional school economy has degenerated into a vulgar farce.' A question is to be asked in the House.

Overhearing a boy say to another, 'The little prig paid me in genuine notes,' a master suspected that the notes may have been among a pile stolen from him on the cricket field.

'I want that boy's name,' he said.

The lad thus addressed said, 'He's not easy to find. His name is Pladding, but he's down on the school roll as Gacker. But, sir, is it a birching offence to pay in real notes?'

'That,' said the master, 'depends on whose notes they are, and where and how he got them.' He smiled as he said it, for only twice before had any Narkover boy ever called him 'Sir'.

Interviewed yesterday, Dr Smart-Allick said, 'So far this term thirty-two boys have run away. Those who go to the races usually return after a day or two. If they are still absent after a week we contact any fathers who are not in prison. Absent masters are usually assumed to be in some sort of trouble and lying low.'

*　　　*　　　*

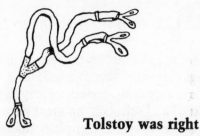

Tolstoy was right

'It is the bursting of braces at a public dinner which makes a man lose face.'   (*Tolstoy*)

The guest of honour rises to reply.
There is a silence broken only by
The swish of falling trousers.
There he stands,
Grabbing the elusive garment in both hands.
The toastmaster, so vigilant and alert,
Hauls up the breeches and tucks in the shirt,
While whispering sternly in the victim's ear:
'Hold them up tight, and you need have no fear.
A lack of braces, though it gives offence,
Is no impediment to eloquence.'

Contretemps

I knew a very nervous man,
Who thought of a peculiar plan
To counter the embarrassment
Of bursting braces. When he went
To dine with friends, he always wore
Two pairs of trousers – never more.
One fatal evening in Mayfair
His braces burst. The second pair
He had mislaid, the silly clown.
Both pairs of trousers tumbled down.

Another tragedy

Diffident Charlie always felt
That if he wore a broad, strong belt
As well as braces, there would be
No risk of a calamity.
Alas! One night in Chislehurst
Both articles of clothing burst,
And in a huff his Uncle Bill
Cut Charlie's name out of his will,
Remarking, 'One thing I abhor
Is trousers trailing on the floor.'

Postscript

You whose trousers never fall
May possibly feel quite secure.
Excuse me if I ask you all,
Are you so absolutely sure
Your confidence is justified?
No. Even you may live to see
The trousers which you wore with pride
Obey the law of gravity.

Tail-piece

'English is a beautiful language. Don't let's louse it up.'
(*American radio commentator*)

9

Roy Footle's Marathon

A Feat Worse Than Death

Tomorrow Roy Footle will try to break the water-ski land record. A traction-engine will tow him on his water-skis from Bibney St Vitus to Byle Hampney. He will live on energising capsules and raw haddock.

Roy, whose father is a Teignmouth dry-salter, has a sister who studied plumbing in Uttoxeter for some months, until she married a Shepton Mallet solicitor's clerk and settled down in Frensham, where her uncle had lived before moving to Appleby. Roy, 23, and a student of Turkish folklore, trains on mulberries soaked in soda-water.

The band of the Bibney St Vitus quarrymen played as Roy Footle started on his 'unorthodox pilgrimage' (I quote Councillor Carbide). As he stood ready to be towed, the rope attaching him to the traction-engine broke and he fell over backwards. The fire brigade, hastily summoned, brought another rope, but when the traction-engine started Roy had not grabbed the rope. He was left shouting at the driver. The engine backed, and Roy deftly grasped the rope and, secure on his water-skis, was dragged from the town amid a cheering multitude while the band played 'Jolly Old Captain Ginger'.

The first eight miles of Roy Footle's journey were covered without incident. But as he went through Scowlham a ploughman, who thought Roy was the victim of an accident and was being dragged along by the traction-engine, cut the rope with his jack-knife. Roy was precipitated into a ditch, and the engine, unaware of the contretemps, proceeded on its way. 'What you got on your feet?' asked the rescuer. Roy explained, and the post-mistress sent a message to the next village. The engine returned, a new rope was procured from a farmer, and the bizarre journey was resumed. 'I never did in all my life!' said the post-mistress.

At King's Knucklefurther a crowd obstructed the traction-engine. Many people carried banners bearing the legend: 'Welcome! Happy landing!' One man held aloft a placard saying, 'Arbitrate, Don't Litigate', and a group of youths representing the Anti-Chinese League handed out leaflets with 'Opium is the Religion of the People' in large red type. One or two local wags yodelled as Roy floundered by on his water-skis, and a fat matron in an upper window cried, 'Bring us back a chamois, matey!' A grocer's assistant struck up 'A Life on the Ocean Wave' but was hushed by the village constable.

Having covered thirty-two miles, the strange team halted outside the Bricklayers' Arms in Lower Hiccough, where rooms had been booked for the driver and for Roy. Unable to unfasten his water-skis, Roy could not get through the narrow inn door. So he slept in them in a barn. A start was made at dawn. About nine o'clock, outside the town of Abbot's Pudding, Roy went off at a tangent while negotiating a roundabout, and the traction-engine had to back into a hedge to rescue him. In the town there was a traffic jam, and Roy and his team had to submit to a ribald chorus while they waited. A little later the engine took a wrong turning down a lane that led only to a girls' school. The headmistress said a few ill-chosen words. The driver backed, forgetting Roy, who flung himself clear, and was bitten by the school dog.

At Nimbleworth there was a fracas. Footle's traction-engine met, in the narrow high street, Elvira Mulch, who is attempting to haul a barge over-land, by a rope clenched in her teeth, from Tavistock to Kendal. The two ropes became entangled. Elvira found herself hauling the traction-engine backwards, and Footle was dragged against the barge. Musclewoman Elvira can bite a telephone directory to bits at one blow of her granite teeth. After a village uproar, during which a draper was nearly strangled by the ropes, Elvira hauled the engine, the barge, and Footle out onto the common, where the muddle was sorted out. Today the plucky Amazon, the Penthesilea of Bumpton Regis, is complaining of toothache.

The entire population of Byle Hampney is preparing to welcome

Roy Footle and the traction-engine on their arrival. The Mayor, born free, but now in the chains of office, will read a speech from the neo-Palladian portico of the Town Hall and little Topsy Turvey, the two-year-old daughter of Sir Derek Turvey, will present Roy Footle with a bouquet of plastic nasturtiums. The Fire Brigade, in new tunics, will form a guard of honour while the Mayor inspects the traction-engine. After that there will be an appalling dinner in the Turvey Arms at which Footle will be presented with an old print of Byle Hampney in 1571 and the driver of the traction-engine with a life-membership of the Byle Hampney Literary Circle.

Yesterday, at 4.15 p.m. (Byle Hampney time), a hoarse roar from 17,346 throats announced the approach of the traction engine. Four minutes later the ugly piece of mechanism nosed its way into the town, and there, on the end of the tow-rope, was Roy Footle on his water-skis. As he came opposite the Town Hall, where the Mayor and the dignitaries awaited him, he slithered, owing to the slowing-down of the engine. There was an intake of 17,346 breaths, like the sound of the sea receding over shingle, as our hero cannoned into a surly Socialist Councillor, and rebounded into the arms of the astonished wife of the Mayor. 'Cannon off the red,' murmured the Mayor, while his wife, overwrought by the significance of the occasion, aimed a ceremonial kiss at Roy's forehead.

*   *   *

May I be steeped in stinking camomile by the demons of St Julien-le-Repos and thwacked by the howling horde of hobgoblins from Prèmanon, whose lives are lived between the dish and the flagon – may they all set upon me if I have not once again read the old boast that this is a hard-headed, unsuperstitious age. Rat me if the whole country is not up to the fetlocks in astrological fish-fash, and those who are not chained to the signs of the zodiac – and what a zodiac! I wouldn't give you a groat for it – are hazarding their lives in the gutter to avoid walking under a ladder at 3.46 on a Tuesday. The great-godmother of Trievel Rasimus, who made such a din in her drinking at the Cheval de Bronze in Remiremont, always wore a *green* jerkin and lived to be 114.

The most enterprising fortune-teller I ever fell in with came into a small restaurant in Bordeaux. He went from table to table handing out little printed leaflets which foretold each recipient's fortune. Nearly everyone bought a leaflet and threw it away. My own informed me that I was destined to win a cycle race. He had chosen probably the only man in Europe who has never ridden a bicycle.

Powerful symbolism

At last English audiences are to see one of Udmer's strange masterpieces. His *Awning Over The Moon* is an attempt to depict in terms of everyday life the despair of a lighthouse-keeper who is convinced that he should have been a jockey. While he and his assistant are discussing the matter the untended light fails and a fog comes down. A ship in distress bangs into the lighthouse, and the only survivors are a beautiful Bulgarian gipsy and a horse. With a cry of joy the frustrated keeper mounts the horse and falls off. In his despair he kills the gipsy, the assistant keeper, a laundress who lives there as his aunt, and the horse. He then shoots himself with the laundress's revolver. There is a moment's silence. Then a foghorn is heard. Curtain.

A sample of the dialogue will reveal its trenchancy.

GIPSY: I think you were never on a horse before.

KEEPER: (*furious and humiliated*) What is that to you? How could you understand that my soul has lived on a horse for years?

ASSISTANT: If your soul rides as badly as your body—

LAUNDRESS: Do not taunt him, Bulzett.

KEEPER: Go on! Laugh at me! (*Advances menacingly on the assistant.*)

GIPSY: We have a saying. 'When there is an awning over the moon, the seagull goes mad.' (*She begins to hum a Balkan lullaby.*)

And so on.

For recitation at parties

While tugging at a glutinous meringue
  His braces burst with a melodious twang.
The hostess, with delightful *savoir-faire*,
  Began to hum a catchy little air;
In his embarrassment, he heard her say,
  'I will sing, Mr Wentworth, if you'll play.'
Angrily he replied: 'I must regret
  That single note is all you're going to get.
An accompanist in this distressing plight,
  Can't burst his braces more than once. Goodnight.'

Tiddlywinks news

The burning question arises: Is Alexander Flobbe an amateur or a professional? As a member of a popular tiddlywinks team, the North Pibsey Rovers, he accepted a cheque for £14 7s. 3d., subscribed by the local branch of the Friends of Asia, and an enamel rose-bowl from Lady Harness, who once donated a set of silver tiddlywink pieces to the club. As a professional, Flobbe would have to enter the tiddlywinks hall by a small side door instead of the main door, which is reserved for amateurs, and he would no longer be entitled to the Mr, with initials, on score-sheets.

Udmer's masterpiece

Rehearsals of Udmer's *Awning Over The Moon* are to start soon. Gwecklick has designed an octagonal lighthouse, the whole of which revolves during the action of the play. Here is another tense scene.

LAUNDRESS: A horse is out of place in a lighthouse.

KEEPER: No. It is the lighthouse that is out of place. A question of adjusting ideas to reality.

LAUNDRESS: What's reality? The lighthouse is real, if it is here. As real as the horse.

KEEPER: There is a reality which we accept as a semblance of reality. Things inanimate lack the full reality of things animate. A stone is not real as a man is real. A building is not real as an animal is real.

And so on.

Twenty years of uproar

Reading of a conductor whose pace was too hot for the singers in an opera, I remembered how Rustiguzzi deals with this sort of thing. She holds up an aria by singing more and more slowly, so that if the conductor does not want to be left with a silent orchestra while the singer finishes the aria, he has to moderate his impatience to get it over. The conductor who finishes ahead of the singer may try to cover his embarrassment by joining in again. In which case Rustiguzzi increases her tempo, making him look a fool for the second time.

Dr Rhubarb's corner

E.F. WRITES: My husband washes his face in the morning with his hat on. Is not this a bad example for the children?
DR RHUBARB SAYS: Not if he washes his hat too while he is about it.

(*Advt.*)

Biter bit

The Italian who bit a dog the other day was apparently not a reporter getting a 'new angle'. He could probably find employment with a butcher to prevent dogs from stealing meat, or by someone living in a remote cottage ('Beware of the man'). There was a man who deliberately encouraged his dog to steal from shops. One victim of this trick ran out of the shop, and shouted at the man: 'Is that your dog?'

'He was,' said the man, 'but he's keeping himself now.'

Mimsie Slopcorner and C. Suet, Esq.

Mimsie Slopcorner has been elected May Queen of Shobbleborough. Her Maids of Honour will be up at dawn on May 1 to present Mimsie with the symbolical nuts gathered for the occasion. A plastic maypole will be erected in the Market Square, and round this the inhabitants will dance a mimba, watched by Mimsie and the Mayor from the roof of the Town Hall. Asked if Charlie Suet would be present, Mimsie said: 'That is for him to decide.' The temporary coolness between them is said to be due to Suet's disapproval of the kiss given to Mimsie by an alderman when she was Plastic Dustbin Queen of North Croydon.

It has been Charlie Suet's custom for many years to call for Mimsie Slopcorner and take her and her aged dog for a walk. A husband and wife have noticed them passing for as long as they can remember. One day the husband said: 'Do you think those two will ever marry? They've been courting long enough.'

'Indeed they have,' replied the wife. 'They've worn out two dogs so far.'

Personal

EX-DEBUTANTE would exchange tiny four-poster bed specially made for budgerigar, for pair of Nampound de luxe adhesive serge eyebrows (green).

Udmer's masterpiece

In a powerful scene the laundress explains herself.

KEEPER: It is the darkness. Always darkness. Not knowing who is there.

LAUNDRESS: Nobody is anywhere. By the time I am here, I have begun to be somewhere else, like your light, which flashes here, and yet is out at sea. Who can reason with that? If those I met knew where they were going, they would turn back, and it would be too late.

KEEPER: Too late for you or for them?

LAUNDRESS: *(with a sudden cry)* For the whole world! *(Sobs.)* That is why it is no good. Perhaps the darkness is better, after all.

How the other half lives

An alarm clock which turns on lights and springs a mouse-trap sounds rather Strabismal. The sage of Waggling Parva once invented an electric pencil-sharpener, which, when connected to a saw, lowered a saucepan from the roof of a shed by a cord fastened to a sieve weighted down with onions. When a lever was reversed, a convertible wheelbarrow overturned, loosening the rope round a trestle on which was a sack of ferrets. 'Picturesque rather than useful,' shrewdly commented a passer-by.

For the ladies

Melisande writes:

> Bodawerbl's *maison* is showing the new semi-fitting cutaway *redingote*, with bubble sleeves and gordings of chamfered twine. This gives an Albanian silhouette, and is worn with a sausage-brown worsted surcoat of ruffled *mingot*, sluttered around the hem with Indonesian *sakri*. Varnished elbows peeping through the slotted sleeves add a sophisticated touch to what is really a simple version of Quagg's foreshortened demi-jabot.

Dementi

I see that a student of theatre has said once again that women do not make good clowns. My dear sir, take a look at the fashion pages of any newspaper today.

Short story

The conversation at the dinner table was mostly about big business, and Sir Ronald Rathouse was rather irritated by the young man next to him, who wanted to talk about art, with a view to his future. 'Have you ever been done in oils?' he asked the wealthy magnate.

'Never,' replied Sir Ronald testily, 'but I lost a packet over the Joxton merger.'

Udmer's masterpiece

LAUNDRESS: These are my great-uncle's braces. He bought them in Swansea.

KEEPER: You live in the past. What use are the braces of a dead uncle to a woman?

LAUNDRESS: (*softly*) What use is a withered rose? It holds the past like an old song.

KEEPER: Whoever tried to keep his breeches up with a withered rose?

LAUNDRESS: You are a utilitarian.

KEEPER: No, no. I have no religion.

LAUNDRESS: (*in a reverie*) My uncle Fred wore these the day my mother took me to Barnstaple Fair.

Open letters to motorists

'Something,' writes a peevish motorist, 'should be done for motorists.'

O fractious monster, is it not enough that whole villages are being demolished and towns replanned to please you? For you the countryside is littered with hideous garages, and the cities become car-parks. Yours is the freedom to drench the air with the stink from your machine, and to harry the pedestrian with impunity. For you are the abominable lamp-standards erected, with their ghoulish light. For your gratification landscapes are reshaped, hedges torn out, quiet valleys desecrated, woods cut

down, winding lanes straightened and broadened. What more do
you want, arch-fool of the world, and pest of every common man?

No harbinger of spring

She flung her window wide
  And in excitement cried,
'So soon! So soon! So soon!
  The cuckoo's call!'
Alas, what she had heard
  Was not that little bird,
But the village postman's hiccough.
  That was all.

10

Before Mr Justice Cocklecarrot

The Case of the Talking Horse, and
The Case of the Erroneous Asphalt

In the Court of Uncommon Pleas yesterday, Mr Justice Cocklecarrot refused a mandatory stay of replevin to restrain the plaintiff,
Mrs E.L. Utterleigh, from starving the defendants, Charles Bobbity
and Henry Lumpe. The defendants, impersonating a horse, had
taken up their quarters in Mrs Utterleigh's stables. Her claim
that while they remain *in situ* they must eat oats or nothing was
characterised as inhumane and unreasonable. Lumpe (the hind legs)
was alleged to have refused with violent oaths to desert Bobbity (the
front legs).

Mr Tinklebury Snapdriver, for the defence, maintained that since
nobody really believed that Messrs Lumpe and Bobbity were a
real horse, to expect them to eat oats was unreasonable. Mr
Honeyweather Gooseboote, for the prosecution, said that unless
the men declared themselves for what they were, by emerging
from the disguise they had adopted, their unwilling hostess could
hardly be expected to serve them in the stables with three-course
meals. Such foolery would demoralise the other horses.

COCKLECARROT: Were they supposed to eat their oats with a knife
and fork, off a plate?

SNAPDRIVER: Or to eat their soup, meat and pudding out of a
manger or a nosebag?

GOOSEBOOTE: Mrs Utterleigh, of Farabole House, Pilcombe, made
the round of her stables and was surprised to find an extra horse
there. She thought its hide looked ill-fitting. She offered it a
handful of oats. The mouth opened and a raucous voice said,
'Bacon an' eggs, miss, please.' She then realised that the horse
was a man, or rather, two men, as a second voice, in the rear,

said, 'And marmalade.' She rang up the local police who verified the human contents of the hide.

COCKLECARROT: Did she evict the tenants?

GOOSEBOOTE: No, m'lud. She was in a daze, as it were.

GOOSEBOOTE: Now, Mrs Utterleigh, when did you first suspect that it was not a horse you were harbouring in your stables?

MRS UTTERLEIGH: When it started laughing, and the two halves came apart.

GOOSEBOOTE: Did all this put the other – the real horses – off their food?

MRS UTTERLEIGH: No. But it put me off mine.

GOOSEBOOTE: What made you think, even for a moment, that they were a horse?

MRS UTTERLEIGH: Well, I'd never seen a four-legged man, with hoofs, a tail and hairy fetlocks.

GOOSEBOOTE: That is understandable.

COCKLECARROT: It passes my understanding how a respectable and educated lady, used to horses, ever came to extend the hospitality of her stables to these two men.

SNAPDRIVER: They arrived by night, m'lud, and neighed, whinnied, and pawed the ground most realistically. The lady is a member of the Homeless Horse League.

GOOSEBOOTE: The boy Charlie Towle will testify that the front part of the horse yawned at him, and the other part hissed, 'Steady, Harry!'

COCKLECARROT: A remarkably unequine reprimand, surely.

SNAPDRIVER: Your name is Charlie Towle?

TOWLE: Yes, thank you.

COCKLECARROT: Thank your parents, not learned counsel.

SNAPDRIVER: When your employer told you to stable these – er – this so-called horse, did you think it was a horse?

TOWLE: No, sir. It winked and whispered, 'Here we go!'

SNAPDRIVER: Why did you not inform your employer of this?

TOWLE: I couldn't disillusion her. She had already christened it – er – them 'Damson'.

Mr Justice Cocklecarrot winced at the intervention of a sailor, who claimed that he, too, had formed part of the horse, but had made his escape, as there wasn't room for three. 'The horse must have had six legs,' said Cocklecarrot.

'No,' said the sailor, 'I sat on Lumpe's shoulders.'

'That must have given the animal a hump,' said Cocklecarrot. 'I wonder nobody said there was a camel in the stables.'

After a whispered consultation, Mrs Utterleigh was asked if she had noticed the hump. 'I thought it was a bump,' she said, 'where the horse had banged itself against something.'

SNAPDRIVER: We have heard the plaintiff assert she thought the hump, made by the intrusion of the sailor, was a bump on the horse's back.

GOOSEBOOTE: To raise a bump on its back a horse would have to bang itself against the stable roof.

COCKLECARROT: That is possible with a very low roof.

GOOSEBOOTE: I submit, m'lud, that the sailor could not have sat on the shoulders of either the hind legs or the forelegs under a very low roof.

COCKLECARROT: So be it. We cannot have a demonstration of this feat in court.

Mr Justice Cocklecarrot said yesterday: 'The introduction of a third party into this human horse contributes an element of farce into what was already a comedy. For Mrs Utterleigh, the sailor represented a third mouth to feed – though, originally, only one mouth was suspected. We must not too hastily blame the plaintiff for taking the alleged horse at its face (and body) value, and restricting the meals to equine fare. How many of us, on discovering that a horse was three men, would continue to allow them the run of our stables? The case is adjourned to allow the collection of further evidence. The three defendants must show cause for their unconventional behaviour.'

The Case of the Erroneous Asphalt

Mr Justice Cocklecarrot has postponed the hearing of the complicated case, Whackstraw Industrial Units, Mrs Rowena Stalt, Canon Crisp, and Wivenham Public Baths versus Commodore Tiller, Renston Gas Undertakings Inc., Alderley Ferret Farm, and Lifeguardsman Stellfurther, Anthony Froyle intervening. The case concerns a shipment of asphalt delivered to a retired lighthouse-keeper in error, but there is a suspicion that the whole thing is a hoax.

Messrs Treacle, Treacle, Treacle & Treacle, solicitors for Alderley Ferret Farm, a company formed by a Mr Gorrickle, have revealed that their client is a Major Hugh Thunder, his alias having been adopted under the terms of his grandfather's will. It was he who denied that Canon Crisp had any financial interest in the Wivenham Public Baths, whose swimming instructor denied all knowledge of the Renston Gas Undertakings.

The application, on behalf of the Wivenham Public Baths, for a writ of sequestration, prompted Mr Justice Cocklecarrot to ask, 'Sequestration of what?'

Mr Tinklebury Snapdriver, for the defence, said, 'My lord, it has come to my notice that Mrs Melcott—'

'And who,' queried the judge, 'may she be?'

There was an outbreak of murmuring, and Mr Honeyweather Gooseboote, for the prosecution, said suavely, the writ should be a writ of *quo warranto*, as in Budge versus Culpepper.

'Plenary?' asked the judge.

'Plenary,' said Gooseboote firmly, adding with a sneer, 'if it please the court.'

Mr Justice Cocklecarrot was informed by Mr Honeyweather Gooseboote that, pending application for a legally enforceable contract, so constituted, *ceteris paribus*, conditional reservations in the matter of the re-examination of witnesses would be subject to a plea of retainder entered by the gasworks manager. The judge replied that the manager, as titular residuary, was entitled to plead *bona fide* discrimination *in toto* within the qualifying period laid down. Mr Tinklebury Snapdriver quoted a corporation by-law of William IV, defining the exact implications of statutory injunctions.

It transpires that the asphalt delivered in error to the retired lighthouse-keeper was the result of a telephone conversation by two people who had each got the wrong number. That is how the public baths attendant, Shrewlake, became involved with the ferret farm run by Colonel Porter, who thought Shrewlake was a representative of Whackstraw Industrial Units. 'All this,' said Cocklecarrot, 'can be settled out of court, given good will, patience, tolerance, *savoir-faire*, common sense, determination, humanity, and a reasonable amount of intelligence – none of which qualities appear to be possessed by anybody concerned in the matter.' (*Case dismissed.*)

The Lighthouse Ruling

Mr Justice Cocklecarrot has been consulted as to the legal position of a man who boards an abandoned lighthouse built half in and half out of territorial waters. The learned judge said: 'The position of a lighthouse in extraterritorial waters may be held to be in maritime territory in contact with the sea or seas. No trespass (*nulla violatio*) can be proven against a person who remains in the coastal portion of this said lighthouse, though both portions are, *sine die necnon cum sostulatione*, deemed to be maritime, in that they are both in contact with the concomitant waters.'

Cocklecarrot went on to explain that a writ of *condimentum*, with stay of replevin, applied for by the Ministry of Bubbleblowing, would be *ultra vires* unless the occupant were not only in the territorial portion, but seen to be in it. (See *Mrs Faffnage v. Protection of Lighthouses Committee, Commodore Marrowfat Intervening.*) In the case of the occupant himself being half in one portion and half in the other, albeit in transit, a writ of *mandamus* may be lodged with the Court of Uncommon Pleas, *coram populo*.

Officials of the Admiralty have asked the Cocklecarrot committee whether a man who sleeps in an abandoned lighthouse, with half his body in territorial waters and half in coastal waters, is subject to puisne capillation. Cocklecarrot replied: 'The body being mobile, such a man could sleep sideways, i.e., latitudinally instead of longitudinally, east to west, instead of north to south, provided that no portion of his *corpus* or body projected over the demarcation line. In such a case, see *Fossgrove v. Maldrick Dredgers and Mrs Mouthe.*'

Mr Justice Cocklecarrot laid down yesterday that a man who sleeps sideways, east to west, in a lighthouse designated as being in territorial waters, is held to be sleeping at sea, the edifice being in contact with the sea or seas. If, however, a portion of his body protrudes into coastal waters, maritime law regards him as sleeping in both coastal and territorial waters, since each portion of his body may be said to be in the edifice, the edifice itself being, for purposes of exact definition, ambivalent, owing to the ambience of the sea or seas, both coastal and territorial.

*   *   *

> Reader, I offer a surprise.
>   These verses of a sort
> Are a convenient disguise
>   For poverty of thought.
> When there is nothing much to say,
>   I like to pass the time
> In an innocuous kind of way
>   By throwing you a rhyme.

PRODNOSE: It seems quite pointless, may I say?
MYSELF: If it amuses you, you may.
(ENTER, *dancing, the fairies* QUARTBOTTLE *and* GROGBLOSSOM.)

The Lentil-Webfold Controversy

Dear Sir,

Mrs Lentil evidently knows little of horses. Her suggestion that a man who rides a horse backwards should face the tail instead of the head shows a pitiful misunderstanding of the whole thing. To turn your back on the horse, as it were, is to lead it to surmise that

94

you are no longer in command of the situation. Nor can you see what is coming along in front, or rather, behind, if you are facing the tail while going backwards.

F.S. Webfold

Dear Sir,

   Neither Mrs Lentil nor Mr Webfold touched on the technique of suspending oneself under the horse's belly instead of sitting on his back. This is a favourite trick of the Ahaha tribesmen when engaged on night raids. The sentries in watch-towers see only riderless horses in the light of their flashlamps. Then, with a yell, the raiders spring to earth.

T.R. Mutterspoon

Dear Sir,

   Surely Mrs Lentil had in mind a horse at a circus going backwards, not the absurd tactics of an African tribe. Nor does Mrs Trott clarify matters by dragging in reference to Major Fawle's famous ride from Shrewsbury to Appleby, kneeling on the saddle. Such things are but tricks and vulgar by-products of equestrianism. No good purpose is served by Mr Webfold's red herring.

George Fafnagle

Dear Sir,

   Mountains are being made out of my humble molehill. I had no intention of decrying hunting or sneering at cavalry officers, as Miss Fopple hints, when I advanced a plea for facing the tail instead of the head when riding backwards. The allegation that I know nothing of horses is refuted by the fact that not only is my niece employed at a livery stables, but my late husband drove for a brewery for twenty-three years.

Agatha Lentil

Dear Sir,
  What on earth has the fact that Mrs Lentil's husband once drove for a brewery got to do with it? Presumably he didn't face the back of the dray while driving. All this about facing the horse's tail is sheer rubbish. If a drayman drove with his face towards the back of the dray, he wouldn't see the horse at all and there would be nothing to drive.

Basil Penfold

Dear Sir,
  I read the correspondence about sitting backwards on a horse and I should like to say that not only was I unable to understand what it was about or to what it referred, but each letter seemed to me completely meaningless. As I cannot believe that the so-called controversy was entirely purposeless, I should like to have an explanation.

F. Wainwright

It was all symbolic, but I don't think so.

★   ★   ★

This does not happen every day

A tailor has said that trousers should be exactly the right length, falling neatly over the shoes. That may be, but I knew a rich man whose trousers were so long that he was followed by pages who held up the ends like a lady's train. In a high wind they billowed, and once he was blown through an open window into a solicitor's office in Kilburn. The pages fell into the basement. The solicitor, noticing the dandy's struggles to disentangle himself, said coldly, 'Why not tighten your braces, sir?'

Onion

Still as a windless night
Till some hand moves it
This way or that, the onion
Reveals its essential reality.
Inanimate being manifested
By an acceptance of subjective
Reality in the beholder.
Paint it, weigh it, it still
Remains an onion.

(Roland Milk)

Mimsie Slopcorner at the
Bottlehurst Pageant

Mimsie Slopcorner will again appear in several tableaux in this summer's Bottlehurst Through The Ages Pageant. It will be remembered (or forgotten, what the deuce do I care?) that last year she got her spear entangled in the wig of Egghed the Bald, and fell off the milk-float into Councillor Fullbright's arms. Being a married man, he passed her, as deftly as any three-quarter, to the Mayor. As the *Bottlehurst Argus* reported: 'She was hoisted back on to the float, unfondled, but dishevelled and squinting a trifle.'

Before the first rehearsal of the Bottlehurst pageant, a local innkeeper announced that drinks for the band were on the house. That may explain, as the Mayor said, why the band turned up an hour late, and why while some were playing a Sousa march others were playing 'The Last Rose of Summer'. A stupefied minority fumbled idiotically with their instruments, and a bassoon made a sound like a frightened walrus. Said Mimsie Slopcorner, 'The poor men are tired out.'

The Mayor spoke plainly to the band yesterday. He said, 'We all know that playing is thirsty work, but there is no excuse for making a parade of thirst before so much as a single note has been blown. At our second rehearsal several instrumentalists were wiping their mouths with their sleeves ostentatiously, and I noticed a clarionettist so overcome with maudlin giggling that he missed four bars of 'Soldiers of the Queen'. This is repellent. As soon as a rehearsal is over, the bandsmen crash into the opening bars – in a strictly non-musical sense.'

In the tableau representing the Return from Agincourt, no armour will be worn this year. The reasons given by the committee for this decision are: that the inexperienced find armour harder to get out of than to get into; that last year there were cries of 'Sardines!' as the warriors trooped past the Bottlehurst Arms; that Councillor Tombs was hit by a spent helmet; and that the villagers in armour looked more like demented amateur actors than like fifteenth-century soldiers.

With the arrival of Mimsie Slopcorner, rehearsals become more orderly. She is already word-perfect. Representing the spirit of Bottlehurst, she declaims a prologue outlining the history of the village from the time when Bottlehurst was but a name:

> From earliest days our quiet Bottlehurst
> Was never tainted by a foolish thirst
> For fame . . .

At the word thirst, an outbreak of coarse laughter from a few men was quickly suppressed.

Yesterday the incident of King Charles's halt for a drink at the village inn after the battle of Worcester was rehearsed. Unfortunately the King found several friends in the inn. Time passed. The royal escort dismounted and went in to fetch the monarch. More time passed. The spectators heard voices singing 'My old man's a fireman'. Mr Gooke, the Master of Ceremonies, finally persuaded the King and his escort to come out and get on with the rehearsal. It was noticed that King Charles mounted his horse uneasily, and sat on it the wrong way round.

'Drink is the enemy of the thirsty class,' said a Bottlehurst solicitor who has followed the rehearsals closely. Yesterday everything went off without a hitch, unless the apple impaled on Mimsie Slopcorner's spear by a youth to whom local history made no appeal, may be called a hitch. Mimsie removed the offending fruit with the grand air of a duchess at a banquet delicately picking a bit of food off her fork.

The news of the victory of Waterloo was brought to Bottlehurst in June, 1815, by a man who rode breakneck from Tiddlecombe. The rehearsal of the incident went wrong. The rider was supposed to shout, as he rode through the village, 'Victory! Victory!' But he had his own ideas. He pulled up outside the Bottlehurst Arms, and declaimed a speech composed by his uncle. 'Our Iron Duke hath hit the foul Caucasian tyrant Boney for six. Mine host inviteth us all to celebrate in a bumper of ale.'

The old, old question has arisen. Shall Mimsie Slopcorner be kissed by the Mayor outside the Town Hall? Mimsie has always disliked the routine. A councillor suggested that the Mayor should kiss her hand. But other councillors objected to the introduction of Continental gestures into an English pageant. The idea of a military salute was abandoned as ridiculous.

At yesterday's rehearsal, the decorated farm-cart in the tableau Bottlehurst Today got one wheel caught in a ditch. Mimsie Slopcorner, holding aloft the Cornucopia filled with flowers and tomatoes, staggered against a shepherd, and both were covered with the contents of the great horn of plenty. A three-piece ladies' orchestra at the back of the cart wavered in a powerful rendering of an Edward German dance. Order was restored by the village policeman, but not before a slight tomato-battle had broken out among the spectators.

Drink continues to play a leading part here in Bottlehurst. Said one of the organisers, 'A dropped clarinet in the middle of "Land of Hope and Glory" augurs ill for the great day, and a rehearsal becomes a music-hall turn when Mimsie Slopcorner, as Britannia, pokes the instrument with her trident, and says loudly, "Melhuish, you have dropped that clarinet again." The obvious mirth of the villagers during such unrehearsed incidents is no guarantee of the approval of the more sophisticated spectators on the day itself.'

*   *   *

A note on a politician who 'has his ears to the ground' is rather startling. One ear is usually enough, owing to the difficulty, admitted even by leading contortionists, of getting more than one ear at a time into that position of vantage. The difficulty is increased by the necessity of keeping the nose to the grindstone. 'If the grindstone is placed in a little hole in the ground,' says the manual, 'the ears can brush the soil on either side at the top of the hole.' Very ingenious, but what public servant would care to be seen by his constituents in such an undignified attitude?

Song

A politician on the fence
Should always sit astride.
This makes it easier to climb down
On one or other side.

What can it mean?

GOAN DBOI LY OU RHE ADI NABUC KETOF TAR

This inscription, in an unknown language, has been found on a palaeolithic stone discovered at Rickmansworth. Archaeologists are trying to decipher it.

No nasal tiddlywinks

An invitation to Evans the Hearse, of Aberbananer, to use his nose in a tiddlywinks championship has been refused. The Welsh

Nasal Pea-Pushing Association has pointed out that: 'The nose is for pushing peas, not for flicking counters into a receptacle. The pressure exerted by the nostrils on a counter would destroy that delicacy of touch which is essential to a nasal pea-pusher.' Evans himself is in training at the moment for an attempt on Cwm Hafod. At his headquarters in Llanlebwrwst he punches a small silk bag with his nose, and practises thrusts with alternate nostrils, using a pea suspended from the ceiling.

The ignoblest Roman of them all

'Organising a pageant requires great patience,' says an article. A village pageant was being rehearsed last year by a gracious lady. Her attention was attracted to an ancient Roman whose clothes didn't fit, and who was evidently not accustomed to handling a spear.

'Webley,' she said, 'are you Appius Claudius?'

'No, mum,' he replied, 'miserable as 'ell.'

Dr Rhubarb's corner

E.N. WIRTES: My daugher's fiancé called the other day with a bottle sticking out of his pocket. He said it was medicine for a sore ankle. My husband said he too had a sore ankle, and they both went into the backroom 'for a talk'. Is he the man my daughter should marry?

DR RHUBARB SAYS: Undoubtedly – if she suffers from a sore ankle.

Folk song

A goldfish sang on a shady bough –

PRODNOSE: Surely you mean a goldfinch?

A goldfinch sang in a shady bowl
    With water up to his neck
And the lyric he chose to soothe his soul
    Was 'The Boy on the Burning Deck'.
Bang! Suddenly and without a sound
    Both bowl and goldfinch burst
And none of the people standing round
    Knew which of the two burst first.
Refrain:
With my dumbledown, dumbledown, di-do,
And who'll wed parson's daughter?

The Rickmansworth Stone

Innumerable letters about the Rickmansworth Stone persuade me
that I have underestimated the interest aroused by the discovery.
I have just heard from Professor Tunnicliffe that a second, almost
obliterated inscription has been found, below the first, on the stone.
It seems to read thus:

A NYBO DYW HO TA KE STHETR OUB
LETODE CIP HERTH ISNO NSE NSEI SAB
IGGE RFOO LTHA NITH OUG HT.

'Iron-Nostril' Balzarotti

'At last it seems that Evans the Hearse will meet his nasal
pea-pushing Waterloo.' Thus the *Aberbananer Argus*. 'Iron-Nostril'
Balzarotti went round the Penmaenmawr stadium yesterday in four
seconds under the four hours, using the alternate nostril technique.
Evans, who brings the entire nose into play, relies more on stamina
than speed. He wears his opponents down, and then spurts. He is
at his best in rugged mountain country, and his Snowdon record of
two hundred and thirteen hours, four minutes and twelve seconds
has never been challenged. When the two champions meet in the
cross-country race from Denbigh to Dolgelly it will be, says the
Brecon Messenger, 'a contest between a thunderbolt and a streak
of lightning.'

A questionable precedent

A man who fixed wheels to his hat so that he could drag it
along behind him in hot weather, stayed too long in a public
house and was arrested for being drunk in charge of a hat. He

pleaded that the hat was not a vehicle within the meaning of the Act. Asked what Act, he said, 'Any Act.' The question then arose as to parking a hat, fixing a rear-light to it for use after dark, and so on. The magistrate said, 'It is only when a hat has a tiny outboard engine that it becomes a vehicle. Nevertheless, if everybody hauled his hat about in this fashion, new regulations would be called for.'

Ninety-four dentists in riot

'He was calmly sucking a stalk of grass while lowering his putt at the last hole.' *(Golf item)*

'The proof of the putting is in the eating,' commented a silly spectator.

Evans *v.* Balzarotti

From 'Iron-Nostril' Balzarotti's training headquarters outside Aber-bananer a report comes that the Perugia virtuoso packs a tremendous left-nostril punch. He buffeted a pea seven inches yesterday, feinting with the right nostril, and then leading with the left. This unorthodox style is more tiring than the rhythmic thrusts of Evans, using the entire nose. Said Evans's trainer, Matt Jones, 'When Evans gets going, the pea won't know what hit it.' For luck Evans wears round his neck the golden pea he won at the contest arranged by the organisers of Swindon's *Semaine gastronomique*.

Molesworth, G.R., etc.

A leading actor is to give readings from the *List of Huntingdonshire Cabmen*. There is much speculation as to the method he will use to make a mere list of names and initials dramatic and moving. 'It can only be done,' he said, 'by emphasising certain names or initials, or by taking a number of names, beginning in a low voice, and gradually raising the pitch until the climax arrives with, say, Clarke, E.N. This second method is more effective and creates more suspense than suddenly thundering out 'Relf, W.' Asked if he would retain the alphabetical order of the original, he said, 'Of course. That is the whole point of such a list.'

Something to do with me

Dear Sir,
   I suppose the *List of Huntingdonshire Cabmen* is intended as a joke. Otherwise I fail to see what possible interest such a list

could be, except to the families of these men. Perhaps there is some satirical meaning in your list. If so, I can only say it must be a very highbrow one, and if the men exist it is surely a joke in very bad taste. It would be kinder to invent names, though I admit that would be even more pointless than a list of real names.

A Constant Reader

A scandalous situation

The revelation that the pea to be used in the great Evans–Balzarotti contest was imported from France has caused an uproar. It is being asked, has this country really fallen so low that we are incapable of producing a pea for use in nasal pea-pushing championships? A spokesman said that a number of English peas were tried during practice, but they all lacked resilience, and one disintegrated when propelled against a boulder on Cader Idris. Nostril House said, 'No comment.' Lord Shortcake said, 'If the pushers care to contaminate their nostrils with a foreign product, it is their own affair.'

'Iron-Nostril' Balzarotti spent yesterday at the punch-pea in his training quarters, lashing out with alternate nostrils. Evans pushed a pea up Cader Idris, using the full-nose or bi-nostril technique. He was paced by Tom Blood, the promising nasal ace from Newport, who has the advantage of a long nose for ferreting the pea out of cracks in rocks. One great nasal drive by Evans sent the pea five and a half inches. Balzarotti favours short, sharp jabs, and a higher rate of striking.

Gracious living

Luxury miniflatlettes with one roomlette are the answer. Attached to the television set are a cooking stove and a chaise fairly longue for a bed, a sink which can be sat in like a chair, and a fold-up bath which can be turned upside down and used as a table. The accommodation is ideal for two people, as there is space between the radio and the cocktail cabinet for a second television set with all the attachments.

Dr Rhubarb's corner

E.N. ASKS: I bought one of those tiny electric cosies for keeping a boiled egg warm, but I dread power-cuts. What can I do?

DR RHUBARB SAYS: Have gas laid on at once.

Balzarotti sprains nostril

'Iron-Nostril' Balzarotti, the challenger of Evans the Hearse, sprained his left nostril while on a trial push at Llangherkin. He was negotiating a tricky corner on a footpath. Evans yesterday pushed his pea up a 234-foot hill in nine hours, four minutes, two seconds. The wind was against him, and the pea blew out of control for twelve minutes.

The char

A headline 'Canada Protects The Char' roused my insatiable curiosity. The story opened with the statement that the char is the pride of the Eskimos. I tried to imagine the Mounties galloping across the ice to protect Eskimo charwomen from the reactionaries who object to them as an innovation. I visualised old men sulking in a corner of the room while fussy women tidied the place up, and then I discovered that the char is a fish. Too late. This survey of the whole situation was already written.

Marginal note

An article about beautiful place-names omitted my favourite: Madrigal de las Altas Torres, the village where Queen Isabella was born. And what of Mooncoin in Co. Waterford, and Fontpédrouse and Fontrabiouse in the Pyrenees? Or Lostwithiel in Cornwall?

Evans v. Balzarotti: the showdown

Gigantic crowds converged—
PRODNOSE: In holiday mood . . .
—in holiday mood on the Aberbananer Stadium at 2 p.m. (Llangherkin time). The two men trotted down to the starting gate and, at a signal from the referee, crouched down on all fours and adjusted their noses to the twin peas placed before them. Evans's nose was off the mark like a bullet from the starting pistol, and at three yards he led Balzarotti by a nostril and a quarter. He had perfect control of the pea, whereas Balzarotti appeared to be feeling his way. His thrusts lacked full nasal power, and once or twice he pushed wildly and too hurriedly. His rate of pushes was 93 to the minute, as against 74 by Evans. At five yards he sliced his shot, and Evans increased his lead.

After six hours, and with only eleven yards to go, Balzarotti, fourteen feet behind Evans, attempted a spurt, but he was obviously tiring. The frenzied crowd roared and threw their hats in the air as Evans neared the winning post. Balzarotti's supporters from Italy shouted advice and encouragement, but Evans hammered away with that nose which is insured for £221,000. Relentlessly he increased his lead and passed the post with a classic jab which almost lifted his pea from the ground. With a gracious speech, the Mayor's wife handed Evans the golden pea and the cup – the latter filled with Welsh champagne. Both men drank greedily from it. Thus ended one more attempt to wrest the championship from – in the words of an arch Druid – 'The greatest nasal pea-pusher of all time'.

N.B. The pea used by Evans the Hearse in his victory over 'Iron-Nostril' Balzarotti is being exhibited in the Town Hall at Aberbananer. The money charged for admission will help train young nasal pea-pushers. Yesterday Evans left the imprint of his nostrils in wet cement on the threshold of the new lending library in Aberbananer. His latest challenger is Tiger Barrington, who won the Prix Sagan at Chantilly last year.

12

Tumbelova and the Trombone

While dancing a *pas de Calais* in Travetino's *Vespa*, Tumbelova fell into the orchestra pit, and got her left leg jammed in the entrance to a trombone. The *corps de ballet* hauled to free the captive limb,

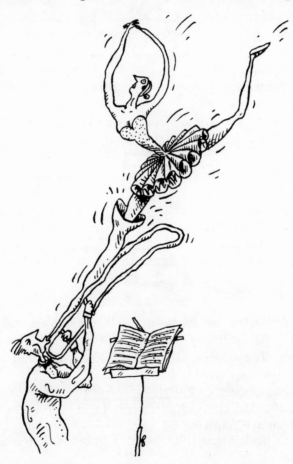

and the musicians pulled her the other way, as in a Metropolitan Police tug-of-war. The audience behaved very well, smothering its laughter. The curtain was lowered, but Tumbelova clutched at it, and when it was raised, there she was, like a minnow on a bent pin, twenty feet above the stage, with the trombone still attached to her leg. A mechanic was lowered from the roof, and he cut the instrument away. A large bit fell on a violinist's head and knocked him out. Tumbelova was lowered on a rope. The audience refused to take its money back, alleging that it had had great fun.

The accident to Tumbelova in the ballet has caused a stir. Apparently the mechanic who cut the instrument from her leg was not a member of the trombone-cutters' union. And even if he had been, he had no right to cut trombones from living matter, but only from furniture or walls. Moreover, the Musicians' Union is accusing its members of taking part in a tug-of-war during working hours, and the musicians reply that they had deposited their instruments to pull the ballerina, and so were not working as musicians, but as private individuals. The Tugs-of-War Union has protested against the use of musicians who are not members of the T.O.W.

In a statement to the Press, Mr Arthur Whackstraw, secretary of the Tugs-of-War Union, said: 'There can be no doubt that the incident of Mme Tumbelova's leg led to a genuine though informal tug-of-war, with grunts, cries of encouragement, and all the accompaniments of such contests. In future we shall picket the scene of such incidents. If there is a tug-of-war strike, full blame will rest with the musicians and the dancers. Let the public judge whether the liberation of a ballerina's leg from a trombone is worth the resulting chaos, and the injury to industrial relations.'

From a leading article:

> A distinguished dancer who, through no fault of her own, finds her leg trapped in the aperture of a trombone may be excused for resenting the subsequent tug-of-war organised for the release of the errant limb. Managements must be compelled by public opinion to safeguard their ballet-dancers by rearranging the orchestra in such a way that instruments capable of trapping a leg are furthest from the footlights. The lesson to be learned from Mme Tumbelova's mischance is

that, as things are at present, no artist, however eminent, is safe from the kind of accident which brings the ballet into discredit.

Mme Sonia Tumbelova has protested against a critic who wrote: 'The show must go on. A dancer with Tumbelova's experience and know-how should have gone on dancing with the trombone on her leg. A sympathetic audience would have cheered her to the echo, however ludicrous a spectacle she presented.'

Tumbelova said yesterday: 'Dancing with one leg caught in a trombone is not my idea of ballet. I am not a low comedian.'

Mr Edgar Lubber (Lib., North Mossick) is to ask the Home Secretary what steps he proposes to take to prevent dancers' legs being engulfed in trombones; whether he intends to allow the Tugs-of-War Union to dictate policy in matters of entertainment; and why a certain famous dancer was allowed to appear without some kind of sheathing-plate to protect her legs from the impact of large instruments.

Nation-wide comment on the *affaire Tumbelova* continues. A lover of ballet asks why the violins cannot be placed closest to the footlights to avoid accidents. 'Nobody could get a leg caught in a violin.' I disagree. One stumble, and a dancer might find her foot entangled in the strings. Even the golden wires of the harp can be a trap for the unwary, as a long-nosed singer discovered when a whack on the proboscis from harpist Gloria Chevening warned him to keep to his own side of the fence.

It was noticed during last night's performance of *Le Baiser du charcutier* that Tumbelova winced every time there was a blast on the trombone. She eyed the musician with undisguised hostility, but the evening passed off without any untoward incident, unless the violent collision of two dancers, during the *culbute* which follows the pork-butcher's *volte face*, be called untoward. After this a jovial stage-hand affixed a large cardboard L to Serge Trouserin's back.

Least said, bassoonist mended
'She lands from a leap with the grace of thistledown.'

(*Ballet critic*)

I threw a dancer into the air,
    She fell to earth I know not where;
But, later, a bassoonist said
    She had crash-landed on his head.
       (Serge Trouserin: 'Salute to Tumbelova')

*　　*　　*

Seesaw at Boulton Wynfevers

From the Filthistan Trio:

... A sekkleterry hath invited us three to play seesaw in the Izelebethan manure house of Lord Shortcake. This pier is lord of the manure, and our seesaw will holp him to show off his prosessions to the pooblick. Phancy us three being the synocure of ivery eye of the assitocracy, ho yes. Ashura is yest now practissing kurtesses and boughs and kissing hands of barrownesses, and Rizamughan hath bort himself a traveeling hamburg hat with a dent in it. Wot a phop, isn't it? ...

The three Persians visited Lord Shortcake to discuss their seesaw demonstration when the grounds are opened to the public this summer. Gazing at the house, Ashura said, 'No wunder the lord of the manure needeth such a large manshoun.'

'He moost have made a took-it-over bid for all the manure in the villidges,' said Rizamughan.

Addressing Shortcake, Kazbulah said, 'If there is mooch more of this manure, your lordmanureship will have to move hout into a barn.'

Shortcake then explained that the word was Manor.

Memo to Lord Shortcake:

We three hartists presenk our complimentz to yore lordsheep. You spake to us of a guyde, we want no guyde, we are knot enny aunchient bildings, stetews, or bitz of meddyevil harmor or bedds hupon wich Kween Birdeseer or Kromwill slep. Yore ownerd bitter arf, her ladisheep Snortcake, said seesaw must be hixplained to the Kommun hurd. We told her that even in Inglund babiz took in seesaw with theire muthers' milk.

Another memo:

... and we sujjost to your lordsheep that upon the perogram
of iventz shood huppear thus: At Larst!!! The Three Wizardz
From Filthistan And There Wunderfull Plonk Wot Has Wun Prays
From Menny Keround Heddz. Hixcluziv Hingragement By Kind
Premisshun Of A Pier Wich Will Be Prowed To Hav His Manure
And Graunds Saved From Rooing By Our Humbil Efforks ...

Lord Shortcake's plans for the coming stately-home season include
a large mat at the entrance to the house, with 'Welcome' embroidered on it, 'to put the crowds at their ease'. Lady Shortcake says
that he might as well serve beer in his shirtsleeves in the Min-
strels' Gallery, and change the name Shortcake Manor to Erewear
or Owerbahtit. 'Such a mat,' said her ladyship, 'would not go with
the bed in which Cromwell slept or the chair on which Queen Anne
sat.'

Nelson's chair, sold by antique-dealer Foulenough to Lord Shortcake, has apparently been sold also to Sir Arthur Jostleham for his
country mansion. Asked to explain, Foulenough said, 'The suggestion that a man in Nelson's position would have only one chair
is ludicrous. As a matter of fact we have several more of them in
stock.'

Privately, Foulenough rang up his head man and said, 'Lay
off the Nelson chairs. Make some of Wellington's.'

Lord Shortcake's decision to throw open Boulton Wynfevers and
its grounds to the public was not made without trepidation. The
offer of a bearded lady by an agency was refused with contumely.
A placard on a suit of armour worn by Sir Adelbert de Shortcayke
at Crécy bears the legend: 'Please do not strike matches on this
armour', and there is a large litter-bin in the Long Gallery. The
seesaw of the three Persians is to be set up on the lawn where,
according to the tradition, an ancestor shot a hedgehog on which
George IV was about to step.

'I trust,' said Lady Shortcake to her sillier half, 'you are not
contemplating dressing up in armour, and having jousts here.'

'It might attract visitors,' said Shortcake.

'So, undoubtedly, would Mr Daniel Kaye or any other comedian,'
she replied. 'And don't expect me to lean from a window and throw

you my gloves to wear in your helmet. If you start any such foolery, I shall tell Mason to get the dustman to take away all our armour.'

From the Filthistan Trio:
. . . We wish we waz never have got in this stattley home bizness. Lord Shortcake wantz oldwurled darncing by tinagerz wile we seesaw. Minaretz, we perzoom, Kort of Lewis Kattauz, Maddem ler Pumpadoor, wot hath orl this to do for Persian seesaw, you tell us, pleez, thang you. We tell his worseship to take arfadozzin runnin jumps at hisselve, ho yes . . .

By the next post:
. . . Seetid in a lucksherry cheeselong with kooshunz in her boudwah Lord Shortcake's bitter harf swore owthz that there would be no folk-dancing near our seesaw. So we kizzed her hand, and she flushed and got wite under her paynt az if we was three dedally koberaz or hoppypittamuses, not hickusstumed waz she to orryuntal kawtizzy. Then a buckler in kawt dressing give eech of us three a bier in a place kawld the servinksawl. So, as you Brittaniers say, awl is hunkerrydory, ho yes.

Interlude

There is an old Indonesian proverb which says—
PRODNOSE: That sort of statement is usually the prelude to one of your lies.
MYSELF: If I sued you for libel it would make legal history.
    Journalist Sues Figment Of His Imagination. You don't exist, you know.
PRODNOSE: Metaphysical twaddle! I am your public.
MYSELF: That is what I have always suspected.

Fun at Boulton Wynfevers

'Pardon me for speaking, your Lordship,' said a demure lady from London, 'but that lily pond of yours badly needs weeding.'
    'Weeding?' thundered Lord Shortcake. 'What do you mean, weeding?'
    'Why,' said she, 'it's thick with weeds.'
    'Allow me to inform you, madam, that those things are not weeds. They are the lilies.'
    'Oh well, then, you should put up a notice. My nephew's on the bank hoiking them out with his umbrella.'

Shortcake turned puce and ran to the lily pond.

The bad men ride again

Thanks to poisonous sprays bees are becoming so rare that bee-rustling is increasing. Masked men in veils drive herds of bees on moonless nights, crying 'Yippee!' and firing water-pistols. One village has appointed a marshal to clean up the neighbourhood, and so strong is the influence of the films that he has already found twelve aces in the stocking of a lady bee-keeper who sings in a local saloon.

Make a note of this

A writer seeks the cure for the widespread nervous irritation of today. The cure is to drink wine. Wine soothes the nerves, strengthens the body, enriches the mind, and rejoices the heart. It restores to the harassed a sense of proportion. For its full enjoyment it demands leisure and companionship, so that it may transmute the prose of a meal into poetry. Pray remember that Bacchus was a warrior, and that his armies had little fighting to do, because wherever he appeared he taught the cultivation of the vine to the grateful and submissive natives.

Storm in a goldfish bowl

In the Long Goldfish Gallery at Boulton Wynfevers a notice saying 'Do Not Spit' is prominently displayed. Lord Shortcake said: 'Among the coachloads of visitors there are bound to be a few spitters, and the noise upsets the little beggars in their bowls. Last July we had a tobacco-chewing sailor who spat like a machine-gun, and two Blackwell Beauties went off their grub for a week.'

Said Sir Gregory Linseed: 'It only shows the kind of riff-raff Shorty attracts. At Linseed Castle the only notice required is "Visitors Are Requested Not To Stub Out Cigarettes On The Louis XVI Chairs".'

Here, there and everywhere

A MONOTYPE keyboard minder, Alfred Kork, 42, of Plott End, was stung on the ankle by a hornet while playing the violin at a television tea. He continued playing and was stung twice more.

AN UTTOXETER school-teacher ate a small bicycle made of sugar at her uncle's birthday party. Her mother works for a butcher in Nottingham.

FOUR HUNDRED tons of parsley were stolen from an outhouse in Carlisle belonging to a pawnbroker. Two anglers were questioned by police.

THREE RAILWAY porters at Nendley Junction got stuck to a passenger's beard when glue was spilled from his suitcase. They were released by Phoebe Caskett, a Doncaster typist, who cut the beard loose with a penknife.

A stationmaster's sang-froid

'The uniforms of three porters were splashed with the oil which flowed along the platform.'   (*News item*)

'That,' vouchsafed the stationmaster, 'is what we of the railways call pouring oil on troubled porters.'

Fun at Boulton Wynfevers

... Lord Shortcake kimplains that our seesaw is droring siteseerz away from the bedstedd in wych Charles the Sekkund slepped. We three repplie art konkerz fernitcher. As we are the startern our names shud be farstind up fore foots hi and nilonlited. Wot erbout songayloomiar, like erbrorde, telling the histeri of seesaw from prohisterick times? Veev ler seesaw as the Frinch wud say. Enny uther hofferz furm launderd gintery with stayterli manchunz? ...

Lord Shortcake has threatened to close his house and grounds to the public if there are any more 'incidents'. Last weekend a huge woman was found boiling water for her tea in a crusader's helmet in the Long Gallery. Two youths were using an early Vaurien landscape as a darts board.

Chez Snibbo

At the Instant Restaurant owned by Snibbo, gourmets will be able to enjoy 'instant' meals in luxurious surroundings. The waiter will bring the food block to the table in a can of tasteful design, and will thaw it in a porcelain bowl. He will then separate the various items of food, scraping the sauce off the cheese, and draining the soup off the lobster. Smaller food-packets for dogs will be supplied. The instant wine accompanying the meal will be thawed more slowly, in tepid water, to preserve the bouquet. Coffee and brandy, in separate urns, will be poured from a tap into hygienic plastic cups.

Anything to oblige

An article about George Moore reminded me of a story they tell in Dublin. Moore and Gogarty were in a train in Kerry. Moore said, 'What a glorious view. I'd give any money to be able to stop and look at it.'

'That can easily be arranged,' said Gogarty, and he pulled the communication cord.

Fun at Boulton Wynfevers

The crowds had departed. Lady Shortcake heard loud snores coming from one of the bedrooms open to the public. Peering in, she saw a man lying asleep on the bed in which Edward III slept after Crécy. In his hand was an empty whisky bottle. She shook him. He opened his eyes and muttered, 'Fill 'em up, Flo.'

'This is not a public house,' she said.

'OK. No closing hours,' said the reveller. 'That suits me,' and he turned over and went to sleep again.

Mimsie Slopcorner's ordeal

There were rowdy scenes at Belching-on-the-Wold when Mimsie Slopcorner opened a new civic centre. A man who stood on one leg on the roof with a miniature model of a dockyard crane in his hand pretended to be giving a running commentary. A newsagent kept on shouting: 'I name this liner Babs.'

When Mimsie inserted the golden key in the door, there were cries of 'Anyone at home?' and 'Don't let the mice out!'

Mimsie said afterwards: 'I would not claim that civic consciousness is to the fore in this place.'

Bowlermanship

'A storm in a hat,' drawled Mr J. B. Morton, when I asked him yesterday for his opinion of a recent correspondence about the correct way to wear a bowler. Said Mr Morton, one of the four best-dressed men in England, 'A hat that fits is a must with me. I have nineteen, and wear them in rotation. They are specially made for me, actually.'

'And what is the correct position for a bowler?' I asked.

He demonstrated the correct angle for me, smiling tolerantly. 'One does feel it does something to one,' he said.

I felt I had talked to a man who will stand no nonsense when it comes to bowlers.

Lord Shortcake gets a letter

Ashura, on behalf of the seesawsters, has thanked Lord Shortcake, in a moving letter, for engaging them. He wrote:

Deer pier, thiz iz a bredanbutta billydoo to yore bitter arf, that dilishus creetur what did give us tees and kake in er roes gardin. We kiz er haund not of orsez play but rispekt. Rizamughan and Kazbulah saith no korz of divvorz, meening a jowk. May yore shiddo and erz neffer bekum smorler az yore profferb saith. We hoape this is oreevwar not goobie. Except our thonks pleez pier no offenz, ho yes. Peesses: if our umbil effurtz brort into you much welth, bi a yot and korl it Seesaw, and reepare yore estaterly ome with the chainje.

Fünfjahrezeiten

Gehort! Die Schwabenspiegel!
O Schnipfelbaum! Gefangen,
Du bist mein Engelskriegl,
Mit Schopfheim und Zustangen.

(Baldur Dasch)

13

How to Look at Cod

The increasing hatlessness of men is a gnawing pain in the vitals of hatters. But instead of moving us to tears by telling us that, unless more hats are bought, they will starve, they cry that no man is well dressed without a hat, that it gives him confidence, helps his career, and endears him to girls. Those who, while feeling guilty, object to wearing hats, carry them gingerly in their hands, and shove them on their heads while passing hat shops. The hatter's last hope is the bowler-wearer. Without a bowler, his neatly-rolled umbrella would be a mere mockery. Therefore, I urge hatters and umbrella-makers to join forces in a last despairing campaign.

Red revenge (I)

Ambrose Detmold scratched the top of his bald head with his elbow. Celery Bapchild had once said, 'Not for nothing is Ambrose double-jointed; well, almost nothing, since the ability to scratch one's head with one's elbow may be justly considered its own reward.'

Blanche Ruggidge's contempt was too deep for silence. 'He does it to attract attention,' she answered, 'like Baron Fombombi, who plays Schumann with the backs of his fingers.'

'They ought to meet,' said Celery. 'How they would entertain each other!'

At that moment, in the crowded drawing-room, a shot rang out, followed by a scream.

Approach shot

'Gently he kissed her cleek.'   (*From a serialised novel*)

In his impetuous way he would have kissed every club in her

bag had not the caddie been looking. Following up the indirect approach, he said to her, 'Will you give me a photograph of your putter to place beside my bed?' She blushed and veiled her glorious eyes with her Stikon lashes (13s. 6d. a pair. All sizes. Write or telephone Maison Ninon.)

Red revenge (II)

We left Mrs Relf by the Zambesi—

PRODNOSE: We did no such thing! We have never heard of Mrs Relf.

MYSELF: Ah, yes. Well, as the shot rang out in the Kensington drawing-room, everybody ducked. Then another rang out, and another; eight shots in all. Each time everybody ducked. But after the eighth shot Paul Brenton bobbed up too soon, was hit by the ninth, and fell as though dead – which he was. Who was the author of this unwonted fusillade? That's exactly what the police asked the terrified survivors when they arrived at the house.

Song

The abandonment of the habit of wearing a hat removes one more distinction between man and the lower animals.

(A hatter)

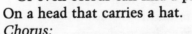

> All is human under the hat,
>> And every decent hatter's plan
>> Is the common brotherhood of man.
> For plebeian or aristocrat,
>> No distinction of class or race
>> Or even colour can find a place
> On a head that carries a hat.
> *Chorus:*
>> For all is human, human, human,
>> Utterly human under the hat.

He will see his brother

Red-moustachioed Ernest Clutterback, 43, a Wantage haulage-contractor who married Agatha Cunning, Nuneaton's Miss Parsley, a 27-year old brunette, whose aunt collects tin ashtrays for her sister's children's dolls' house, is flying out to Ecuador to visit his brother whom he has not seen since 1933.

(Beachcomber News Agency)

The Strabismus bed

Why not sleep in comfort? The Strabismus bed to end all beds has a built-in cocktail cabinet at one end and a refrigerator at the other. Along one side of the chinchilla mattress there is a washing-machine, a revolving book-case, two television screens and two radios; along the other side, an electronic brain with long-playing records, a Dictaphone, a telephone, a fog-horn, a stamping-machine and a rack for luggage. Under the cocktail cabinet there is a set of tools for carpentry, and above the refrigerator a miniature billiard table. Affixed to the mink pillows there is a cedar cabinet containing playing cards, pipe-cleaners, casseroles, string, a bird-cage, gardening tools, a camera, a false beard, a meat-chopper, glue, golf-balls, a tuning fork, a tiny lightning-conductor, blotting paper, a shooting-stick, and a saxophone.

Song

I am asked if there are any more verses to that stirring song, 'All is human under the hat'. There are seventy-one verses in all. Here is verse II.

> All is human under the hat,
>> Whatever its texture or design –
>> Even a tattered hat like mine,
> Which might have been brought in by the cat.
> For beneath a hat is a human face,
>> Whatever the colour or creed or race,
> The hat can never be out of place.
> *Chorus:*
>> For all is human, human, human,
>> Utterly human under the hat.

Red revenge (XLIV)

The Zambesi is navigable for nearly 1,700 miles. Lance Fuddington had done the 300 miles between the Supuma cataract and the Gonye Falls in his Luabo canoe, intent on some ratting in the Chipiwamba hinterland. A sack of ferrets was slung over his shoulder, as he moored his canoe to the trunk of a huge eucalyptus, and struck westwards into the Kebabungu desert. Lance—

PRODNOSE: What on earth has all this to do with your story?

MYSELF: A story has many strands, which are woven into a pattern. Patience, fleas, the night is long, as the Spaniards say.

He got the bird

'The thrush flew through an open window and bruised his forehead.' 		(*News item*)

'A missile thrush,' said a well-known ornithologist.

Twenty years of uproar

'Singers,' says an article, 'are very touchy and temperamental.' A critic once wrote that Rustiguzzi was the only singer who could fill Covent Garden. The diva interpreted this as a reference to her gross tonnage rather than as a tribute to her vocal talent. Semolina had more cause for complaint when, under a photograph of a rhinoceros at the zoo, appeared the caption, 'Coloratura flies in.' And Tapioca was once referred to as 'The lady whose vice has won the applause of millions.'

Dernier cri

For those who require something more luxurious than the Strabismus bed, which I described recently, the sage has devised a diesel bed, which will transport the occupant from room to room. It has a built-in helicopter, in which the lazy can deposit themselves on the floor, a hen-house attached to the head of the bed, an electric organ, a stereophonic typewriter, a steam-saw, a diving helmet, a binnacle with compass, a hose-pipe, a windvane, a raft for use in floods, a Japanese waste-paper basket, nutcrackers, a horse collar, and an adjustable bacon-slicer.

Red revenge (XXI)

'Will Colonel Sprott please come to the purser's office on B deck?' The *Briny Ocean Star* was bucketing in a dirty sea off Cadiz, her rudder awash, her sham funnels dripping with salt spray. In the Assyrian-style cocktail lounge the hardier travellers were pretending to enjoy the vile concoctions handed out by a bartender dressed as a surgeon in an operating theatre. Colonel Sprott, alias Toby Roofe, staggered into the purser's office.

'We have received a wireless message,' said the purser. Visions of incarceration, torture, and what not assailed the vile imposter. 'You have won £336,428 9s. 4½d. on the pools,' continued the purser.

The 'colonel' fell in a swoon of relief. Far away in Islington an anonymous widow sat grinning by the fire.

How to look at cod

A writer on food says: 'Cod is usually a sore subject. It depends on how you look at it.'

Yes, yes. You can focus a telescope on it, creep up to it by night with an electric torch, come at it suddenly round corners, sight it with one eye through a hole in an umbrella or a broken bucket, put it on a high shelf and go down on all fours to look up at it, get on the roof and lean over the edge to look down at it, bicycle past it with a sideways glance. And all to no purpose.

A question of status

The amateur status of Evans the Hearse is being questioned. Grateful citizens of Aberbananer presented him with a golden pea mounted on teak. As the *Aberbananer Argus* said: 'If the man whose nostrils have brought fame to his native place accepts presents, he will be bringing this amateur sport into world-wide discredit.'

Dr Rhubarb's corner

H.L. WRITES: A cousin of mine has his family's coat of arms on the front of his bowler hat. As he is not a Conservative, but votes Labour, is not this vulgar ostentation?

DR RHUBARB SAYS: The family should try to persuade him to transfer the coat of arms to the lining of the bowler. Cloakroom attendants would be suitably impressed.

The 'Abstract Concerto'

The first performance in this country of Nammelwint's Abstract Concerto was received with wild applause. The second movement, an adagio for three frying-pans, summed up the monotony which reflects Nammelwint's conception of intellectual music. Barbauld's playing of the saucepan produced sounds new to the concert hall, and musical purists were puzzled by the overpowering interruptions of the hammers as they flogged the sheets of tin. Those who expected a strong melody were disappointed. Said one member of the audience, 'There was no tune to whistle or hum, but one came away with the impression of having heard something strange and new.'

Aberbananer flares up

Yesterday 364 citizens of Aberbananer lay down in the road outside the Town Hall, as a protest against the disqualification of Evans the Hearse as an amateur, because he accepted a golden pea from the Llanbwilth Sports Committee. The protesters carried banners on which were photographs of Evans's nostrils. A deputation which attempted to push peas with its noses into the Town Hall was refused admission. 'It is a storm in a peacup,' laughed the Mayor.

Viscount's niece swallows two orchids

'Her see-through blouse shone like glass.'   (*Fashion note*)

As the proverb says: People who live in glass blouses shouldn't show bones.

Red revenge (XIX)

Far away from the Zambesi, in Islington, to be precise, a stamp-collector sat over his album, dazed. By the fire stood Detective Inspector Jack Malpractice, a stern smile on his handsome face. 'Where were you, Mr Gulf, on the morning of the third?' he asked.
   'Littlehampton,' replied the collector.
   'Why?' he queried.
   'To purchase an unperforated Turkish stamp,' replied Gulf.
   'From a sailor?' pursued the inspector.
   'Yes,' faltered Gulf.
   'You know that sailor is dead?'
   'I read about it in my paper.' During the pause you could have heard a tin of fish drop. Both men did hear it, and turned to the door.
   There, trembling, stood Mrs Upchurch herself.

Encounter in Bucharest

The worm-eaten phrase about travellers abroad being ambassadors caught my eye.

One day, in a restaurant in Bucharest, I complained about a meal. An Englishman who overheard me said: 'You know, you ought to remember that we are, in a sense, unofficial ambassadors of our country, and ought to behave as such.'

I gave him the glance of the basilisk. 'Sir,' I replied, 'I happen to be your Ambassador in this country – the official one. Kindly address me with more respect.'

He slunk away like a whipped cur with a mammoth flea in each ear.

Snibbo does it again!

The controversy about froth on stout is good publicity for Snibbo-fome, the plastic froth supplied in neat, if gaudy, packets. Each bit of froth is the standard size required, nine-seventeenths of a fluid dram. All the barman has to do is affix the froth to the top of the drink without being observed by his customer. The plastic froth is quite harmless, and can be blown off if unwanted. Blindfold tests made on forty-two people showed that only two of them could tell Snibbofome from genuine froth, and they were accused of cheating.

How bats keep fit

A vet has said that animals keep fit in far more sensible ways than human beings. I hope he sings to the bats in the belfries:

> What makes the humble flittermouse
>   A sturdier and fitter mouse?
> A course of exercises on the
>   Very latest plan.
> He bends to touch his little toes
>   While breathing deeply through his nose.
> It must be good for flittermice
>   If it is good for man.

Interlude

PRODNOSE: What has happened to your serial 'Red Revenge'?
MYSELF: The matter is rather complicated. It ended at Chapter
   IV which was printed after Chapter XIII, and then continued

with a few previous chapters. This unconventional treatment was an attempt to keep up the suspense by sharpening the reader's curiosity. Nobody knew what would happen next or what had happened before or even what was happening at the moment.

PRODNOSE: How true!

Earwiga

In the eighth century there was a Saxon queen called Earwiga, who wore tin garters once a year. Today the tiny Gloucestershire village of Sudby holds the traditional tin garter ceremony. A young man dressed as a hrothman ties a tin garter to the flagpole on the village hall. The villagers sing the garter song: 'A garter! A garter! And a beetroot pudding for you.' Each man hands each woman a beetroot pudding, while the oldest inhabitant pretends to bite a dog. The origin of this latter ceremony is lost in the mists of antiquity.

Nothing to do with me

A man who claims that he has been trying for eighteen months to teach a whiting to fly has abandoned the attempt. The fish, he complains, 'took absolutely no notice of my patient work.' There's ingratitude for you! Spoilsports who ask who or what would benefit from the capacity of whiting (or, for that matter, mullet) to fly are referred to Sir Henry Flatton's failure to induce hornets to eat wall-paper, described in *The Hornets in my Life*.

Here, there and everywhere

A MAN stood on a red-hot egg for forty minutes for a bet at Wivenhoe early yesterday morning. The egg was found to be quite cold, and to have been painted red-hot.

A THRUSH'S NEST was found in a gigantic model of a hat in a hatter's window by a sailor. 'It should have been an ostrich,' said the hatter, with a wry smile.

FOURTEEN THOUSAND BRICKS were delivered in error to the local post-mistress at Stubbs End yesterday. 'Someone has dropped several bricks,' she said laughingly.

I let you into a secret

A correspondent asks me why I often start serials without continuing them. It is a trick, sir, to create suspense, promote interest, and pass the time. It also explains why I sometimes begin with 'Chapter XVI.' Millions of readers write for back copies, believing they have missed fifteen chapters. Lastly, it is a way of filling up space.

Zagrooter strikes again (Ch. 1)

Inspector Farragut was shown into Lady Parboyle's drawing-room. He at once sensed that something was wrong. There were eleven people in the room, and every single one of them was dead, not counting an Aberdeen terrier, a Siamese cat, and a mouse. There were no signs of a struggle, but the floor was littered with daggers and bottles of poison.

Summoning the butler, Transom, Farragut barked, 'No one must leave this house.'

'There's only me left to leave it,' said the butler. 'Cook's dead, the maids are dead, and I – I'm not feeling too well myself.' With these words Transom staggered and fell dead.

Song

They questioned him in accents mild:
  'Why did you stab your parents, child?'
The surly lad responded, pouting:
  'So I could join the orphans' outing.'

14

The Motheton Mystery

Jack Malpractice Investigates

It was a Thursday, and why should it not have been? Mavis Kindlewoode had been arranging flowers in her boudoir at Motheton Manor. Hearing a thud in the drawing-room, she went to investigate. The door was closed, but not locked. Some heavy object resisted her efforts to open it. Finally, she was able to squeeze her way into the room. With a gasp, she stopped dead. She had expected to see her husband, Sir Miles, practising golf-shots. What she saw, recumbent on the floor, was a full-grown elephant, lying on its side. It seemed to be dead.

Mavis Kindlewoode prodded the great beast timidly with her foot. Then she withdrew. Calling her husband from his study, she said: 'Miles, there's an elephant in the drawing-room!'

'What have you been drinking, old girl?' he replied.

'Tea,' she said. 'But, Miles, it's true.'

To humour her, he accompanied her to the drawing-room. 'By Jove,' he cried, 'it *is* an elephant!'

'We must ring up Scotland Yard,' said Mavis.

'Nonsense,' snorted Sir Miles, and then, addressing the monster, he shouted: 'Come up there, Jumbo!' Not a muscle of the animal moved.

'Perhaps it's murder,' said Mavis.

'Who would want to murder an elephant?' replied Sir Miles. 'At least, not in a drawing-room.'

'This,' said burly George Mulph, the village constable, 'is a matter for the Yard . . .'

'Scotland Yard. Detective Inspector Malpractice speaking . . . Yes, Constable. A what? . . . In the drawing-room? Are you sure it's an elephant? . . . Yes, but how did it get there? . . . Perhaps it has just fainted . . . No, no. Get a vet . . . Try the zoo . . . Murdered? Any marks of violence? . . . Right. Don't let anyone touch anything in the house. Question the staff . . . I'll be right along.'

Five minutes later, Jack Malpractice was on his way to Motheton in his Thanatos Six.

The vet bent over the huge beast. 'Stone dead,' he said. 'No pulse. No sign of breath on my little mirror. The autopsy may reveal a rare Venezuelan poison.'

Close questioning by Malpractice failed to reveal how the animal had got into the drawing-room. The gardener was sure that he had not seen an elephant in the garden. The housekeeper was equally sure it had not been in the room on the previous night. There had been a cocktail party and plenty of strange creatures had come, but not an elephant. Lady Kindlewoode's psychic aunt suggested that it was a ghost.

'Elephants don't have ghosts,' said Sir Miles.

'Cover it with a sheet,' snapped Malpractice, 'or, rather, several sheets.'

Murder? By further questioning, Malpractice discovered that every occupant of the house hated elephants. Therefore every one of them had a motive. As the detective ruminated, his technical assistants were spilling powder all over the room, and discovering hoof-prints, tusk-prints, trunk-prints, tail-prints, and ear-prints.

'It was trying to get out,' said Mavis Kindlewoode, in a sentimental whisper.

'Could it have died of old age?' asked Malpractice.

'No,' said the vet, 'it wasn't old enough.'

'Any Indians in the neighbourhood?' was his next shrewd question.

'Only Anglo-Indians,' said Sir Miles. 'Myself, and two colonels. None of us ever owned an elephant.'

Suddenly the sheets covering the great beast moved slightly. The women screamed. The vet muttered: 'It was only a coma.' Slowly the alleged corpse rose to its feet, and gazed round the room with a puzzled frown. Then, with all the majesty of a lord of the jungle, it ambled towards the door, where it stuck. Malpractice and the vet pushed at its stern. The Kindlewoodes, their aunt, and the gardener pulled at the prow. It was like a Metropolitan Police tug-of-war in reverse, each team aiding the other. Finally they got it clear. It stumped across the hall, and through the entrance door thrown wide, down the drive and out of the gates. 'Follow that elephant!' shouted Malpractice to his chauffeur.

Jack Malpractice, failing to overtake the quarry, remarked that it appeared to have vanished into astonishingly thin air for a beast of such proportions. The family psychiatrist declared that there had never been an elephant in the drawing-room.

'What, then, did we all see?' asked Lady Kindlewoode.

'It was a collective hallucination,' replied the expert, 'the result, among a group who dislike elephants, of unwishful thinking.'

'But the detective rather liked elephants,' said Sir Miles.

'He,' retorted the psychiatrist, 'was affected by the total ambient reaction.'

To this day, whenever Lady Kindlewoode enters her drawing-room, she carries a bun — just in case. There the matter, but not the elephant, rests at present.

*   *   *

The Strabismus Lunatik moon rocket

'The emancipation of women,' writes Professor Skurge of Uppsala, 'will not be complete until they take their part in space travel.' It is known that Dr Strabismus (Whom God Preserve) of Utrecht, with rare old-world courtesy, has suggested that his first passenger in his Lunatik should be a woman. 'Women,' he once said, 'are more sensitive to atmosphere than men.' And his choice has fallen on that English rose, Mimsie Slopcorner. If she accepts the honour, the great question is: Who will sponsor her attempt to land like thistledown on the moon? In other words, what firm's products will she advertise?

When Mrs Slopcorner heard of the sage's suggestion, she said: 'I wouldn't put it beyond Mimsie. She was always fidgety and restless, and when we lived in Wolverhampton nothing would suit her but to go off to Walsall, and even to West Bromwich.'

Slopcorner *père* said: 'I don't want any daughter of mine mixed up with the moon, fidgety though she may be.'

Asked if she would be prepared to train as an astronautette or glamourcosmogirl, Mimsie said: 'I do so think girls have their part to play in the expanding universe, if only to get rid of Victorian prejudices which prevent them from being archbishops or billiard-markers. My cousin Enid, billiards champion of Barnet, was refused permission to mark in the Edgware Shield final. That is not the way to open woman's road to the planets.'

Life is like that

A stranded touring company had to take passage to their next destination in an old coaster carrying chemical manure. As they left the harbour another boat hailed them, and asked what cargo they carried. 'Chemical manure and actors,' was the reply.

A lugubrious actor turned to a colleague and said: 'Godfrey, shall we never top the bill?'

Fun in court

'It seems,' said the magistrate, 'that you sat on this horse in the yard all night. May one ask why?'

'I have knock-knees,' answered the man shamefacedly, 'so I was stuck there.'

'You mean you couldn't dislodge your knees from the horse's flanks?' queried the magistrate.

'That's about it,' replied the man. 'They were clipped as in a vice.'

'It was the horse that was clipped,' riposted the magistrate. 'But we will let that pass. How did you contrive to dismount in the morning?'

'I shouted to some workmen,' said the man, 'and they lifted the horse and turned us both upside down, and I was shaken off, natural like.'

'Anything less natural,' said the magistrate, 'I cannot imagine. I advise you to give up riding.'

'I'd hardly call it riding,' said the man in a surly tone.

Encouragement from a male

Dear Sir,

Now that girls are no longer expected to sit in their boudoirs doing embroidery, I think it is an excellent idea that they should get out and about. The sky's the limit, so far, but who knows what new worlds are waiting beyond the ken of our most powerful telescopes? Let British girls show the stuff they are made of, and we men will be the first to take off our hats to them. Therefore I say, go to it, Mimsie! More power to your rocket!

Richard Trowle

Is Foulenough going North?

The question being asked in shooting circles is whether Captain Foulenough intends to travel North for the drinking this August. Last year the moor owned by the Macaroon of Macaroon was a disgrace to grouse-lovers. Thanks to a merry party, which included Foulenough, at the end of the week the moor looked like an abandoned cellar, and the birds, completely ignored by the sportsmen, had become so tame that they were pecking biscuits in the Laird o'Kilcockrobbin's pocket. On one occasion the laird, in an absent-minded moment, raised his gun and potted a grouse. He missed, and the Macaroon shouted: 'Give him the other barrel.'

Foulenough, whose mind was on the only remaining barrel of whisky, cried, 'Don't be a fool! We shall need it ourselves.'

A woman's point of view

Dear Sir,

The spectacle of such men as Mr Trowle skulking behind
the petticoats of space-borne girls is a pitiable one. Has Britain
lost her manhood? Can smug complacency go further than to
urge a delicately nurtured girl to get herself shot to the moon?
It may be true that the spirit of Florence Nightingale, Boadicea,
and Grace Darling is to be found in certain dedicated women, but
is an apprenticeship to public life, culminating in being chosen as
Miss Plastic Dustbin, really a qualification for gambolling among
the planets? One doubts it.

(Mrs) Eva Bildillow

Mayor's foghorn stolen

The hedgehog, says a writer on nature, has a very inferior brain
development. At any rate it has enough sense to make itself into
a small fortress and shoot out its spines when in danger, which is
more than you and I can do. It also shows good sense in sleeping
out the winter in a comfortable bed of dry leaves. I am always
moved by its lonely look. As the poet has written:

> A hedgehog, roaming in its lonely way,
>   Lost in the dark of night, had wandered far,
> And bumped into a cactus. 'Hi! I say!'
>   He shouted, 'Mind where you are going, Ma!'

Interlude

PRODNOSE: Why do you often give a paragraph an utterly
  meaningless headline?

MYSELF: To excite interest. Most people who read 'Clergyman's
  Niece Bites Dog' or 'Duke Hidden in Chimney' will read on
  avidly.

PRODNOSE: You must have a pretty low opinion of your readers.

MYSELF: Who has a better right to such an opinion?

The controversy rages

Dear Sir,

If reactionaries like Mrs Bildillow had their way, British girls
would still be playing croquet, fainting at the sight of a mouse, and
singing drawing-room ballads. Miss Slopcorner is made of sterner

stuff, as her refusal to be photographed inside the winning dustbin at the Wynchcombe Gala proves. May she be the first ambassadress of our earth on the moon, instead of settling down to a humdrum life as Mrs Suet. We women are solidly behind her.

Eva Dubble

Foulenough will be there

To the moors! To the moors!

'At any moment now,' writes my sporting correspondent, 'the ping of the rifle will reverberate from butt to butt, and cries of 'Pot him, Gregson!' will rouse the marksman rooting in his hamper for the bubbly.' West End restauranteurs will prepare to shove extra shot into last year's birds 'flown in' so that every mouthful may contain evidence of an expert kill.

'The little moor, and how much it is,' as Browning said when overcharged for a season's fun.

'Among those present' at this season is always Foulenough. Lurking in plebeian dress among the sportsmen, he cries to the most successful, 'Carry your bag, sir?' Thus the table of the Macaroon of Macaroon is always plentifully furnished. No dog, however well trained, picks up as many birds as this diligent interloper.

A note on holidays

When travel was more difficult than it is today, and therefore more of an adventure, a man decided where he wanted to go, and went there. Nowadays he is told where he ought to want to go, and even what he is to do when he gets there. Here is a tip for the eccentric who likes to be independent. By studying all the travel literature, he can find out what places the agencies ignore, and can enjoy a peaceful holiday. In every country there are vast areas, off the main routes, where nobody goes. This means meeting foreigners, but that is not so terrible when you get used to it.

Much ado about nothing

Dr Strabismus (Whom God Preserve) of Utrecht is much disturbed. By every post he receives offers from dress-makers and dress-designers to supply Mimsie with space costumes for day and evening wear. One firm has sent her a backless space gown in breath-grey *chabrette*. Sparks & Fillett have sent a fine-woven duster for dusting the gadgets inside the Lunatik. Strabismus said last night that all the fuss is premature. The Lunatik is still being modified, and Mimsie pleads a prior engagement at Torquay. 'The moon can wait,' said her mother.

On the moors

Without firing a single shot in anger, Foulenough had provided a feast for the Macaroon of Macaroon and the Laird o' Kilcockrobbin. Many toasts were drunk, and Foulenough piped the birds aboard with a bagpipe interlude. He became entangled in the instrument, and old Angus Turagh released him, while the laird, for lack of swords, did a knife-and-fork dance on the table.

'This,' said the Macaroon, 'is better than slogging across the moors or skulking in the butts.'

'To the moors, to the moors!' they roared in chorus, somewhat inconsequently.

Dr Rhubarb's corner

E.L. WRITES: Is it true that gin stops parrots from being seasick?
DR RHUBARB SAYS: No. It is merely a trick to get gin.

Heir to the Sausage throne

A reference to someone as the Packaged Food King reminded me of James Allison's story. A man was introduced to guests at dinner as 'Mr—, the Sausage King.'

His Highness in turn introduced his son, saying, 'This is the Sausage Prince of Wales.'

News of the Lunatik

Dr Strabismus (Whom God Preserve) of Utrecht now hopes to land three dozen ferrets on the moon when his Lunatik is ready. Those who are already talking of colonising the moon ('the foul imperialists': *Peking Argus*) are asking what purpose the little creatures could serve, except to incommode the first men to land on the moon. The Sage of Waggling Parva replies that by means of the ferrets we shall know whether there are any lunar rabbits up there. Pictures of the ferrets, sniffing about the place, will be transmitted to earth.

Top secret

So closely guarded, day and night,
Is this mysterious rocket site.
So jealously the secret's kept
That no one knows it's there – except
Those who repeatedly declare
That nobody suspects it's there.

Turn to Page Two for the first photograph ever published of the Indian rope-trick. Both climber and rope have disappeared.

15

The Filthistan Trio

Seesaw at the Fête

An invitation sent to the three Persian seesawsters to take part in the Bibney St Vitus Summer Fête has been accepted.

Deer organhizers,
We three's dillite nose no bownderies with the onner of being part of yore feete. Wood the klurgy man who wull interuduse us like our hortigeraffes? We noate from yore pogromme that the wait of a inormouse caik is to be gest. What phun to putt it on Ashura's belli like the seesaw plonk, his mussels is of steal, ho yes. Hott riggardz for orl of yew, from Ashura, Kazbulah, Rizamughan.
                                THE FILTHISTAN TRIO

On arriving at Bibney St Vitus for the fête, the three Persians selected for their rehearsal the foyer of the County Hotel. Observing the plank, the people in the reception office thought that the manager had sent for carpenters. But when one of the carpenters lay down and balanced the plank on his belly, curiosity became alarm. Two maiden ladies protested, and the manager, hastily summoned, rang up the police to ask if any escaped lunatics were in the neighbourhood. He then requested the intruders to leave.

'We hare here for your feet,' said Kazbulah.

'Where can we rehorse?' asked Ashura.

A colonel standing by said, 'You have lost some horses? Is that it?'

'Mongseenyor,' said Rizamughan, 'we do not play seesaw on horseback.'

A puzzled silence fell.

On learning the truth about the three mysterious visitors to his hotel, the manager, in the interests of the Bibney St Vitus fête, allowed the rehearsal to continue.

A guest, emerging from the lift, immediately rang up his psychiatrist. 'There are three foreigners playing seesaw here,' he said.

The psychiatrist hurried round. 'It is all in the mind,' he said.

'You mean they are not there?'

'Of course not.'

At that moment Rizamughan sneezed, the plank shifted on his belly, and Ashura's end caught the psychiatrist a crack on the leg.

As he cursed and swore, the patient said, 'It's all in the mind. You only imagined it.'

The three Persians were surprised to learn that they are to take part in the Bibney St Vitus procession through the village on a milk float, seesawing as they go, and with Vikings around them.

'Who the devil is Wiking?' shouted Ashura. 'And what doeth he on our cart?'

It was explained that the Scandinavian pirates landed at Bibney in olden times.

'Aha!' said Kazbulah, 'did these Scandinavian robbers land on a float of cows' milk, and was they come to watch seesaw?'

Said Rizamughan: 'We want no prehistoric thiefs for stealing our plonk. We pertest to the mare.'

In a letter of unparalleled dignity Mimsie Slopcorner has refused an invitation to take part in the Bibney St Vitus fête. It is believed that she hesitates to become involved in the pranks of the three Persians. Misfortune has dogged her lately. At the Bilgewater Agricultural Show she trod on a big cheese, and sank in over the ankles.

'Hard cheese!' cried the mayor laughingly.

'You mean soft cheese,' riposted a clergyman, wiping the Slopcorner feet with his sexton's hat.

A letter to the *Bibney St Vitus Messenger and Clarion* says:

Dear Sir,

As a lifelong resident of our lovely little town I must protest against the introduction of a vulgar note into our fête. Seesaw, when played by children, is a beautiful sight, but I see nothing edifying in a seesaw balanced on the stomach of a grown-up alien, with a fellow-alien at each end. Do we pay our rates for this sort of thing?

The Filthistan Trio reply:

Sir,

We three was brort up saying yore konntry was the erbode of libberty and tolderashun, and now we was ittact in the Press korling us alyunz, ho yes. Seesaw is hart and nose no frunteerz, it was an oonimversul langgwidj of hinteranashunial frenships. Peesses: their is nothing vulger erbout Kazbulah's belly, which hath tattued on it a onion jack.

(The Bibney fête was eventually rained off.)

*   *   *

Song (verse XXIX)

All is human under the hat,
  We are brothers under our skins;
From the penniless tramp to the plutocrat
  The respect which the wearer wins
Is a fount of joy that never runs dry.
  The hatless cheer as he passes by,
And the sceptic is given the swift reply:
  'All is human under the hat.'
Chorus:
  All is human, human, human,
  Utterly human under the hat.

Still on the moors

Captain Foulenough lay in wait for stray birds uncollected on Chulish Moor. A lady on her way to join her party discoverd him in a fold of the ground and uttered a cry. 'You gave me quite a fright,' she said.

'I never shoot a walking bird,' said Foulenough. 'Joke,' he added, as she looked puzzled.

'Why,' she said, 'you haven't got a gun.'

'I stalk 'em,' he replied, 'and my dog brings me my gun when I've cornered a bird.'

'Extraordinary!' said the lady.

'It is rather,' agreed Foulenough.

When Foulenough related this encounter to the Macaroon of Macaroon, the Laird o'Kilcockrobbin said, 'Supplies are rather low. This is no time to be stalking ladies.'

'Considering that it is I who stock the larder, that remark is in bad taste. Now biff me with your claymore,' answered Foulenough.

Said the Macaroon, 'You should take a gun, for appearances' sake, when you go out. People will get suspicious.'

'They are already suspicious, Mac,' replied our hero. 'Yesterday Sir James Buttock saw me exercising your poodle, and my pockets were stuffed with birds.'

'Wrong dog,' said the laird.

Secrets of the trade

A hatter has said that in choosing a hat the customer should never jam it hastily on his head. It should be eased into place slowly. At one West End hattery the customer is held upside down by two assistants and slowly lowered into the hat, which is placed on the floor. This ensures a perfect fit, on the egg into egg-cup principle. In the case of the Cad's Cap, with no peak, the cap is held ten feet away from the customer, who, with head outstretched like a tortoise, crawls towards it on all fours.

A powerful allegory

Udmer continues his amazing experiments. He is at work on a play the action of which takes place on a tightrope. A sailor with a wooden leg starts to walk across the rope, but halfway across he meets a Welsh fireman who has started from the other side of the stage. No words are exchanged, but a lorry-driver enters and holds a bucket beneath the rope. The fireman steps into it, and is carried off. The sailor continues his journey along the tightrope.

Curtain. And that's only Act I: an allegory of the futility of life.

On the moors

Odd though it may sound, the Macaroon's bag yesterday was one lobster. Apparently the Laird o'Kilcockrobbin, warned of an early start for Shrillwillie Moor, came down in the half-light of dawn and saw a bird-like object at the kitchen window. He ran for his gun crying, as to the manner born, 'Mark over!'

The Macaroon of Macaroon thought he was shouting 'Narkover!' and that the place was being invaded by urchins from the famous school. He rushed from his bedroom, snatched the laird's gun, and fired at the object in the window, winging, or, rather, clawing it – for it was a dead lobster.

Roused by the noise, Foulenough rubbed what it is charitable to call the sleep from his bloodshot eyes and came downstairs. He was able to explain that before going to bed he had noticed a hole in the kitchen window, and had bunged it to stop the draught with a lobster he had found under a chair in the library; part of an impromptu meal during the day. The three men, each looking extremely silly, then went back to bed.

Tiara boom-de-ay!

The news that Emilia Rustiguzzi is to sing (sic) again in this country is a signal for frantic polishing of tiaras and many a stealthy tap on the pawnbroker's door where the family fal-lals are housed. She is to play the Fairy Queen in the Spanish opera *Cuento de Hadas* by the Basque composer Zugarramurdi. As befits a fairy, even a big one, she has to fly now and then. A strong cable is to be substituted for the usual wire, and she will land on a kind of miniature runway. The producer's job is to see that none of the cast is within striking distance when she lands. Unusually strong scenery is being made, in case of accidents.

Away from it all

Dear Bob,

Here we are in Paris at last. Our plane was hijacked by someone who demanded to be taken to Lisbon. We got away from Lisbon after a lot of fuss, but another couple of hijackers, who wanted to go to Nicaragua, were themselves hijacked by rivals, and we found ourselves in Stockholm. On leaving Stockholm luck was with us. We were hijacked by a couple of men who had not inquired where we were going, and demanded to be taken to Paris. So here we are at last.

Yours ever,
Stan

Something attempted, something done

Determined not to give people a wrong idea of what goes on on the moors, the three Musketeers, Foulenough, Kilcockrobbin, and the Macaroon, set off yesterday in businesslike fashion for Shrillwillie with plenty of food and drink, four packs of marked cards, two bloodhounds, and a large sack for the grouse. At the close of play, one bloodhound, shot by Kilcockrobbin, was in the sack; the Macaroon had lost £127 15s. 9d., and had written out an IOU and hidden it in his wallet; Foulenough was having a heated argument in the wrong butt.

Rustiguzzi is airborne

At the first rehearsal of *Cuento de Hadas* the cable which enabled the Fairy Queen to fly became entangled in the wires of two minor fairies. The diva, dangling like a hooked fish, was 'talked down' by the stage-manager, an ex-airman. But halfway through the aria *'Tempestad y Truenos'*, owing to the carelessness of a stagehand, Rustiguzzi was whisked off her feet again and up into the air. From this position of disadvantage she addressed to the flinching producer a few ill-chosen words from a vocabulary which would have done honour to the Genoa docks. An interpreter translated this outburst for the composer into the slang of the Paralelo quarter of Barcelona.

Printer's frolic

'Foreigners like to watch people throwing bits of beard to the pigeons in Trafalgar Square.'   (*News item*)

It should be explained to them that the bits of beard are either bought cheap from theatrical costumiers, or stolen from barbers' shops. Even bearded men who love pigeons are loth to mutilate their own beards to amuse the birds.

Woodland idyll

I passed beneath a tall beech tree
Whereon a small bird sang to me.
The rascal, not content with that,
Left a memento on my hat.
A tiresome prank, but, anyhow,
I'm thankful it was not a cow.

(ENTER, *dancing, the fairies* GROGBLOSSOM *and* QUARTBOTTLE.)

PRODNOSE: Cows don't sing in trees.
MYSELF: So I have often noticed, idiot.

On the moors

Captain Foulenough strayed far from his party yesterday to do a
bit of freelance work, and was discovered disputing a grouse with
a dog belonging to Lord Shortcake, who had shot the bird. To the
protests Foulenough replied that he happened to be crossing the

moor on business, and he had stopped to adjust the bird more firmly in the dog's mouth. Shortcake seemed incredulous until he noticed that the intruder was wearing an MCC tie.

A generous offer

The tourist who got into trouble because he insisted on driving the taxi he had hailed in Piccadilly reminded me of an old story of Tristan Bernard, the French wit. Bernard asked a taxi-driver, 'How much to the Rue Taitbout?'

'One hundred francs,' said the driver.

'Jump in,' said Bernard, 'I'll drive you there myself for fifty.'

Enter the Fairy Queen

At yesterday's rehearsal Rustiguzzi crash-landed. The Italian tenor Broccoli was singing about the tranquillity of the forest glade where the fairies hold their revels. The Spanish baritone, Montemayor, waiting in the wings, rushed out to help the Fairy Queen to her feet. Two fairies, played by Semolina and Tapioca, went into screaming hysterics. The Basque composer Zugarramurdi broke his baton across his knee in a tantrum, and Rustiguzzi showed a command of Spanish and Italian which would have made the entire Berlitz staff clap its hands to its ears.

Dr Rhubarb's corner

H.L. WRITES: My house is overrun with mice. Yesterday a herd of them rushed across our sitting-room and drove the cat back against the wall. As a supporter of the RSPCA, what should I do?

DR RHUBARB SAYS: That depends on whether you are on the side of the cat or of the mice.

The Huntingdonshire cabmen

A holidaymaker who was in Huntingdonshire writes to tell me that he traced several of the cabmen who figure in the *List* (fourth edition). He suggests that in the next edition addresses should be given, and that it should include half a dozen Cabmen of the Year. I am passing on the suggestion to the Trustees of the Sutterbury Foundation. It may interest them to know that in M. Marc Vaurien's French translation of the *List*, *Les Cochers de Huntingdonshire*, the addresses are given in English. An Italian translation, *Le Cocchiere di Huntingdonshire,* is in preparation. There is also a German translation: *Die Mitschuldigen Ausgeschon-köpfe im Teufelsglocke Wahl-wehrwandschutz Gesellschaft Verlangen.*

a useful book.

Puzzle corner

Arrange eight matches in four lines, so that the fifth and the seventh are next to the third and the first, counting backwards from the second line.

Travelling hopefully and arriving

Having decided that, though it has been a good season for drinking in the North, it has been a bad one for grouse, Captain Foulenough has returned to London, 'somewhat the better for wear', as he put it. The Macaroon of Macaroon and the Laird o'Kilcockrobbin will remain at the castle as long as the cellar holds out. Foulenough travelled to London on a platform ticket, angrily protesting to the authorities that he was looking for his aunt to say goodbye to her, when the train started. He was put off at the first stop, bought another platform ticket for the next train, told the same story, and was put off at the next stop. In this way he finally reached London, where he was put off grumbling loudly about having to return to Scotland.

Railway song

'He said that you could break a tooth on some of those railway buns.' *(News item)*

Little Miss Muffet
Sat in a buffet,
  Cramming a bun in her maw.
But, alas and alack,
There came a loud crack.
  Miss Muffet had fractured her jaw.

16

Charlie Suet, Civil Servant

An Office-Worker and a Gentleman

The election of Mimsie Slopcorner as Sliced Bread Empress of Little Sniffington will no doubt delay the words that have been trembling on the tip of Charlie Suet's tongue for so long. It is known that he is reluctant to interfere with her career. 'A career devoted to social utility,' said Suet, 'is a preparation for a steady marriage, giving one a sense of responsibility, service, and self-denial. Even a deputy carnival queen is an ornament to the female sex.'

By an amazing irony Suet's new secretary, Vanilla Darling, is last year's Tupton Tracy Beauty Queen. The surname alone terrifies poor Suet. And when she looks at him with her large blue eyes he flinches as though menaced by a hornet. He dictates his letters from a distant corner of the room, in the lee of a protective filing cabinet. When she hands him a cup of tea he backs away like a shying horse, and then reaches out, as though they were standing on opposite banks of a stream. 'Mimsie Slopcorner,' said a friend, 'is the only girl in Suet's life – and she is only just in it.'

Yesterday Suet was engrossed in a pile of documents. He heard his secretary approach his desk, and without looking up, extended his hand, expecting to receive a memorandum he had sent for. Vanilla Darling, accustomed to friendly gestures, placed her little hand in his. Suet jumped nervously and abandoned the hand as though it had been a poisoned arrow.

Vanilla's eyes said plainly, 'If you prefer a rotten old memorandum, here you are!' and deposited it on his desk.

Suet said to himself, 'What did I do to lead her on like this? I must be more circumspect.'

When she brought his tea, he was standing with his back

to the wall, like a man about to be shot.

'Playing hard to get,' muttered the beauty.

Mimsie Slopcorner called at Suet's office to return a book he had lent her – *Aspects of Departmental Administration*.

When Vanilla Darling swayed across the room, Mimsie stared as though Cleopatra had appeared.

When Vanilla had gone, Mimsie attempted sarcasm. 'Your aunt, I presume,' she said.

'No, no relation,' said Suet absent-mindedly.

'Well, thanks for the book. Don't let me detain you from the bathing-pool.'

Suet gaped. 'What bathing-pool?' he asked.

'The one,' said Mimsie haughtily, 'which is not mentioned in your thrilling book about departmental administration. Good day, Mr Suet.'

Suet laid his finger horizontally along his upper lip and breathed down his nose. 'I shall never understand women,' he said to himself.

Suet's colleagues are much amused at his hesitant and ponderous manner of speech. When he addresses his secretary, Vanilla Darling, he says: 'Miss – er – Darling,' and the accent seems to fall on the embarrassing surname.

Eyes glinting with mischief, Vanilla said one say, 'You may call me Vanilla, if you like. It would avoid having to use the word Darling, wouldn't it?'

Said Suet, 'The – er – that word used in reference to – er – you is used by me not as a word but as a name.'

'What a pity,' she replied. Suet looked aghast. 'I mean,' she added, 'what a pity I have such an awkward name.'

'Most people,' said Vanilla, 'call me Darling, because Vanilla is such an odd name, and I'm no relative of the well-known ice. Far from it.'

'To avoid misunderstanding,' mumbled Suet, 'I prefer to use the prefix "Miss" when addressing you.'

'I don't think I should ever misunderstand you if you dropped the "Miss" now and then,' replied the secretary.

'My colleagues might,' said Suet.

'Onny swar ke mally pence,' riposted the siren. 'Here's the statement from Mr Clodd.'

'Thank you, Miss – er – Darling,' said Suet.

'Unless you drop that "er", foul tongues will wag,' said Vanilla. 'It sounds as though you were calling me darling.'

Suet flushed, and made no reply.

On her way through London, Miss Araminta Suet, Charlie's aunt, called at her nephew's office. One glance at Vanilla Darling bore out all she had ever heard about secretaries.

Seeing his aunt's disapproval, Suet became confused. 'Aunt Araminta,' he said, 'this is my darling, Miss Secretary – er – my secretary—.'

Vanilla left the room, helpless with laughter.

Miss Suet addressed her nephew with withering scorn. 'So, Charles,' she said, 'this is what goes on! Your belated attempt to conceal what is no doubt your customary term of endearment does not hoodwink *me*. Good-day, Charles.'

Miss Araminta Suet to her brother:

... And in Charlie's office there was a sort of film-star creature whom he addressed as 'darling'. Of course, he said she was his secretary. Who would ever have thought that his mask of shy innocence was a cloak for the antics of a libertine? He seems not to care two straws for the family name. What poor Miss Slopcorner's feelings must be I tremble to think after the way he has led her to expect an honest proposal. I am too upset to write more. The so-called secretary's outlandish costume seemed to be designed rather for some dreadful bathing-pool than for a properly-conducted office ...

A voice over the telephone said: 'Is that Vanilla?'

'No,' said Suet, 'it's not Vanilla. It's Mr Suet.' And he handed the telephone to her.

Later, she said: 'You know, that was the first time you've used my Christian name, and in office hours too!'

'I – er – it was – er – ' stammered Suet.

'Don't spoil our friendship,' said Vanilla, with a wicked, sarcastic smile.

Suggestions of a more decisive approach to matrimony pour off Suet like water off a duck's back or champagne off an actress's. Every year the Slopcorner parents hope for a happy ending to the interminable courtship, the monotony of which is broken only by an invitation to a lecture on civic consciousness or the gift of a pamphlet about departmental co-ordination. On one occasion, Mrs Slopcorner suggested to her husband that Suet should be asked firmly if his intentions were honourable.

Mr Slopcorner replied, 'My dear, judging by the progress made over the years, he must have a pretty dull notion of dishonourable intentions.'

A blush mantled his wife's cheek as she uttered the monosyllabic reproof: 'Arthur!'

Charlie Suet called on the Slopcorners yesterday. The parents thought that, at last, Suet was about to ask for Mimsie's hand in marriage. He was left alone with Slopcorner *père*.

'I will come straight to the point,' said Suet. 'My godson's niece has a cousin who collects the labels of marmalade-tins. It is an obsession. Would you, as the father of a family, allow this to go on? The boy is fifteen and big for his age. I have advised his mother to stop buying marmalade.'

Said Mr Slopcorner to Mrs Slopcorner, 'I wonder, bearing in mind that this Suet may one day propose to our Mimsie, whether he believes in long engagements?'

'Nobody,' replied Mrs Slopcorner, 'can say that she has led him on.'

'Only once,' said the proud father, 'when, as she admits, she let the Mayor of Snadgehurst kiss her at the fête, to make Suet jealous. All Suet said was "That was very nice of the Mayor." As for leading him on, she might as well try to lead on a stuffed mackerel.'

Rumour ran well-nigh rife in the Slopcorner residence last week. Charlie Suet had called, and on leaving had handed Mimsie what looked like a *billet doux*. It was assumed that the painfully shy bureaucrat had proposed in writing. Mimsie opened it when he had gone, and her parents gathered round. Blushing like a Lincoln beetroot, Mimsie extracted a ticket for a lecture on Co-ordination. The accompanying note said: 'This may interest you. I shall be on the platform.'

A bunch of daffodils arrived yesterday for Mimsie Slopcorner from the impetuous Charlie Suet.

'Any day now,' said Mr Slopcorner, 'he'll touch her hand, as though by accident, during some accursed lecture on departmental co-operation. And when she falters, "Mr Suet! You really shouldn't!" the oaf will move his own hand away as though stung by a maddened scorpion.'

Said Mrs Slopcorner, 'It was a kindly thought. She can wear one of them at the Luton Vegetable Rally if she is elected Miss Cauliflower.'

Looking not only spick, but span, Charlie Suet called at the Slopcorner residence yesterday to take Mimsie to a lecture on departmental co-operation. Slopcorner *père* said sarcastically, 'No chaperon?'

Suet replied: 'There will be 1,750 people at the lecture, sir. Your daughter will be amply protected from unwelcome attentions.'

Said Slopcorner *mère*, 'Dad, I think, was joking, Mr Suet.'

'Ah,' said Charlie, at a loss for more words. As for Mimsie, a wild-rose blush, mantling her cheeks, spoke more than words.

'Mr Suet called me his Persian rose,' said Mimsie to her father.

'My word!' said Mr Slopcorner. 'He's stepping out. When I was courting your mother, I whispered once, "My little wood-pigeon." And she replied, "My big hippopotamus." That was how it all began. What did you reply?'

'I was so flustered,' said Mimsie, 'that I dropped my handbag. He picked it up and said, "Keep this in memory of today." '

'He's daft,' said Mr Slopcorner.

Lovelorn Charlie Suet

What do the cuckoo's two notes say?
  'Mimsie.'
The beech trees in the copse
  mutter 'Slopcorner' as they sway.
The bluebells nod their azure tops
In time to her enchanting name.
Even the farmer's creaking cart
  squeaks 'Slopcorner', and feeds the flame
That doth consume poor Suet's heart.

These lines were sent by Suet to his love after he had spent a weekend in the country.

Mimsie's father comments

Dear Mr Suet,

I read your poem. I am not a poet, but I can hardly believe that you really think a farmer's cart squeaked 'Slopcorner' as it went by, or that a cuckoo called 'Mimsie.' You must have a diseased imagination. What would you think if I said that the rain falling into our water-barrel said 'Mrs Slopcorner'? My wife would have me certified.

Yours faithfully,
Henry Slopcorner

Suet tries again

The stars are her golden tiara,
They are only there to adorn her.
They trace a delicate pattern
Which forms the word 'Slopcorner'.
Those who have never loved
Will doubtless accuse me of whimsy,
But the Great Bear writes in the sky
A capital M for Mimsie.

Mimsie replies

I'd have thought, wouldn't you,
That the stars had something better to do
    Than spell my name?
    All the same,
Hard though I try,
I can't see SUET written in the sky.

Suet to his love

Over a second cup of tea
Mimsie Slopcorner sighed at me,
And the accompanying sigh
Pierced my heart like an assegai.
But then I heard her softly mutter,
'Charlie, your elbow's in the butter.'
I suppose I had been too presumptuous,
To expect from her a phrase less bumptious.

Mimsie gives a hint

If ever I marry Suet
   I hope he will change his name.
I should certainly urge him to do it.
   Imagine my feelings of shame
Were I photographed as 'Miss Factory Bread',
   And they called me 'Mrs Suet' instead.

The riposte

Suet is a more rational name
Than Slopcorner, one must agree.
And 'Mimsie' is sillier than 'Charles',
Or so it seems to me.
The sneers of my potential bride
Are tasteless and unjustified.

*   *   *

'Brief Idyll' – A Story of Love
Two Hearts That Beat Carpets As One

Mr Epaminondas Peristhenes was richer than even the Inland Revenue authorities suspected, but he was unhappy. As he sauntered along the Croisette at Cannes, followed at a respectful distance by a corps of secretaries, the taste in his mouth was not of caviar, but of unripe Dead Sea fruit and ashes. His yacht, described by more than one chronicler as a veritable floating palace, rode at anchor as only she could ride. His wardrobes were reputed to contain 734 suits of clothes, and he never wore the same hat twice, and seldom even once. Yet there was a fly, or rather an elephant, in the ointment. Epaminondas was in love, and contemplating marriage, but the course of his fairly true love was running about as smoothly as a Rumanian mountain-bus.

It had happened in a flash. Epaminondas had been about to enter a shop in the Allée de la Liberté, when Mabel Bottle, the simple unassuming tea-hostess with an East Anglian firm of steam carpet beaters, collided with him, prodding his chin with her sunshade. A blush of embarrassment mantled the damask of her cheek, and she apologised in a voice which twanged like the guitars of Paradise.

The stricken millionaire, with Cupid's arrow firmly embedded in his heart, conversed with her awhile, and invited her to partake of refreshment at a café on the next morning. Mabel, out of compassion for one who seemed to be a lonely magnate, accepted the invitation demurely. Epaminondas went on his way, murmuring 'Mabel Bottle' as though it were a line of exquisite poetry.

Epaminondas had always vowed that he longed to be loved for himself, not for his money; a whim which had often sent his parasites into screams of laughter. But Mabel was apparently unwilling to love him either for himself or for his money. When he spoke of marriage, she said, 'I hardly know you.' Many people would have envied her that singular good fortune, since Epaminondas was a terrible bore. Yet he persisted. He found her, he said, 'different'. He who was so accustomed to a babel of chatter was refreshed by her economy of words, and attributed to delicacy and refinement what was merely the expression of an empty mind. One day, as he spoke of his enormous villa on the slopes of the Estérel, which awaited his bride, she interjected, 'There's a fly on your nose.' He found that charming.

Mabel Bottle dreamed of love in a cottage, and it was in vain that Epaminondas protested that his tastes were simple. He was contradicted by three enormous motor-cars, with chauffeurs better dressed than her father; by the yacht, with its Assyrian decorations and smart crew; by his friends, who seemed so vulgar and ostentatious to her; and by his corps of secretaries. When he first took her to a luxurious restaurant, he was touched when she asked for a cup of tea and a boiled egg, with a slice of cake to follow.

When he asked her if she liked champagne, she said: 'No. It's like getting pins and needles on your tongue.'

'You are adorable,' he replied.

And for the first time in his life this phrase was met with the astonishing reply: 'You really ought not to say such things.'

The courtship made no progress. When he sent her orchids, she said her favourite flower was the woodland primrose. She would accept no presents, and every time she drank grenadine while he was drinking champagne he felt it as a kind of tacit criticism of his way of life.

At a party in his yacht she said to a glittering woman: 'Those pearls must have cost you hundreds of pounds.'

'They didn't cost a penny,' said the woman.

And Mabel thought, 'She is no doubt the wife of some jeweller.'

When invited to play poker she said she would rather go upstairs and lean over the railings to look at the sea. Epaminondas began to hate his wealth. And one day he had a brilliant idea.

Epaminondas said to himself: 'I really believe she would marry me if I was a poor man. So I will be a poor man for the present.' He asked her to meet him in the port, and come out to the yacht for some dancing. What was her amazement when he arrived in a dirty old rowing-boat, which he was rowing himself. He was in rags, and unshaven. 'I'm broke,' he explained. 'I've sold the yacht to pay my debts.'

Tears of compassion came into her eyes. 'Oh, you poor Epimanidondas!' she cried (she could never get his name right, the little ass). From that moment she softened towards him, even offering to lend him 1,173 francs (all that was in her purse).

Deeply moved, he accepted the loan. 'I suppose,' he said, 'you would never marry me, now that I am ruined?'

'Of course not,' she answered, 'what would we live on?'

'Have you no money?' he asked.

The moment Epaminondas asked Mabel, 'Have you no money?' she said to herself, 'Now that he is poor, he no longer loves me for myself. He is after my money.' She flushed with humiliation and said rather coldly, 'Do not spoil our beautiful friendship.'

Her suitor, with a memory of the last film he had seen, replied, 'This thing is bigger than both of us. We can't fight it.'

'I can,' said Mabel, and walked off in high dudgeon.

The rejected magnate rowed himself back to his yacht, discarded his rags, howled for champagne, and resumed the normal life of a millionaire. Mabel Bottle returned to England and married the manager of a public baths in the Midlands.

Song (verse LXIV)

All is human under the hat,
  So do not judge by the face.
Even the stockbroker with his pose
Of a bowler tilted over the nose
  Belongs to the human race,
  For the simple reason that –
Chorus:
  All is human, human, human,
  Utterly human under the hat.

17

Peas in the East

The Tibetan Venus Again

Word has come to the Foreign Office of a secret rocket-site in the Afghan hinterland. The site was said to be disguised as a factory for canning peas, and there was talk of a mysterious Tibetan woman of surpassing beauty who was in some way involved. The choice of an emissary to penetrate the secret naturally fell on Colonel Egham, who had so often been outwitted by Dingi-Poos. Nobody doubted that she was the mysterious lady concerned. Thus it was that the colonel found himself in the village of Furzah, stained with walnut juice and the dirt of travel, half hoping to find once more the Tibetan Venus, and half dreading her poisonous beauty.

Colonel Egham's parachute had deposited him with a dull thud, on a moonless night, in a field of turnips on the outskirts of Sabzawar. Hiding the tell-tale gadget under a *buzwari* bush, he felt his way northwards. The colonel was disguised as a water-carrier, but he had forgotten the water, and when he entered the village of Furzah shortly after dawn he was surrounded by a thirsty crowd. Luckily he spoke the dialect. He told them he had been robbed of their water by bandits. He was given a breakfast of *showjah*, and mountain *zuls*, washed down with *kuri*. Casually he asked if they knew anything of a canning factory in the district. Silence fell. One old rogue asked how a cannery could concern a water-carrier. 'Times are bad,' said Egham, 'and canning peas is a thirsty business.' Insincere laughter greeted this quip.

While Egham was guzzling in the village, a lean-faced herdsman slipped away. Three hours later Dingi-Poos, reclining on a divan, was betting all China to a blood-orange that the mysterious water-carrier was none other than her old antagonist Egham. Her eyes narrowed. Her exquisite knuckles showed white as she gripped her fan. She rewarded the herdsman with a pile of counterfeit coins, changed into something comfortable, and hummed a Tibetan folk-song. Presently she slunk across the room to a green marble telephone. 'Give me Kabul 83719,' she drawled. In her eyes was a lazy, cruel smile. Outside the Afghan stars shone down. In the distance a Gowji howled and was answered by its mate.

When Egham came into Koh-Safed he had discarded his water-carrier's rags and was now dressed as a prosperous Kashmiri merchant. He left his string of camels on the outskirts and saun-tered through the town. At the hotel where he booked a room, he signed his name Kaga Zahari, and gave out that he had come to purchase canned peas. 'In that case,' they said (having been instructed by Dingi-Poos), 'you should go to see the great lady who has an interest in this cannery.' Within an hour Egham was at the gates of the magnificent mansion from which Dingi-Poos spun her web of intrigue and beastliness. His heart beat faster as the *jabah* announced him. 'Sit down, Mr Zahari,' she said suavely.

'I understand,' said the Serpent of Old Brahmapootra, 'that you are interested in our cannery.'

'Passionately,' replied the merchant. 'My camels await their loads. I am mad about canned peas, and the fame of your cannery has gone far and wide, beauteous lady.'

'I will take you to see the manager,' said Dingi-Poos. 'The factory is near at hand. But first we will drink to our deal.' She clapped her hands, and a girl brought in brick tea and rancid butter on a yakskin trolley.

'Afghan food disagrees with me,' she said. 'This is our own Tibetan snack. Whenever I partake of it I think of a certain Englishman, an old friend of mine named Egham.'

The merchant jumped and spilled his brick tea.

'This Englishman,' she went on, 'couldn't stomach it. He used to pour the tea into a flowerpot when he thought I wasn't looking.'

'Indeed,' said the merchant, feeling sick already.

Despite himself, Egham was falling once more under the spell of her beauty. She passed him a lump of rancid butter, and their hands touched. He shuddered, seized her hand and kissed it loudly. She smiled. 'Mr Zahari!' she breathed languorously.

'Call me Kaga,' said Egham in a hoarse undertone.

'Silly Gaga! Silly boy!' she whispered, 'Don't spoil our friendship.'

Egham stroked her cheek. 'Oh, you merchants!' she cried, wondering how he could be fool enough to imagine that she had not penetrated his disguise.

'One little kiss,' he pleaded in fluent Afghan.

'Canned peas before pleasure,' riposted the enchantress. 'Come! We will go to the factory before your ardour sweeps me off my feet.'

Egham grinned like an oaf.

'The warmongers of the West,' said Dingi-Poos, 'pretend to believe that this canning factory is a rocket site! Well, here are the rockets, Mr Zahari.' She and Egham were walking round the factory. She pointed to a shed filled with enormous packing-cases labelled 'Peas'. A bespectacled man who looked more like a scientist than a canner came out of a large room crammed with instruments. Egham was on the alert. The man said to Dingi-Poos, 'We have an order for sixty gross of cans from Pakistan, and tins have arrived for the Turkish consignment.'

'Very warlike, isn't it?' she said to Egham, who was puzzled. Why had he been sent on this wild-goose chase? Everywhere he looked, he saw nothing but receptacles labelled 'Peas'.

'What,' asked Egham, 'is that thing over there – it looks like a warhead.'

Dingi-Poos uttered a squeal of melodious laughter. 'What would tinned peas want of a warhead?' she asked. 'That is the swivel-faucet, which dehydrates and processes the peas when they cascade down the shoot from the hardening room. Did you imagine we were preparing to shoot a tin of peas to the moon? Suspicion persists in rearing its ugly head, eh?'

'My suspicion,' answered Egham, 'had the loveliest head in Afghanistan.' And he darted an ardent glance at her glossy mane. Then, remembering to play his part, he said, 'May

I have some cans loaded on my camels?'

'Certainly,' riposted the belle of Dung, who had taken care to have some tinned peas ready for such an emergency.

Egham's camels pawed the ground peevishly. They were loaded with tins of peas. Egham, reassured as to the rocket-site, was saying goodbye to Dingi-Poos. The Kashmiri merchant had forgotten his part, and the Tibetan Venus recognised his brand of wooing. 'One kiss for auld lang syne,' he pleaded, slipping into English.

'Whoever old Lang Zyne may be,' replied Dingi-Poos, 'I know my dear old Egham.'

'Dingi!' cried the warrior. 'Who would have thought of you being interested in tinned peas?'

'Or you,' she replied.

Folding her in his arms, he planted a kiss on her upturned nose.

'Make a favourable report to your masters,' she said.

'About you?' he asked.

'Of course,' said she. 'Tell them our peas have no designs on outer space.' Thus they parted.

'What the devil am I to do with all these camel-loads of peas?' Egham asked himself.

'Afghan Tinned Pea Site.' 'Egham Solves Mystery.' 'Tibetan Beauty In The Clear.' So ran the headlines. And in Koh-Safed the 'manager' of the 'factory' took the dust covers off the intercontinental missiles.

In Whitehall a puzzled Foreign Office spokesman asked Egham, 'You're sure it is only a cannery?'

'I saw it with my own eyes,' said Egham, 'and I took away a load of tins and sold them to tribesmen.'

'That seems to prove it,' said the official, 'but Dingi-Poos must have turned over a new leaf. You don't suspect her?'

'I would as soon suspect myself,' replied Egham gallantly.

'Perhaps you ought to,' muttered the uneasy official.

*   *   *

Clarion call

The nation must face the facts. What those facts are it would not be in the public interest to reveal. There are certain aspects of the situation which, though they do arise, or have already arisen, or not, complicate whatever is to be done, however or whenever it is to be done, or whatever it is, which make it essential to consider the whole situation in its entirety, without, however, taking any premature action, or prejudicing any steps which might or might not be deemed advisable or inadvisable under certain conditions, which may or may not obtain then or now.

Lucky dip

'The words he used seemed surprisingly cryptic, but one must concentrate on their presumed meaning.'   (*Report of speech*)

> We must presume he had not said
>   Precisely what he meant to mean,
> And that he meant to say, instead,
>   What he had meant to say. Between
> The meaning and the words there lies
>   Whatever *we* care to surmise.

The autoyacht

The Automobile Association says that our motorways are too windy, and warns drivers to reduce speed in a high wind. The answer is the Strabismus autoyacht, a car fitted with sails, and an outboard motor for use in oily calms. This saves petrol and adds a touch of the picturesque to those dull roads. The Sage points out that if an autoyacht capsizes in a sudden gust there is no danger of drowning.

Come into the kitchen

How to unpickle gherkins.
Reverse the pickling process.

For the discerning

You can always pick out the girl who drinks Snibbonac, the Sparkling British Brandy. She has poise and charm, and is always seen about town with top people. Snibbonac is non-alcoholic and is prepared from a secret recipe in our laboratories by trained chemists. It cures insomnia, coughs, bandy legs, nerve-strain, freckles on the soles of the feet, baldness, and blushing. It can be used to remove grease-stains from felt hats. It is an All Purpose Drink.

Con brio

'Some of the heavier chords were played with more than the forearm or arm weight. They were played with the whole body, the pianist rising in her seat for better effect.' (*Music critic*)

The Norwegian pianist Sledjhammer often jumps into the air and comes crashing down on the keys. He boasts that with one blow of his fist he can stove in a whole octave. To preserve the delicacy of his hands, Kurt Peildreiver plays the more ferocious kinds of music in special boxing gloves. The blurring effect of this is rather fun. 'He will stand no nonsense from the piano,' wrote a critic, 'and very little sense.'

Feed your gnats on fish scales

A painstaking apiarist has discovered that bees fed on tomato skins buzz more loudly. I hope that their honey tastes of tomatoes. What should we feed bluebottles on to increase the volume of their carefree song? It is such questions as this which—

PRODNOSE: You might as well say that mice fed on dandelions squeak more loudly.

MYSELF: You took the words out of my mouth. I was about to say something like that.

PRODNOSE: Are you paid by the word? If so, I can understand this drivelling.

MYSELF: Indeed, yes. And let me tell you I am paid extra for commas,,, and often use three where one would satisfy an inferior stylist.

Further clarification

It is now quite clear that, having regard to all or many of the circumstances obtaining, and making allowance for the potential factors which form an integral part of the question, viewed in whatever light, no clear-cut decision can be attempted until a more exhaustive probing of the overall position has resulted in some elucidation of every aspect, resulting in the possibility of an understanding being reached as to exactly what it is that is being considered.

Wellington

On a recent list of the Duke of Wellington's sayings I missed his reply to Louis XVIII when the king apologised for the French marshals who had turned their backs on him and walked out of a reception. 'Pray do not distress yourself, sire,' said the duke. 'It is not the first time they have shown me their backs.'

Here, there and everywhere

A WINDOW-CLEANER who went into a bank and asked the cashier for a return ticket to Aylesbury tried to sell the assistant manager a ball of twine.

A BOY stole a prawn from an Edgware fish-shop. He said he wanted to tickle a dormouse with the prawn's whiskers.

CLAIMING to be a viscount on his mother's side, a night-watchman bored holes in a drum, filled it with sand, and left it on the doorstep of a Tarporley barrister.

Lady Annabella Steps Out: An Egalitarian Tale

'Chalk up that last brown ale to my father,' said Lady Annabella Floote-Gawdreigh to old Mumpy, the rubicund landlord of the Cuddlingham Arms. As the Earl of Cuddlingham's daughter left the inn, and was about to get into her Thanatos Twelve, she fell over a bucket. A policeman approached, and, with a courteous, nay, deferential air produced from his pocket a breathalyser. 'And what,' queried her ladyship, 'may that disgusting object be?'

Apologetically the constable replied, 'It detects any alcohol fumes remaining in the breath, my lady.'

Withering the minion of the law with a look of scorn, the apple of the earl's eye riposted, with a curling lip, 'My breath is my own affair, Carter. Go take a running jump at yourself.' And she drove off, as though to the manner born.

'Annabella,' vouchsafed the earl, as he sat on his shooting-stick in the sunken garden, 'idle tongues are wagging. They say that you frequent the village inn. Is not this house capable of satisfying even the most inordinate thirst? When the desire for drink overwhelms you, is there no bell with which to summon Mason, Travers, or Rawlins to minister to your needs? Must I live to hear one day that you have been roaring vulgar choruses with my labourers?'

'Father,' replied the spirited girl, 'the inn is a home from home, where I meet real people.'

The earl pondered this information in gloomy silence.

'Monstrous!' cried the earl. 'Here is a bill from the Cuddlingham Arms for £7 14s. 3d. for beer. I trust you did not consume this ghastly sea of drink unaided.'

'I have to stand my whack,' retorted Annabella sulkily.

'Could you not stand what you are pleased to call your whack in the Royal Hotel?'

'Do you think the herdsmen and ploughmen would go to that morgue? Imagine them with the Castle crowd!'

'I would hardly call our neighbours a crowd,' said the earl, 'but they are more fitting company for my daughter than the villagers. It is all this damned democracy. You will be bringing my gardeners to dinner next.'

'I think,' said the Lady Annabella slyly, 'that if you got a bill for champagne from the Royal Hotel, you would raise no objection.'

'That depends,' said the earl. 'If I thought you had been teaching the villagers to drink champagne I should feel as if you had stood on a soap-box in the market place preaching sedition.'

'Suppose I taught our wealthier friends to drink beer in the inn?'

'Inverted snobbery,' shouted her father.

'Suppose I stood beer to the villagers in the Royal Hotel and champagne to our friends in the inn?'

The earl pouted, sighed, and groaned. 'You are trying,' he said, 'to turn the world upside down.'

Under the earl's flashy waistcoat there pounded a human heart. Annabella was his daughter – or so he had been led to believe. One day he entered the Cuddlingham Arms. A hush of embarrassment rather than respect fell on the assembled company. A kindly word here, a smile there, a slap on the back, and all was well. Lady Annabella, tankard in hand, could hardly believe her eyes. 'Name your poison, dad,' she screamed.

The earl rose to the occasion like a trout under a cloudy sky. 'Magnums all round, Mumpy,' he bellowed at the landlord, who at once unearthed a dozen of Roederer kept for the pageant. 'Mud in every eye!' said the earl.

'And in yours, dear dad,' replied Annabella, grinning through her tears of happiness.

'With knobs on,' muttered a cowman.

Ah, democracy!

18

French Leave

Foulenough on the Riviera

It is reported that Captain Foulenough, travelling fairly incognito as Sir Helmsley Spadwell-Gadleigh, has arrived at Cannes. In a bar frequented by yachtsmen he was heard to say, 'My damned boat hasn't arrived yet.' A newt-faced social climber, hoping to get in with another wealthy ne'er-do-well, introduced him to the owner of a yacht, who, for reasons we need not go into, was unpopular among the moneyed crowd. He at once invited Sir Helmsley to stay on his yacht for a day or two. Sir Helmsley won £127 15s. at poker, swam ashore during the night, and turned up next day at Fréjus as Major Fauconwell.

The police of Fréjus, alerted after a card-party, which ended in a brawl, have received from Foulenough his usual holiday picture-postcard saying: 'Wish you were not here,' signed 'Ron'.

In the Coucou bar at Cannes Captain Foulenough came face to face with Vita Brevis. Hearing him addressed as Bigg-Nunkerley, she raised her Phiton eyebrows (£3 15s. a set) a good inch or two. Hastily he explained that his aunt had left him money in her will on condition that he took her name.

'How much money?' she asked sceptically.

Sensing the danger, as a thirsty crowd closed in, Foulenough said jauntily: 'Only about fourteen shillings after death duties and taxes. Anyhow, the poor old girl was never well off.'

A gentleman in Cannes accused Foulenough of looking at his opponents' cards during a dispute.

'I have a terrible squint,' said the warrior. 'I can never be sure what I am looking at. It's hereditary. My father could see round corners. Without wanting to, of course.'

Seeing Foulenough with a cheque-book sticking out of his pocket, Vita Brevis asked sarcastically: 'May one ask what *you* are doing with a cheque-book?'

'One may, delightful morsel,' he replied. 'The sight of such an implement provokes confidence. Recently, when a barman seemed disinclined to give me credit, I took out this book, wrote a cheque for £150, addressed the envelope to a peer of the realm, and asked for the nearest post-box. Next day the barman positively encouraged me to drink.'

In a crowded café in Cannes a young couple announced their engagement. Captain Foulenough, who was with the large party, noticed a waiter within earshot, and whispered to the banker next to him, 'This calls for champagne all round, don't you think?'

'Yes, rather. Splendid idea,' said the banker, and repeated, 'Champagne all round – the very thing.'

The waiter heard the words and obeyed. 'That was really very decent of you,' said Foulenough to the astonished banker, who was too timid to make any protest.

'Help! Help!' The cry came from a man who had fallen into Villefranche harbour. Foulenough, who happened to be there, seized a life-belt and threw it to him. A crowd collected and the man was hauled ashore. 'Why, it's Lord Horsecroft!' exclaimed Foulenough. 'Monty, old boy, that was a near thing.' Willing hands escorted rescuer and rescued to a café, and willing voices ordered drink. It took his lordship a long time (and many drinks) to recover. Foulenough also appeared to be much shaken and in need of stimulants. When the two finally left, arm in arm, Lord Horsecroft ('Flash' Scudmole to us) said, 'This trick will only work once, de Courcy. Think up something else.'

A stroke of luck at the tables in Monte Carlo posed a problem for Foulenough: how to deal with all the people to whom he owed money. The other day he picked out in a bar an acquaintance to whom he owed a trifling sum, lured him into a corner away from all the others, and repaid him with a flourish. At that moment, a well-coached attendant summoned him to the telephone, before the lucky creditor could spread the news of the warrior's generous impulse.

'Your luck,' said a newly-made friend to Foulenough, 'is phenomenal. Anyone would think the cards were marked.'

'Not anyone,' riposted the warrior. 'Only a man with a very suspicious mind, surely.'

'I was joking,' said the owner of the yacht.

'Of course, of course,' replied Foulenough, draining his glass of champagne, and looking round furtively for the ice-bucket.

'Do you ever play in championships?' asked Lady Funneigh.

'Oh, no,' said Foulenough. 'It's all too formal, if you see what I mean.' And he added under his breath, 'I hope you don't.'

Vita Brevis, invited to lunch on the *Ocean Sprite*, owner Mr Hector Koruthaiolos, was dumb-founded when her host introduced her to the Marquis de St Pol, and she found herself confronted by Foulenough. He kissed her hand and was half-way along her arm before she could extricate herself. She said coldly, 'I believe we have met before.'

'Zat eese so, Madame,' was the reply. 'Eet wass at my château orn ze Loire.'

'Probably,' said Vita, 'I wouldn't be surprised.'

'Your name seems familiar, but I cannot recollect your face,' said Foulenough to a lady in a café.

'But you don't *know* my name,' she replied.

'It is the face that matters,' retorted the warrior, emotionally.

'You must be drunk,' said the lady, moving away.

'Intoxicated with beauty,' cried Foulenough, 'but I have enough self-restraint to cut you dead from now on. Goodbye for ever, heart of stone.' And he strode away, wondering what the devil he had been talking about.

Foulenough had drunk just enough to make him touchy. One of a large party in a café said to Vita Brevis, 'Who is that vulgar friend of yours?'

Foulenough leaped to his feet, and, with a knightly gesture, snatched Vita's glove and fixed it to his panama. 'Sir,' he said, 'any insult to me is, *per se*, an insult to this lady. We have no horses and lances, but I would throw this drink in your face were I not too thirsty to waste it. Consider yourself unhorsed and wounded.'

An embarrassed silence, broken only by the sound of the knight-errant's drinking, followed this outburst.

Minetti's Bar at St Tropez was crowded. Foulenough noticed a pretty girl drinking alone, and joined her. 'Cheer up,' he said, 'it may not be true.'

'It is true,' she said. 'My boyfriend has left me.'

'How much has he left you?' asked the warrior.

'Don't be silly,' said the girl, laughing. Five drinks later, all paid for by Foulenough, she said, 'Buy me another drink.'

'No wonder he left you,' muttered Foulenough. 'I must go and telephone. Excuse me.'

Vita Brevis's aunt, who disapproved of Foulenough, frowned when she saw him coming towards her at St Tropez. She said, with malicious pleasure, 'Vita has gone with some people to Rapallo.' At that moment Foulenough pulled out his handkerchief to blow his nose, and out came a pack of cards. The aunt winced, as though he had produced a cobra.

'I often play patience to pass the time,' said Foulenough.

'So I've heard,' she replied in her glacier-voice.

He could not resist replying, 'Don't believe all you hear.'

'I don't,' said she.

The curious-looking, flashy ring which Foulenough wore had been bought outside a public-house in Holborn for eightpence. The wealthy American widow in a café in Nice asked its history.

'It belonged,' said he, 'to my grandfather, and was given him by Palmerston. Take it, dear one, as a memento.'

'No, I couldn't,' said the widow.

'Perhaps you couldn't. Idle tongues might wag. Give me ten thousand of the new francs for it, and thus disown at birth the raucous voice of scandal.'

The money changed hands.

'Think of me sometimes, when you look at the ring,' said Foulenough. 'I must now get back to my aunt, the dowager.'

Foulenough sat in a café, watching a gay party of a dozen people. Presently one of the men came over to him. 'Surely it's Tom Graham?' he said.

'That's right,' said Foulenough, to whom names are a trivial matter.

'You remember me – Paul Sellick?'

'Of course. How are things, Paul?'

The warrior was taken over and introduced to the rest of the party, wondering who the deuce this man was.

'We're all going up to Felicity's place in the hills,' said Paul. 'You'd better join up.'

The cavalcade of cars set off, and 'Graham' discovered that he was supposed to have been in Sellick's regiment years ago.

It was a nice luxurious villa, well-stocked with champagne, in the hills above Nice. Then Phyllis Nudgem arrived, an adventuress whom they all seemed to know.

'Hello, de Courcy,' said she.

'Hello, Phyllis,' said he.

'Why,' asked Paul, 'do you call Tom "de Courcy", and why does he call you Phyllis?'

'Just an old joke of ours,' replied Phyllis, whose name at the moment appeared to be Jonquil Shelton-Armitage.

When the party broke up, Foulenough whispered to her: 'We'd better stick together.' So she drove him back to Nice.

It was rather a staid company to which Foulenough had attached himself. Some of them were discussing their properties in the Bahamas. Angry at being ignored, the captain, stimulated by several cocktails, sang in a fruity voice to a lady who seemed to be less wealthy than the rest the old song, 'Yes, We Have No Bahamas'. They all moved away from him, including the lady.

His parting words were: 'Ring me up at my place in Marbella. I shall be at my other place in Majorca. Thank me very much for having you.'

While strolling through the lounge of an hotel in Nice, Foulenough saw Vita Brevis. His heart leaped like a salmon going over a weir. 'Vita!' he cried, 'so you followed me here!'

'Don't be a fool,' said Vita, 'I'm waiting for my aunt.'

'Surely,' said he, 'we need no chaperone. However, shall I lunch with the two of you?'

'We're going to Ste Maxime,' she replied.

'What a coincidence!' said the warrior. 'I too am bound thither. Can I cadge a lift?' Vita smiled ruefully, 'I've never known you unable to cadge anything,' she said. 'I made a mistake,' she added, 'we're going to Le Lavandou.'

'So did I,' said Foulenough, 'that's where I'm going.'

*   *   *

Les Cochers de Huntingdonshire

My music critic writes: 'The production of the French opera based on the famous *List* has puzzled audiences. Some are obviously bored by the singing of the cabmen's names during three acts, others are baffled by the absence of a plot. The foreign singers are unable to give the full significance or even the correct pronunciation of some of the names. Nor does the libretto, consisting solely of these names and initials, lend itself to sustained melodies. This explains the excessive use of recitative, as in the over-long passage which opens with the murmured "Gackwynd, C.F.L."'

When the curtain rises on the first act, the cabmen are assembled outside their shelter. They move about, laughing, and singing with verve the opening chorus:

TALL CABMEN: Jimpson, W., Mockpudding, C.F., Ralston, E., Bumcombe, R.J., Upchurch, C.L.K.
SMALL CABMEN: Walters, O.R., et cetera, et cetera, et cet-er-aaaa.
(*Enter* MIFFCOTE, H., FAFFNAGE, B.B., *and* SCRAMPLE, G.)

Should farmers shoot moths?

'Women hunted a silkworm moth from the Far East and caught it in a back garden.' (*News item*)

Taking their fences with all the finesse one associates with blood sports, the women picked up the scent near a cucumber frame. Sighting a moth on a compost heap, they gave tongue, closed in, and one of them threw a stone at it, and missed. 'A rolling stone gatherth no moth,' lisped a member of the hunt. The quarry was finally captured in Mrs Pooble's sun-hat.

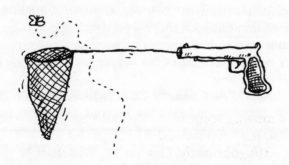

Is it too advanced?

Dear Sir,

Opera must not be the Cinderella of the arts. Your music critic's lofty attitude to *Les Cochers de Huntingdonshire* only proves that he is incapable of appreciating novel experiments. The great chorus in Act II, with each cabman singing the name and initials of another cabman, was an ingenious idea, and the music, hushed and expectant, lifted commonplace names into the realm of poetry. Fourier's gravity as Keigwin, P.A., was most moving, and the touch of humour given by André Mésquin to Rickthorpe, G.S.E., was not at all out of place.

J.R. Gutt

The trumpeter of Cracow

An article on Poland made me wonder if the trumpeter of Cracow still blows his trumpet every day from the highest tower of the church in the market square. I heard the call between the wars – a call to arms which had been sounded every day for many centuries. Long ago the watcher on the tower saw the Tartar horsemen riding in on a raid. He blew the call to arms, but it broke off when an arrow pierced his throat, and ever since then the call had broken off unfinished, to commemorate his death.

A new laid stair-rod

The stair-rod laid by a Sheffield hen,
after a diet of brass filings.

A spokesman commented, 'Even if old-fashioned eggs could be substituted for stair-rods there would still remain the impossibility of utilising stair-rods for human consumption.' A chef added: 'You wouldn't be able to make omelets without breaking stair-rods.'

Les Cochers de Huntingdonshire

Here is a moving scene from Maboul's opera (libretto by Vaurien):
THURSTON, H.A.: (*vivaciously*) Snagget, R.L.?
BOLTON, P.: (*lugubriously*) Erskine, W., Whackstraw, N.E., Milton, J.
Then follows the duet, 'Bapchild, C.T., Mulf, O., Quilch, R.R.'

Nothing to do with me

I am used to grotesque misprints, but tears of joy came into my eyes when I saw these extraordinary words: 'She was wearing an ankle-length hat.' Even if she was a midget, she must have felt silly. I hope there were slits in the upper portion of the hat, to enable her to see where she was going; not that it matters much where she was going, dressed up like that. Yet I trust that when she sat down she pulled up her hat, to disclose a shapely leg.

The Faffgrove method

Mr Eugene Faffgrove is a go-ahead photographer. His method is to persuade well-known people to stand on one leg, with the knee of the other leg bent back at a right angle, while digging both elbows into the stomach, and twisting the neck sideways. He claims that by consenting to adopt this pose people reveal their mentality. I think he is right.

Quelle liste, grand-mémé?

A music critic writes: 'M. Maboul and M. Vaurien have succeeded in doing something never attempted before. The librettist, depending for his effect entirely on names and initials, has made full use of his material. The composer has created an atmosphere of romantic mystery. One is haunted by the feeling that one has crossed a frontier into a strange world where nothing, not even a cabman's name and initials, is what it seems. I can still hear the ringing challenge in Act II, when Pockett, M.R., apostrophises Bibblethwaite, T.'

A Narkover report

The headmaster who has abolished end-of-term reports because they worry parents and boys, might adopt the Narkover type of report. I quote a typical one:

> Thorpestone has had a prosperous term. His card-sense is improving. If he devoted as much time to the school casino as he does to the school betting-shop, he would soon be in the school bridge four. His cribbing during the history lessons is a little timid at present, but it is better to make history later on than to learn it. He should keep his money in a safer place, if there is such a place. He makes friends easily, but is clever enough not to trust any of them.

Beeflam is here!

Have you tried the new meat, Beeflam? It is a composite shoulder of the best beef and lamb, the various pieces being welded together by a new system, and gives you two tastes where there was only one before. This is but one of the amazing highlights of the Snibbo campaign to revolutionise meat.

Two to one on Nibbler

The recent mouse-race in Dorsetshire has not gone unobserved by sportsmen. Floodlit mouse-racing at Wembley, with an electric cheese as the quarry, would be an exciting novelty. Measures must be taken to protect the mouse-stables from dopers. A request from a suspicious-looking stranger to 'Give Flyaway a piece of cheese' must be refused.

Captious critic

An indignant opera-lover asks why the librettist M. Vaurien could not have invented names and initials of cabmen, since such names as Babblebotham are difficult to sing in any language. Surely the answer is that realism was the goal aimed at, nor would the millions who have read the famous *List* take easily to invented names.

What is one to do?

'Why,' asked the magistrate, 'were you wearing only one shoe?'

'I was hopping,' replied the man.

'Why?'

'To keep fit.'

'But,' said the magistrate, 'you were hopping on the shoeless foot.'

'That was the one I was keeping fit,' replied the man.

'Keeping it fit for what?' queried the magistrate.

'A hopping contest,' riposted the man.

'I give it up,' groaned the magistrate.

Mouse-racing

Mouse-racing is catching on. The Somerset mice were in great form yesterday at Shepton Mallet, but owing to last-minute confusion a singing mouse was entered in a race. It stopped after a few yards to squeak what passes for a song in mouse circles. The other mice, thinking this was *de rigueur*, squeaked in chorus, and

so entranced were the spectators that nobody asked for his money back. The proud owner of the soloist joined in, beating time with his hat.

Toujours la politesse

The liner was in mid-Atlantic. A passenger, Mr Harris, said to his friend: 'Last night I was having a drink and a snack in the lounge, when the chap next to me suddenly told me his name – Bonapetty, or something like that. So I told him my name just to be matey.'

'You ass!' said his friend. 'He was obviously a Frenchman and was wishing you good appetite – *bon appétit*.'

The next night the man found himself with the Frenchman. Wishing to be polite, he said 'Bong appetit.'

The Frenchman, anxious to show that he had learned the correct English reply, said: 'Harris.'

The captain comes home

Foulenough has returned to England. His departure was hastened by the news that the police were looking for a man who had appeared in various towns and villages as Admiral Sir Charles Ragwort-Grey, Comte St Rémy de Chamaillot, Colonel Blade, Sir Percy Lawndrey, and Hon. Montague Buttersham.

'Infinite resource and sagacity'

The ex-tailor who ran away to sea the other day will be useful to the crew. Billy Bennett used to sing:

> There are no tailor's shops in mid-ocean,
>   They don't do repairs on the deck.
> So for three years he fastened his braces
>   To a wart on the back of his neck.

19

Before Mr Justice Cocklecarrot

Henchman *v.* Wefthouse, and the
Goriketta Fisheries Case

An action for slander has been brought by Mrs Olga Wefthouse against Mrs Euphemia Henchman. Mrs Wefthouse asserts that Mrs Henchman said to her, 'You are so low that if you were a serpent, a baby eel trying to wriggle under you would bang its head.' This defamatory imputation, constituting a putative slander, *ipso facto*, *coram populo* and *horribile dictu*, exposed Mrs Wefthouse to ridicule, catcalls and sarcasm. In his opening address, Mr Justice Cocklecarrot said that the words used need not be taken in a strictly literal sense. They were, at the best or worst, a metaphorical indication of depravity, a poetic flight of an unbridled imagination.

Mr Honeyweather Gooseboote, for the prosecution, asked Mrs Henchman if she had ever seen a baby eel trying to wriggle its way under a serpent.

Mrs Henchman said, 'I am not a naturalist.'

'You must answer Yes or No,' said Cocklecarrot.

'No,' said Mrs Henchman.

'Then,' said Mr Gooseboote, 'your words were not based on personal experience.'

Mr Tinklebury Snapdriver, for the defence, intervened to say, 'The defence concedes that, though the words, taken literally, were a hypothetical assumption, they did convey the suggestion of depravity by a figure of speech.'

Mr Gooseboote replied that the words used were, 'If you were a serpent', not 'You are a serpent'.

'A somewhat important distinction,' said Cocklecarrot.

GOOSEBOOTE: Now, Mrs Henchman, would it not be possible for a baby eel to pass quite comfortably under a serpent, if the serpent were on the branch of a tree?

MRS HENCHMAN: I suppose so, but Mrs Wefthouse does not sit on branches of trees.

GOOSEBOOTE: Of course not. But, 'if she were a serpent' – I use your own words – a baby eel could wriggle under the branch she was on without banging its head. I put it to you that this would not reflect on her moral character.

MRS HENCHMAN: Not if she was a serpent, but she isn't. And she could still be on a very low branch.

(Lunch interval.)

SNAPDRIVER: My learned friend has ingeniously suggested a method by which a baby eel could pass under a serpent. May I remind him that Mrs Henchman did not use the word 'low' in a literary sense, denoting physical stature. A lady can sit at the bottom of a quarry without being low in any but a physical sense.

COCKLECARROT: Mr Snapdriver, Mrs Wefthouse's arboreal eccentricities are irrelevant to the case. Even more irrelevant is the gratuitous assumption that she might take it into her head to sit at the bottom of a quarry. Any discussion on these lines is as ludicrous as it is immaterial to the main consideration, whatever that may be supposed to be. By the way, how could the eel pass under her at the bottom of a quarry?

GOOSEBOOTE: Mrs Henchman, what was your motive in likening my client to a baby eel attempting to go under a serpent?

MRS HENCHMAN: She threw all her rubbish into my back yard.

COCKLECARROT: (sarcastically) Thus emulating the normal activities of eels and serpents. (Laughter.)

SNAPDRIVER: M'lud, with respect, we seem to be getting nowhere.

COCKLECARROT: Mr Snapdriver, without respect, you took the words out of my mouth. Can we not forget these eels and serpents, and move on to yet more entrancing balderdash? Mr Gooseboote, we hang on your words like an eel hanging from a tree.

GOOSEBOOTE: As y'ludship pleases.

COCKLECARROT: Do I understand that Mrs Henchman threw a quantity of rubbish into Mrs Wefthouse's yard?

GOOSEBOOTE: The other way about, m'lud. And this, m'lud, is exhibit A.

COCKLECARROT: What on earth is it?

GOOSEBOOTE: A castor from an old bedstead, m'lud. I have here also further exhibits, from B to W.

COCKLECARROT: Mr Gooseboote, this is a court of law, not a refuse dump.

SNAPDRIVER: I submit, m'lud, that all this trash has nothing to do with the allegation that a baby eel—

COCKLECARROT: I feared that someone would bring in that infernal eel again.

SNAPDRIVER: Mrs Wefthouse, why did you throw your rubbish into Mrs Henchman's yard?

MRS WEFTHOUSE: It was her rubbish. She threw it. I threw it back.

A VOICE: Fifteen all.

COCKLECARROT: Then it appears that any baby eel could have crept under either of you, had you been serpents.

GOOSEBOOTE: It is the pot calling the kettle black.

MRS WEFTHOUSE: M'lud, is it in order for counsel to call me a pot?

MRS HENCHMAN: Or me a kettle?

COCKLECARROT: It's better than being called a serpent, and it is but yet another figure of speech.

Addressing the court, Cocklecarrot said: 'The core, pith, and marrow of this case lies in the words "if you were a serpent". Note that Mrs Henchman did not call Mrs Wefthouse a serpent. Now if I say to a man: "If you were an elephant no rajah would touch you with a barge-pole," can I be held to be slandering that man? Since Mrs Wefthouse is not a serpent, and was never accused of being one, the question of a baby eel crawling beneath her does not arise. It is absurd cases like this which lead zealots and fanatics to cry, "Arbitrate, don't litigate." This case could so easily have been settled out of court.'

Whereupon rose Mrs Wefthouse and cried: 'Ma Henchman, you are so foul-tongued that if you were a rajah no elephant would touch you with a barge-pole.'

The Goriketta Fisheries Case

In the Court of Uncommon Pleas, Fisheries and Agriculture, before Mr Justice Cocklecarrot, a contested case concerning the validity of proceedings for the transference of the unliquidated assets of the Goriketta Sea Fisheries Association to a person or persons named or unnamed, had its first hearing yesterday. Mr Tinklebury Snapdriver, for the defence, remarked that the whole case seemed to turn on the definition of the word 'registration'. Mr Honeyweather Gooseboote, for the persecution, demurred, and quoted a statutory provision of the Oyster, Crab, and Lobster Act of 1877, dealing with the measurement of crans and the labelling of barrels. Mr Justice Cocklecarrot said he intended to reserve his judgement until such a time as he knew what the case was about.

In cross-examining Mrs Whackstraw, a director of the Goriketta Sea Fisheries, Mr Gooseboote elicited the information that all documents connected with the transference of the unliquidated assets had been confiscated by a man named Snopliffe, who represented himself as acting for an anonymous subsidiary group. Snopliffe, alias Cowfold-Wright, was understood to be a Major Bloodhouse, who, posing as Jack Zobbo, had tinkered with the books. 'I had no confidence in him,' said the weeping Mrs Whackstraw. Mrs Charles Folder then deposed that the Major was a certain Jeremy Goldacre who ran a harmonium factory in Uttoxeter.

COCKLECARROT: Is anything in this mass of obscurity relevant
   to whatever it is you are trying to find out, Mr Gooseboote?
GOOSEBOOTE: M'lud, that's what I hope to discover.

There was a sensation when Mr Honeyweather Gooseboote revealed that the Goriketta Sea Fisheries Association had been taken over, in 1957, by Jermold & Wynch, and taken back from them by the GSFA two months later. Sir Henry Jermold was on the board of both concerns, in the one case under his own name Arlo Dhusch, in the other under the fictitious name of Roderick Hump. Cross-questioned as to the assets of each firm, Dhusch said there were none. Mr Tinklebury Snapdriver at once demanded a stay of replevin, on the grounds of insufficient evidence and plenary incomprehensibility. A Miss Julia Witcraft fainted and was dragged out by the heels.

In a masterly speech Mr Honeyweather Gooseboote drew attention to the difference between the natural construction put upon commercial usage in the matter of a detailed interpretation of unliquidated assets as applied to a negotiated settlement with an anonymous beneficee, and the legal construction put upon the same operation when subject to a constitutional clarification of what might be termed a precedent without precedent. Mr Tinklebury Snapdriver retorted by quoting *Volpin and Mrs Gregson versus Associated Telescopes Ltd*. There it was held that a claim to unliquidated assets is an infringement of incorporeal rights, and is therefore subject to a Vindicatio, regardless of the Statute of Maintenance.

'Assets,' said Mr Justice Cocklecarrot, 'may be deferred, current, fixed, or working. In this case it appears that these assets, whether liquidated or unliquidated, were in part organisational and in part carried over to operational costs.'

Mr Gooseboote intervened to say that he was instructed that no obligation had been assumed in relation to the accounting period.

Mr Snapdriver objected that this ignored preliminary charges on miscellaneous expenditure, itemised on a purely theoretical basis of consecutive accounting advances, predetermined by adding the residuary amounts to a chargeable interest.

Cocklecarrot asked for an explanation of all this to be prepared.

SNAPDRIVER: Mr Turmoyle, you spoke of unliquidated assets. The process of the Law applies only to liquidated assets in the case of joint-stock companies.
TURMOYLE: Is there no machinery for getting assets unliquidated?
SNAPDRIVER: The term is meaningless in law. Nobody can appoint an unliquidator or an official non-receiver.
TURMOYLE: Then why am I here?
GOOSEBOOTE: Why, indeed?
COCKLECARROT: Why are any of us here, if it comes to that?
(*Dead silence.*)

Mr Tinklebury Snapdriver read from a document: 'A joint-stock Company being, *per se*, an incorporated association founded to pursue what may be briefly designated as commercial transactions of a nature determined by the activities undertaken and the enterprises promulgated and proclaimed in the articles, deeds, registrations, and prospectuses of the said Company or Association ...' Here the learned counsel broke off to refer to Goriketta Sea Fisheries Association. Cocklecarrot intervened to ask if the share capital had been registered. Mr Gooseboote claimed that two of the promoters had used the same alias. 'Obviously unintentionally,' commented the learned judge.

Addressing the stupefied jury, Mr Justice Cocklecarrot said: 'This is a classic example of a case which is not even faintly intelligible to the legal luminaries employed. What you, ladies and gentlemen of the jury, make of it is anybody's guess. For my part, with all my experience of the intricacies of the Law, I confess that, for all the proceedings have meant to me, the case might have been conducted in some Bessarabian dialect. The purpose, implications, general trend and particular applications of this confused tangle of absurdities are a jealously guarded secret. Learned counsel on both sides have failed to extract anything comprehensible from anybody. I therefore find myself compelled to adjourn the case, *sine die* and *coram populo*, in order that, at some future date, justice may be done, or, at any rate, may seem to be done.'

* * *

Oi be thaat glad

A townee politician who was trying to ingratiate himself with his country constituency, moves me to sing:

> It gave the villagers a shock
> When he addressed them in a smock.
> And there were many startled looks
> When, in an accent learned from books,
> He tried, and with the worst effect,
> To imitate their dialect.
> And not content with tricks like that,
> He even thatched his bowler hat.

The Hatting

'Surbiton council,' says my paper, 'is to buy a new ceremonial hat for the mayor.'

Surbiton is one of the few places where the traditional Hatting takes place in the town hall. As the bareheaded mayor enters, an usher cries: 'A hat! A hat! Haro, my lord mayor!' The mayor is then handed his old hat by the clerk, and he presents it to the usher. Then four councillors carry the new hat to the mayor on a black velvet cushion, while the town band plays 'Come to the fair'. The senior councillor places the hat on the mayor's head, while all present (especially the rate-payers) cry: 'Long live the mayoral hat, the hat of our mayor!'

Les Cochers de Huntingdonshire

It may be remembered (or forgotten, I care not a farthing rushlight) that when the *List of Huntingdonshire Cabmen* was translated into French, there was disappointment that no attempt had been made to Gallicise the names and initials. What could the French make of 'Owlsblood, P.W.'? A new edition remedies this. The names are printed as the French would pronounce them. As an example, 'Vibbleton' becomes 'Veebellton'.

Round the town

A bounder gate-crashed a swilling jamboree in Mayfair. Approaching Lady Cabstanleigh, known to her intimate London friends as Mount Unpleasant, he said: 'Your eyes are like the jellied eels they sell at Brighton.' Seeing that she was somewhat startled, he added: 'But even lovelier.'

Chemist's hat confiscated

When Mrs Fabble, 42, of 9 The Lilacs, Huff End, answered a knock on her door, she saw her godmother, whom she had not met for twenty-three years. As she did not like her, she at once shut the door, but her godmother climbed in the scullery window. Mrs Fabble locked her in, but she got out through the window by which she had entered, crying as she left, 'Good riddance, Myra.'

'Same to you,' retorted Mrs Fabble.

PRODNOSE: What is the point of this?

MYSELF: It's news, isn't it? Well, then.

Song

A country unexpectedly destroyed
   Can now enjoy the final consolation
Of knowing its defences had employed
   The latest methods of retaliation.

Mutual annihilation, it's agreed,
   Is the best weapon science can invent
To banish war and very quickly lead
   To total peace and full disarmament.

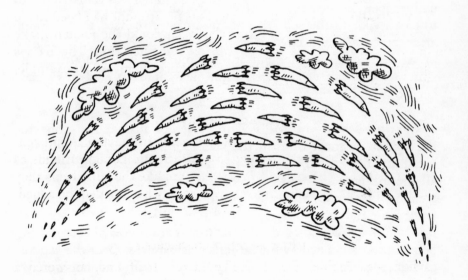

20

The Transformation of Narkover School

A certain influential MP noted for his interest in education and his puritanical opinions, had, in a moment of mental aberration, sent his son to Narkover. Disturbed by the vendetta against the school carried on by a scurrilous, self-righteous columnist in a daily paper, he decided to investigate for himself, and arranged to pay a visit to the school. The headmaster realised that certain arrangements would have to be made to impress him favourably, or, as one senior master put it, 'We must stop his mouth with jam.' As the day of the visit drew near, masters and boys had been coached in the parts they were to play.

It was the day of the MP's visit. A senior master had gone to the station to meet him. In the classrooms ink had been substituted for the red wine (which the boys called *encre ordinaire*) in all the ink-pots and bottles. Swearing, betting, forging signatures, stealing, blackmail, and other youthful exuberances had been forbidden for the day, to masters and boys alike. The MP's son, by now acclimatised, entered into the fun as readily as his comrades, being rather sickened by his father's priggishness. Over the school casino appeared the words 'Divinity School', and the school moneylender had become, according to a plate on his door, a solicitor and commissioner of oaths. All the fourteen pawnbrokers were now antique dealers. The scene was set for the anxious parent.

As the visiting parent entered the headmaster's study, it chanced that Dr Smart-Allick had his back to the door and was, of course, taken unawares, as arranged. The head was saying to a new master: 'It is our privilege here, Mr Stott, to give a new generation armour against the evils of modern life, and—' At this point Mr

Stott indicated the presence of the visitor.

'Ah, Mr Whickeringe,' said the head, 'welcome to our humble academy.'

'I could not help overhearing your inspiring words,' replied Mr Whickeringe. 'I was touched.'

'You will be,' muttered Mr Stott to himself.

'Now,' said Smart-Allick, 'we will go and see the dear boys at their work.'

The headmaster and Mr Whickeringe first visited a form which was undergoing a history lesson. The boys, well rehearsed, showed an enthusiasm worthy of a worse cause. The parent was so impressed by the discipline and deference and eager spirit of the boys that Smart-Allick got him away before either master or boys could blow the gaff. As they entered a second room, the master was saying, 'Now, Whickeringe, was the criminal lie of this man justified?'

'A lie, sir,' came the reply in a ringing voice, 'is never justified.'

The proud parent, overcome with emotion, beamed at his son, and heard the headmaster say fervently, 'God bless the dear boy – and the father of such a son.'

During a visit to the Upper Sixth, Mr Whickeringe noticed an ace of spades at the feet of a boy in the back row. The headmaster had seen it too. 'Vince,' he said sternly, 'we all know you like a game of patience, but you should not bring your cards here. You will remain behind when the form is dismissed.'

At that moment a junior master burst open the door, and shouted, 'He's won! Good old gee!'

The headmaster said quietly to Mr Whickeringe, 'One of our boys, young Gee, has a brother who was competing in a Civil Defence competition. Apparently he has won. That makes us rather proud.'

While touring the various school buildings Mr Whickeringe suddenly missed his wallet. 'Tck, tck,' said the headmaster. 'You must have dropped it. I will have a search made.'

'Careless of me,' said the MP.

'Accidents will happen,' replied Smart-Allick, under his breath, 'in the worst regulated schools.'

'I will offer a reward of five pounds to the finder,' announced the visitor.

By a lucky chance, a boy 'found' the wallet. The visitor was so pleased that he did not bother to count the contents, but handed over a fiver, one of three which, for appearance's sake, the boy had returned to the wallet.

'Good, honest boy!' said the MP. Smart-Allick winked at the science master.

'I trust,' said Smart-Allick, 'that you have now seen enough to dispel any anxiety caused you by the disreputable Press vendetta against this school?'

'Indeed,' replied Mr Whickeringe. 'I go away satisfied that my boy is in good hands.' As the parent turned to a text on the wall of the headmaster's study (Ideals Are The Poetry Of Life) a hoarse cry rang out, 'Where's that bookie got to?'

The MP gave a start of surprise.

'That's one of our masters,' said Smart-Allick, 'looking for Ramsden major. They call him "booky", because he's such a bookworm. Quite a brilliant boy.'

When Mr Whickeringe related his experiences at Narkover to his wife, she said: 'It sounds as though those boys were all milksops. I hope our lad is not going to turn out too much of a goody-goody.'

At that moment her lad, with other milksops, was playing a game of excessively unconventional poker.

'That columnist,' continued Mrs Whickeringe, 'has certainly misled everyone with his lies.'

Said her husband: 'I have told the headmaster to bring him into the courts, but, being a kindly man, the Doctor is reluctant to take any action; he dislikes publicity.'

So great was the strain on the boys and masters of Narkover of trying to behave with reasonable restraint that the headmaster granted a whole holiday, expressing the hope that everyone would soon get back into the normal routine of school life. At the end of this gala day the school Lost Property office (which is the scholastic term for the school fence's office) was so crowded with goods that, in the confusion, many boys found they had bought back, at current rates, things which they had themselves stolen and sold to the receiver of temporarily appropriated goods.

The Narkover tradition

In the first weeks of the current term at Narkover so much money was stolen from masters' pockets that suspects were made to wear boxing gloves. The thieving continued, with the result that the whole school was treated as suspect and put into boxing gloves. Now several boys complain that this gives an unfair advantage to the masters; that five prefects have been robbed, obviously by masters, in the last week; and that two of the poorest masters seem to have come suddenly into money. One boy said: 'When my father visits the school it is humiliating not to be able to get at his pockets, especially when one knows that he has made a good haul from some rich boy or master.'

Experiments are being made with small, steel finger-traps which are placed in the pocket where money is kept. But the more experienced boys have discovered that, by going to work carefully, when the trap closes on the glove, the hand can be withdrawn, leaving the glove in the trap. There have been several cases of a master attacking a pocket and finding only a boxing glove.

A Narkover father has complained that a recent house group-photograph shows all the boys in boxing gloves. 'Has this savage and barbaric sport been made compulsory?' he asks the headmaster in a letter.

Dr Smart-Allick explained that the gloves are intended merely to discourage the picking of pockets.

The father replied: 'I am relieved by your explanation, but surely any boy worth his salt can slip off the gloves before beginning to operate.'

It is not every day that a headmaster's pocket is picked by the smallest new boy in the school. This happened at Narkover yesterday. Reproached by the Governors for his carelessness, Dr Smart-Allick said, 'How could I imagine that the little fellow would have the nerve, during his first term, to do what even the prefects hesitate to do to their headmaster? Luckily, he only got a few forged notes which I was carrying in order to trap a history master.'

Asked why a boy's name cannot be put down for Narkover some

years before his entry into the school, the headmaster said: 'Many parents are forced by circumstances to effect a slight change of name, not necessarily officially. We like a boy to arrive at Narkover under the most recent of his father's names. It simplifies matters for all concerned, and saves both boy and father embarrassment.'

The music master at Narkover laid a subtle trap. He stuffed his wallet with forged notes. In due course he was robbed by a prefect. The prefect was robbed by a new boy, the new boy by a science master, the science master by the cricket captain, the cricket captain by a card-sharper. During a game of whist the music master lost heavily, and could not resist picking the pocket of the card-sharper, a rich boy. Alas! On examining his haul the master found himself landed with his own forged notes.

A rather undersized new boy with a deep voice and adult features has puzzled the masters during this term. He is very popular, but nobody can find any document which attests his admission to the school. Yesterday the headmaster's private detective startled the masters by revealing that he was a thirty-year-old bookie who had smuggled himself in at the beginning of the term and was doing a roaring trade among the boys.

Surprise is always expressed that Narkover is the only school of any standing which never raises its fees. Dr Smart-Allick has said more than once that the peculiar economic administration of the school makes the question of fees a minor one. 'All our masters are well-to-do, so that they need not be paid,' said the headmaster, 'and any boy who is in a lower income bracket has either his father or himself to blame, taking into account the facilities at Narkover for enterprise and initiative.'

The Sixth Form at Narkover walked out yesterday because two boys responsible for sawing a leg off a history master's chair were fined. There was further trouble in the Upper Fifth when boys, whose job it is to pour ink over essays, filled the form master's mortar-board with dirty water. The mortar-board fillers protested that the ink-pourers had infringed their rights, and went on strike.

'Fire! Fire!' The new housemaster woke with a start at 2 a.m., threw on some clothes, and dashed out of his bedroom. The coast was clear. The sixth-form boy who had given the alarm got away with two silver hairbrushes, eight pound notes, some small change, a gold watch, and an electric razor. When the housemaster discovered the losses, he complained to the headmaster. 'It was a false alarm,' he said, 'deliberately given by the thief.'

Said Dr Smart-Allick: 'One of the oldest Narkover tricks, Mr Relf. You have a lot to learn and experience is the best teacher in these matters.'

A Narkover parent has taken exception to the headmaster's recent assertion that all the masters are unpaid. He reveals that many parents, including himself, who are engaged in activities of a somewhat secret nature, have to meet blackmail demands from masters who are aware of these activities. 'My brother,' he writes, 'is in this unfortunate position with regard to Dr Smart-Allick himself. And his boy, now in his second year at the school, has to surrender a percentage of his winnings at cards, in order to protect his father, who is high up in a smuggling racket.'

Dr Smart-Allick has replied to the accusations of the indignant parent. He says: 'Blackmail is an ugly name for the weapon of fear which is used to induce wrongdoers to mend their ways. If the parent who is engaged in the smuggling business had not engaged in that business, nobody would have a hold over him. By letting him know that I am wise to him, I am giving him a chance to go straight, and by confiscating a percentage of his son's card-winnings, I am teaching the boy that his misfortunes are due to his father's wickedness.'

Five nights after the new housemaster had been robbed, he was again awakened in the small hours. 'Please, sir,' said a half-dressed boy, 'I think there's a thief prowling about.' The boy then led the master to a corridor, and each study door was opened, and in each bed lay a boy peacefully sleeping. Meanwhile a boy had emerged from a study on the floor below, and had filled a sack with various articles in the housemaster's dining-room. Later the housemaster discovered his losses, and again complained to Smart-Allick.

'Will you never learn?' said the headmaster. 'If you do a bit of night prowling yourself, you might be able to recover some of your lost property, if it hasn't already been disposed of. Anyway, you could confiscate something of equal value.'

The caning of a small mathematics master by an overgrown boy at Narkover has led to a protest by the master's parents. Dr Smart-Allick told the indignant father: 'Most of our masters are capable of looking after themselves. Your son, being undersized, is naturally a target for any high-spirited boy who is big enough to bully him. When you think of the privileged position of a master, and of how often it is he who does the bullying, you can hardly be surprised when some boy tries to get his own back.'

By order of the headmaster a list of card-debts, with names attached, was posted up in every form-room. Next day, by agreement among the boys, a list of masters' card-debts, with names attached, appeared in the same place. The masters retaliated by stealing and burning the IOUs they had given to boys. The boys retaliated by stealing and burning the IOUs they had given to the masters. 'Now we can all start again,' said the headmaster, 'with a clean – or, rather, dirty – slate.'

After the card-debts incident the masters posted up a list of the boys whose fathers are at present in prison. The boys retaliated by posting up a list of twelve masters who are old lags. In an address to the school Dr Smart-Allick called for a truce. 'If,' he said, 'every time our pots call our kettles black, our kettles call our pots black, school life will become a farce. Every boy and every master has something to conceal. Let it rest at that. Toleration is the mark of a civilised community.'

*　　*　　*

I *was* at Waterloo

As a little boy I was present at the first night of *Peter Pan*. When I told a child this, he looked at me as though I had just come from the battle of Agincourt. Then he said, 'Did you ever see Napoleon?'

I said I had fought with the Guards at Waterloo.

His mother said, 'Don't fill his head with nonsense.'

'It's true,' I said. 'The row was because I had lost my ticket for Epsom.'

The boy looked puzzled.

A curious contest

In Aberbananer they are very excited about the attempt of Evans the Hearse to race a snail, using only one nostril to push the pea. At a stormy council meeting one councillor said: 'Is there not something ludicrous in the spectacle of a middle-aged man crawling along and butting a pea with one nostril, while beside him creeps a snail? Have our citizens nothing else to do? If everyone went on like this, foreigners would think we had gone mad.' He was reminded by the chairman that there is no question of everyone going on like this.

The glowing hat

Another complaint about men's dull clothing can be easily met. The sensation of the Hat Exhibition at the Roanoke Hall in Kilburn is an incandescent bowler. The bowler is transparent, so that the glow from the lining lights up the entire hat and adds brilliance to style. A shagreen peakless cap with tiny fairy-lights round the brim is intended to be worn with the new octagonal waistcoat.

I am embarrassed

Dear Sir,
   Do you really think that the best way to set a good example to schoolboys is to give publicity to what happens at Narkover? My boy said yesterday, 'Gee, dad, I wish our school was like that.' I told him that Narkover was not a real school but an invention, and he said, 'Whoever invented it ought to be a headmaster.'

Dr Rhubarb's corner

D.L. WRITES: My husband's idea of a joke is to shout 'Miaou'
   outside the door when we have guests. It gets on our nerves.
DR RHUBARB SAYS: Open the door quietly and throw him a mouse.

Rustiguzzi with a nosebag

It is not every opera that calls for a bearded diva, as does Stravinsky's *Rake's Progress*. In Grimaldi's *Il Strèpito*, the heroine has to wear a nosebag in Act II, when the magician has tried to change her into a horse, but has only succeeded in giving her a horse's head on a human being's body. Rustiguzzi's singing (through a hole in the nosebag) of the aria *'Rimpianto! Rimpianto!'* brought the house down.

Glossop

If anybody comes across a Victorian municipal building dumped in a ditch or loaded onto an enormous abandoned lorry it will probably be the one that has disappeared 'mysteriously' from Glossop. Since the stealing of an elephant from a zoo, thieves have concentrated on larger and larger objects. Someone must have dug up the Glossop building on a moonless night, working quietly so as not to attract attention. Perhaps there is some unfortunate night-watchman still inside it.

For your album

She was stewing eels in the kitchen,
  And he kissed her before she could move.
Leaning across the pan to salute her,
  He was head over eels in love.

21

Good Gravy!

A Second Portion of Rissole Mio

Mrs McGurgle has received an anonymous letter, evidently from an ex-boarder. It says: 'Madam, your gravy is modernised nectar, your vegetables ambrosia-plus, your puddings have to be eaten to be believed. Even your dog Mortimer has the perpetual grin of the satisfied gourmet. I still treasure the memory of your rebuke to the man who pasted his bacon on the parlour wall, pencilled a frame round it, and called it "Nightmare".'

'What about a second go of pudden?' asked a new boarder.
'Mr Godger,' replied the chatelaine, 'I presume you mean a second portion of "pudding".'
'What I really mean,' said the boarder, 'is that I would be infinitely obliged if you, of your largesse, could see your way to donating me a supplementary amount of that succulent dish, so amply ornamented with half-buried raisins.'
Said Mrs McGurgle, 'There is, Mr Godger, a happy medium between the coarse and vulgar language of the gutter and the artificial though courtly circumlocutions of the Court of Lewis Kattorz.'

Mr Mill was spitting out his grape-pips noisily and viciously on to his plate.
Said Mrs McGurgle, 'The only excusable spitting is the quiet and undemonstrative kind, which distinguishes human beings from wild animals. Glance round the table, Mr Mill, and you will observe that the custom of this establishment is a sophisticated approach to grape-consumption, and a management and control of the indigenous pips which would not bring a blush to the cheeks of a peeress of the realm. A truce to this vulgar method of ejection, I beg.'

'Mr Webb,' said Mrs McGurgle scathingly, 'Miss Wychett has complained twice that you have splashed your gravy over her jumper at lunch. If you cannot confine the gravy within the limits of your plate, I shall be compelled to serve your meat in a deep pudding-bowl. No self-respecting person likes to be showered with gravy.'

'Give him a bucket,' interjected Mr Relf.

'Mr Relf,' said the chatelaine, 'that barbarous suggestion comes ill from one who but yesterday sliced a piece of gristle, striking Mrs Gawkell a glancing blow upon the cheek.'

Pale with fear, Mr Roofe said to Mrs McGurgle, 'There's a ghastly dwarf on the lawn, with a beard.'

The chatelaine explained that it was a stone hobgoblin she had purchased to set off the lupins.

'I thought I was seeing things,' said the much-relieved lodger. 'My uncle, after a night out, once complained that he had been followed home by a tiny Turkish milkman on a camel wearing a tartan fez.'

'When such things occur in a family,' replied the chatelaine, 'one should hush them up.'

A morsel of mutton, propelled from Mr Whiffle's plate, owing to a too aggressive thrust of his fork, landed in the salt-cellar.

'Hole in one!' murmured Mr Kellett.

The chatelaine breathed deeply. Then she said, 'The control of such meat as is on the plate should not be beyond the meanest intelligence. Nothing incommodes the lodgers so much as flying particles of food. The technique of food-handling is only difficult for those whose selfish disregard of their neighbours denotes a temperament unbalanced and a clod-hopping approach to the delights of the table.'

'Mr Gibble,' said Mrs McGurgle, 'if your telescope is to be used for contemplating the planets, or for sweeping the horizon in search of shipping, well and good. If, however, it is to serve the vulgar purpose of spying on ladies on the beach, you have come to the wrong establishment. The phrase, "What cheer, Nelson!" uttered by Mr Lumley, leads me to suspect a not strictly astronomical purpose on your part. Pray remember that a straying telescope in degraded hands might focus on one of our own lady boarders.'

Mr Webb still tends to splash his gravy about.

'Mr Webb,' said the chatelaine, 'may I remind you that you are not bathing on the Reveerer? I must once more request you to keep your gravy to yourself. Mrs Fangett has complained in writing that last Tuesday she was squirted in the eye, and that you shouted "Fore!" as the errant liquid cascaded.'

'Tell him to use his beard as a mop,' said Mr Relf.

'Sound advice, though somewhat vulgarly expressed,' said Mrs McGurgle.

Mrs McGurgle, despairing of her lodgers' ability to rationalise the management of gravy, has pinned up in the hall a notice. It says:

> Gravy is not a kind of bird-bath to splash about in like starlings. It is part of a civilised meal, to be treated as seriously and as carefully as one treats one's portion of meat and vegetables. Discoloured tablecloths too often tell a tale of clumsiness at the best; at the worst, of utter disregard for propriety. Let elegant eating be our slogan.

Mrs McGurgle's campaign for Elegant Eating is not having much success. A commercial gentleman was observed, at lunch, to be licking the back of his soup-spoon.

Miss Relf, his vis-à-vis, drew in her breath sharply.

'One is glad,' said the chatelaine, 'that you like the soup, but there is no need to borrow a technique of appreciation from the lower animals.'

'Waste not, want not,' replied the offender surlily.

'The amount of soup saved by licking the back of a spoon,' riposted Mrs McGurgle, 'would not feed a fly.'

The vegetarian known as the herbaceous boarder was drinking his soup with a noise like the sea breaking on a rocky shore.

'Mr Tufford,' said Mrs McGurgle, with a frown, 'an aversion to meat is no excuse for a barbarous solo on the soup. You are not, I believe, a wild beast at a water-hole. Miss Renton's remarks on the weather are rendered almost inaudible by the tumult you create. Silence is golden, even when imbibing soup.'

Mr Tufford flushed, and confined himself to delicate sipping.

The herbaceous boarder continues to offend. The very soup itself seems to be vocal, as he wields his spoon like a spade. One boarder, in mock alarm, puts his hands to his ears. Another cries, 'Serve out the oilskins!' A third flinches as though menaced by the backwash. A fourth mumbles, 'Try a bulldozer, old man.'

'Pray do not encourage him to more frenzied efforts,' says the chatelaine.

Impervious to mockery and contumely, Mr Tufford toils at his spoon like a galley-slave at his oar, producing sounds that would not disgrace a wallowing hippotamus or a modern concert-hall.

Says the chatelaine, 'Mr Tufford, we can hardly hear ourselves eating.'

Soup came off the menu yesterday. Mrs McGurgle could stand no more of the ribald jests which began as Mr Tufford tuned up, as it were, and continued all through the performance. The boarders are now nervous. Any stray noise made by an eater makes him painfully self-conscious. Miss Gilke, champing a bit of tough mutton, left the table in confusion when a commercial gentleman put his hand to his ear, and said, 'Ah! The first cuckoo!'

The merriment at meal times has got out of hand. It is difficult to eat biscuits quietly. One boarder spread his fingers over a piece of cheese, and said to his neighbour who was eating a biscuit, 'Shall I play your accompaniment on the cheesi-ano?'

Mrs McGurgle turned her head away and clicked her lips. Then she said, 'While not demanding a Trappist silence, I must insist on the decencies. Such music-hall jests in mixed company contribute nothing to a desirable social atmosphere. Fingering cheese may suit an African jungle. In a civilised establishment it is a disgrace.'

The sound of whispered endearments, followed by a kiss, made Mrs McGurgle wince. She rose from her chair in her sitting-room, and prepared to open the door. Suspicion had fastened on Mr Gluddon, a raffish commercial gentleman, who was the cause of frequent complaints by the female boarders. She tiptoed to the door, determined to put an end to Mr Gluddon's outrageous conduct. She would give him notice.

With a rapid movement she flung the door open, and there crouched Miss Wigge, fondling the ear of the house dog, Mortimer, and about to repeat the kiss she had heard. 'Isn't he a treasure?' said Miss Wigge.

The chatelaine, speechless with relief, bent to fondle the dog's other ear.

*　　*　　*

The Waggling Parva Spy School

At Waggling Parva, and not far from the Strabismus laboratories, a new training centre for counter-espionage has opened. For reasons of security a large board says 'Snidder & Fulcrow, Coal Merchants'. From time to time bits of coal are strewn about near the front gate. Here the students are taught how to detect rocket warheads hidden in crates of vegetables, how to look like an Albanian schoolmaster with one eye, how to jam the microphone in the lining of an attaché's hat, and so on.

To keep the students on the alert, frequent surprises are arranged. One day a Chinese was found lurking in a lane near the house. A very smart student pounced on him and cried, 'Ha! George Rigstone! You're always doing this sort of thing.'

The Chinese freed himself and ran away.

Laughingly the student related the incident.

'You fool!' said the chief instructor. 'That was Bung Ho. We've been after him for weeks.'

An important part of the spy course at Waggling Parva is a lesson by an expert in how to masticate and swallow secret documents. I am told that it is almost laughable to watch the students trying

to eat blueprints, charts, and secret messages in code. Novices are allowed a little gravy to make the stuff more palatable. To start with, they are given the formula for a nerve-gas, on very thin paper, to swallow. Later they go on to blueprints for rocket-sites as a full meal.

Dr Strabismus (Whom God Preserve) of Utrecht takes a great interest in the training centre at Waggling Parva. It was he who drew the attention of instructors to an infallible way of detecting a drugged cigarette. The secret agent abroad carries a small dog in his overcoat pocket. When offered the cigarette he says, 'I will give Fido a few puffs. He loves smoking.' Then he lights the cigarette and gives it to the dog. If the dog goes into a coma, the agent pleads a sudden engagement and rushes away.

The secret face

Her unconventional hat almost obscured her face.

(Gossip column)

> Imagination will supply
> All that is hidden from the eye,
> In spite of obstacles like that.
> > Respect her secret. As you know –
> > For I have often told you so –
> All is human under the hat.
> *Chorus:*
> > All is human, utterly human,
> > All is human under the hat.

Aboard the houseboat

Said Mrs Withersedge: 'The boss said 'e thought our ship's cat was ill. I say "What do you expect? The poor little blighter wonders what the 'ell 'e's doin' aboard this lugger. 'E longs for the city lights, an' a bit o' night life and 'igh livin'. Get 'im a fiancy an' 'e'll soon brighten up."

'The boss replied, "This isn't a 'ome for stray cats."

'I says, "You wait. One day 'e will go berzerks an' serve us right for goin' on like musical-comedy sailors in a morgue. Or praps if we ever come apart from our blasted moorin's, 'e may get 'is sea-legs an' cheer up a bit. What a 'ope!!" '

Ballet criticism

A plea that criticisms of ballet should be written in plain English instead of in a jargon has my enthusiastic support ... 'While Tumbelova is mincing about on her toes, Serge Trouserin charges her like a Spurs halfback and, for no apparent reason, hoists her on to his shoulder. Struck by the absurdity of his action, he lifts her down from her perch. Whereupon she stands on one leg like a stork and waves her arms about. Threatened with more shoulder-sitting, she swoons. Knokisblokov emerges from the wings, pots him with a toy bow and arrow, and misses ...'

My mistake

A reader asks why I so often ridicule ballet. It is sour grapes. As an all-in wrestler (Bristol will remember me as Tiger Travoglio) I got a job in a *corps de ballet*. At a dress rehearsal I put a Hackenschmidt lock on a ballerina, and threw her into the stalls. I was disqualified.

Cocklecarrot's ruling

It has been decided that a mobile garage, with wheels under it, does not require planning permission. This reminds me of Cocklecarrot's famous ruling that a bungalow on wheels counts as a house, and therefore the owner, if he is found drunk in charge of a bungalow, is in his home, unless the bungalow is in movement along a road, in which case the bungalow is a vehicle on the public highway. 'But,' added the learned judge, 'a lighthouse on wheels is not a ship.'

Dr Rhubarb's corner

M.J.L. WRITES: My husband came home from a party in a false nose, a very red one. As our vicar had called, he took it off, but his real nose was even redder. How can I explain to the outraged clergyman?

DR RHUBARB SAYS: Say that the false nose was too small and pinched the real nose, thus making it red.

The Basques

There is a Basque saying: 'Give me today's meat, yesterday's bread, and last year's wine, and then, doctor, you can go to the deuce!' An article about travel in the Basque provinces recalled it to me. Where did the Basques get their language? Nobody knows. A priest once told me that he had found traces of it in the Japanese language. If you are thinking of learning it, beware. Everywhere you go you hear a different dialect. Hear them singing in their churches the *Veni, Creator Spiritus*, and you will know a great deal about these strange people.

The impetuous lover

Mimsie Slopcorner has been elected Miss Instant Oysters at Whitstable, having abdicated and laid down her crown as Scrap Iron Queen of Sopping Overcote. From Suet she received congratulations and a pamphlet on Civic Consciousness. 'Sentimentalist,' sneered Mimsie's father. 'Does he expect you to sleep with it under your pillow? How long is this whirlwind courtship going on?' Mimsie blushed as she underlined in pencil a paragraph about litter-bins, with a footnote on rubbish.

Facing fearful odds

Lines to a gentleman who boasted of his feats on the hunting-field:

> See how defenceless and unarmed they go
>   To meet the onset of the deadly foe,
>   Protected only by the loyal pack
>   Against the fox's terrible attack.

Incident at rehearsal

While rehearsing the part of Anisette in the opera of that name, Rustiguzzi put such feeling into her singing that she blew out the eight candles in her boudoir. Broccoli, playing her suitor, said: 'Even in the dark I could follow her movements by the sound of her voice. It was like the foghorn on a lighthouse, only more so.'

Peer steals waistcoast

'She said the gingerbread had made her sick, but her husband said it was her own fault.'   (*Morning paper*)

This is called taking the guilt off the gingerbread.
PRODNOSE: What is the point of that idiotic headline?
MYSELF: It arouses curiosity and overcomes sales resistance.

Fairly short story

Night was falling on the Mhoovi mountains. In a sordid street in Nayazin, Rex Barrington, disguised as a native water-carrier, was talking to a man whom he believed to be Koksnookh. Moving stealthily behind Barrington came Ogoaweh, and behind him an anonymous tribesman, and behind him, etc., etc., etc. Koksnookh turned into a yard, and Barrington quickened his pace and overtook him.

'Get your hands up!' he cried in the Mhoovi dialect.

Koksnookh turned. 'Barrington!' he exclaimed.

'Travers-Gray!' replied Barrington.

'Fancy meeting you here!' they both remarked.

While Barrington and Travers-Gray were exchanging memories of old days, Ogoaweh crept into the yard, covering them with his two sten-guns. The two agents turned to face him.

'Elmslow!' they cried.

'Barrington! Travers-Gray!' exclaimed Elmslow.

'What are we all doing here?' asked Barrington.

'Search me,' replied Elmslow.

'Not necessary. I'll do it,' said a voice in an ugly Japanese patois.

'It's Wotalotahui,' muttered Elmslow.

'Thought I'd surprise you,' drawled an English voice.

'Gutteridge!' cried the three agents.

The four agents left the yard stealthily and took to the fields. They had not gone far when they saw a lion approaching. They were about to shoot it when the mouth opened and a head appeared.

'It's Ravenscroft!' exclaimed Barrington.

'And Reynolds as the hind legs,' said Ravenscroft.

The two agents climbed out of the 'lion' and shook hands, and the six men continued on their way, until they met a tiger.

'This'll be Cattermole and Crawford,' said Elmslow.

It wasn't. It was a real tiger and it killed them all.

22

How to Measure Lard

'Journalists should always acknowledge quotations,' says a novelist. The story is told of a leader-writer who was always late with his copy. One day, when he was later than ever, the editor found him asleep at his desk. He awakened him and goaded him to action. When the copy was delivered, it consisted of an entire leading article from *The Times*, cut out and pasted onto sheets of paper, and prefaced by the words: 'What does *The Times* mean by this?'

The poets at play

The Gorium Possia Group met yesterday in their basement headquarters. Neth Gorium himself started the proceedings by saying the word 'bumblebee' thirty-four times in varying tones of voice. Rampton Glapiron then played a prolonged growling sound on a gramophone, and held up a yellow dishcloth. A young man in a yellow mask, with three pads hanging from it, recited a short 'Salute to Nothing', which consisted of numerals from sixty-four to ninety-three. Finally Eugene Thasko wrote on a blackboard: None go where all stay.

Dr Rhubarb's corner

E.G. WRITES: I want my wife to look her best at a party, but she sticks to her old-fashioned hat. Which of the new models should I buy for her?

DR RHUBARB SAYS: Try the chimney-brim bowler in gherkin-green laipou with a quarter-band Belgian riffet of snitched grosgrain; or the demi-coal-scuttle, steeple-crowned halo in hash-grey *rat-mort*, with a turnover of tufted *flamenco*, and a serge backbow in elephant's-breath-grey.

Do it yourself

The manufacturers of crooked egg-cups will surely protest against a device of which I have just read: 'A Rack and Pinion Egg Straightener fitted with solid rubber rollers.' We now come to steam-driven grindstones for keeping false noses in shape, large-mesh sieves for sifting fluff, electric gimlets for boring holes in rafts, pneumatic bellows for blowing rust off foghorn-containers, rotating clippers for shearing porcupines, miniature pocket-hoses for putting out lighted cigarettes and matches, clamps for holding jellies still in a high wind, detachable snouts for rocking-horses, and gigantic fly-papers for immobilising starlings.

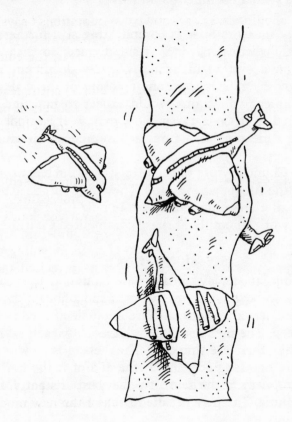

Practical hints for the home

To extricate a rasher of bacon stuck in the slot of a child's money-box use a small shoehorn or glove-stretcher as a lever, holding the box firmly in the left hand and levering gently with the right hand.

C. Suet, Esq.

Is there a spy in Charlie Suet's department of the Ministry of Bubbleblowing? Foreign agents must be well aware that Suet's filing system is the most up-to-date and the most complicated of all. Without the key to this system, which is in a code of Suet's own devising, not even his colleagues could hope to find anything. How comes it, then, that Suet himself has reported the loss of two letters about rafts for coal in flooded cellars? Who could have wanted such a document, and why?

As a security measure Suet is complicating still further his system. Each alphabetical heading is sub-divided, so that, working backwards on a system of averages, every document must be treble-checked by reference to one or other of the codes in use. Thus a document which one would expect to find under C.274 and is referred to in code 12 as H.93, may well be under W.625, the 93 being a meaningless figure used to mislead file-grubbers.

Larracombe Council wrote to the Ministry of Bubbleblowing with reference to the site for a bandstand. They were surprised to receive in reply a leaflet about dung-heaps. 'No new filing system can be expected to work smoothly at first,' commented Charlie Suet.

'Horse Sense'

Udmer, in his latest play, breaks new ground. The scene is the top of a large iceberg. On it are five men and a horse. The men are dressed in mediaeval armour, and are entangled in red twine. The horse is asleep. The men speak simultaneously, each saying what he thinks the others are thinking. The iceberg is slowly melting. There is only one long act, and at the end of it the horse wakes up and swims away to the shore, twenty yards distant, leaving the men still talking. The play is called *Horse Sense*.

At the theatre

Act Two, but the stalls are empty.
No wonder the barmaids grouse.
By the time the last curtain had fallen,
There was not a dry mouth in the house.

Suet under fire

The confusion in Suet's office is pitiful. 'Documents,' said a secretary, 'might just as well be filed by the throw of a dice. Our filing and counter-filing has become a game of chance. By no stretch of the imagination could a foreign agent or his accomplice be interested in ascertaining that a memo about socks for lighthouse-keepers is listed under C.42/9b/S1741/21/12, which deals solely with nylon milk-floats.'

A controversy breaks out

Dear Sir,

Mrs Carpett's boast that she can waggle her ears is in bad taste. Even men look foolish and undignified when they do this to amuse children. Women should have nothing to do with such antics even in the privacy of the home.

(Mrs) Amanda Bulbe

Twenty years of uproar

'Interloping trombonists should be in position at the start of any symphony.' Thus writes a music critic after a concert. The audience were agog for the final movement of the symphony when 'suddenly three trombonists, not hitherto needed, filed onto the platform. The effect was unsettling and ludicrous.' It might have been worse. Last year, in the very middle of the second movement of a symphony, two men carrying a ladder made their appearance.

'Where shall we put it?' shouted one of them above the music.

'Take it away!' yelled the conductor.

The violins, thinking this was their cue, crashed in in the wrong place. During the ensuing chaos an oboist had hysterics.

Is Mrs Bulbe a prude?

Dear Sir,

Mrs Bulbe's squeamish Victorian prudery as to ear-waggling is out of date in this Jet Age. More power to Mrs Carpett's elbow, or, rather ears.

E.F. Morplesdon

Nothing to do with me

'There is no evidence that standing on the head as an exercise
makes women any slimmer.'   (*Note on keeping fit*)

> To become as slim as a wafer,
>   She rises at dawn from her bed,
> Takes a deep breath, turns upside down
>   And stands for a while on her head.
> To avoid a subsequent headache
>   While reducing superfluous fat,
> She wears, at a jaunty angle,
>   A smart little rope-soled hat.

Fun in court

Wearing a false beard of unusual design, a welder of Pershore
admitted that he had stolen it from a goat. He told the magistrate
that he intended to buy the goat a false beard.

'You could have bought yourself one,' said the magistrate, 'while
you were about it. And if it comes to that, judging by the abundance
of your moustache, you could have grown a real beard.'

'My moustache is false,' replied the welder. 'I stole it off a walrus.'

'How preposterous!' said the magistrate. 'If you sheared a yak
you could wear a false wig.'

'The hair on my head,' said the welder with dignity, 'is at
least my own.'

Interlude

PRODNOSE: What on earth did the magistrate mean by a 'false wig'?

MYSELF: I imagine that he wished to underline the fact that
wigs are not usually made from the hair of yaks.

PRODNOSE: Well, why did the man want a false moustache and
beard?

MYSELF: Oh, obviously he was going to a fancy-dress dance, dressed
as a man in a false beard and moustache, like most Pershore
welders.

A plea for mothers

Dear Sir,

Why should men be privileged to wag their ears, but not women? It is the women who run the homes, and are the mothers of the men of the future. Without us there would be no men to boast of this masculine achievement.

(Mrs) Bertha Whackstraw

Feeling the pinch

'Even in the great houses the food is not what it used to be.'

(*Article on food*)

'What is this noxious lump of meat?'
Lord Shortcake cried, 'It seems to me
Such stuff's not really fit to eat;
One wonders what it's meant to be.'
It tasted nastier than it looked,
There were inquiries in due course.
The loyal old family chef had cooked
A superannuated horse.
'In making our economies,'
Said Shortcake, 'we must spare the gees.'

Now, Mrs Bulbe!

Dear Sir,

My grandmother can waggle her ears one at a time. This alternation varies the monotony of her only parlour trick.

H.J. Glapiron

Let the mystery remain

The illustrated edition of the *List of Huntingdonshire Cabmen* has not been an unqualified success. As one critic wrote: 'The appeal of such a book lies largely in the mystery of the names and initials. To see photographs of the cabmen is to lose the illusion. One finds that they are, after all, ordinary people, like you and me.' The suggested anthology of the *List* is an absurd idea. On what principle would one reject or elect? Has Owlsblood, H., a prior claim over Nobbleton, B.J.?

Virtuoso

Dear Sir,

Having been away in Essex, I have only just seen the controversy about ear-waggling. My grandmother once told me that she had known a chemist who could waggle his ears and twitch his nose simultaneously. She used to add 'Much good it did him!'

F.L.B. Morley

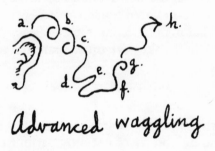

Advanced waggling

Good news

I have secured for serialisation next week in this column Mr Bernard Kender's book *How To Measure Lard*. Mr Kender, who was once a member of the crew of a lifeboat, claims to have rationalised lard-measurement after living for two years in Ghent. The book includes diagrams by Elmer Frank, the American art-collector, and photographs of the actual measurements of lard done at Tarporley by a team of lard-measurers. Restrain your excitement for a few days.

Strabismus does it again!

The Strabismus domestic hoovercraft goes through a house like a bullet through rotten cheese. Whizzing along from room to room, a foot above the floor, it sucks in dirt, dust, bits of food, beetles, and flies, at the rate of two kilos a minute. There is a comfortable aluminium seat for the housewife-driver. A larger model for use in gardens sucks weeds out by the roots, at the same time spraying fruit-trees with poison.

Postman boils egg in letterbox

A journalist has said: 'The object of a headline is to arouse the reader's interest.' That explains my addition to intriguing headlines. Italian Walks Tightrope On His Elbows. Camel Falls Through Croydon Roof. Peer's Cousin Hijacks Cyclist.

PRODNOSE: Presumably a headline should have some connection with what follows.

MYSELF: How very dull! Beauty Queen Marries Again.

Earl pawns his gaiters

Alice Marrowfat, who won £75 by beating Butcher Rose Twyle in a wrestling match which took place in a pit filled with fish, will dive from a height of 42 feet into a tank of treacle next Thursday at the Lodenham Scout Hall. Two of her uncles were in the Air Force during the war, but her mother was once the only female milkman in Creswick, where the famous hen with a striped beak laid a triangular egg in 1949.   (*Beachcomber News Agency*)

23

Before Mr Justice Cocklecarrot

The Case of the Starling's Egg

The cheque written on a pillow-case and accepted by a bank recalls Mr Justice Cocklecarrot's ruling that there is no obligation on the bank, in such cases, to have the pillow-case laundered before returning it with the monthly statement.

At the beginning of this month an extremely absent-minded man wrote a cheque on a starling's egg. The bank cashed it and

returned it with the monthly statement. The man put the egg in a nest, and the mother bird hatched it. The bank claimed the baby birds, on the grounds that they had been included in the egg-cheque, albeit in embryo. The man then wrote cheques on the three little starlings and presented them at his bank. While the cashier was with the manager the birds flew away, and the man accused the bank of wanton carelessness, and sued for 6d., the value of the cheques. The bank retorted that it had not issued the bird-cheques. The case is to come before Cocklecarrot shortly.

The hearing begins:

In the case of *Mrs Harrick and Vagmyre Endowment Trusts versus Commodore Bursting*, Mr Justice Cocklecarrot had laid down that a cheque written on the hide of a rhinoceros would be legal tender. The rhinoceros, by the laws of nature, would be incapable of giving or withholding its consent to any such financial transaction, whereas a human being could protest at being used as a cheque. A bank manager might well prefer his clients to use less mobile and grotesque material for cheques.

Cocklecarrot went on to say that if the rhinoceros were to be lost in transit when returned with the monthly statement to the client, *habeas corpus* would apply in any further proceedings.

Mr Tinklebury Snapdriver, for the defence, talked so much of wivenage, feoffment, gavelkind, cormandry, pithex, etc., that Mr Honeyweather Gooseboote, for the prosecution, demanded a writ of *sic nos non nobis*. The learned judge replied: '*Sic transit gloria rhinocerotis.*' (Laughter and catcalls.)

Mr Tinklebury Snapdriver said yesterday: 'There would appear to be no legal definition of what object, article, beast, or bird may not be used as a cheque. I submit that it would be ridiculous to present a cheque written on a drainpipe. Ridiculous, yes. But, illegal? I can imagine eccentrics writing cheques on old overcoats, merely to get rid of them, or on stuffed fish, or slabs of frozen glue or horse collars, or—'

Here Mr Honeyweather Gooseboote interjected, 'Or on electroplated boilers. Some cheque!'

Cocklecarrot ruled that none of this was germane to the issue, whatever the issue might be.

Mr Howle, cashier at Hufnagle's Bank, asked by Mr Gooseboote if he was surprised when the three starlings were presented inscribed as cheques, replied that he had already cashed the egg, and was getting used to this sort of thing.

GOOSEBOOTE: The point is that Mr Akimbo, the manager, regarded the bird which would eventually emerge from the egg as part of the cheque.

SNAPDRIVER: Cheques do not lay eggs. An oven door is part of an oven. If a man wrote a cheque on the door, would he expect the bank to claim the whole oven?

GOOSEBOOTE: The oven does not lay doors, nor vice versa.

SNAPDRIVER: An oven does not fly. So what? Nor does a rhinoceros.

'Prolonged and inconclusive discussions,' said Cocklecarrot, 'have diverted attention from the three vanished starlings. It may be thought that the little fugitives from justice, having fulfilled their temporary functions as cheques, were justified in resuming the habits of birds. It cannot, I think, be claimed that either little birds, or big ones, constitute an essential part of the assets of a self-respecting bank. Having emerged into the avian world they can no longer be described as a bank's nest-egg. Case adjourned, *sine die* and *coram populo*.'

BUT:

Hufnagle's Bank was beginning to forget the incident of the cheque written on the starling's egg when one of those twelve red-bearded dwarfs rushed in and tried to thrust his left leg through a grille. On it was written the facsimile of a cheque signed Frums

Gillygottle. 'There is more money here,' said the intruder, 'than meets the eye. Legal tender is the cry, therefore pray do not stand on ceremony. Keep withered apples for a rainy day.'

The cashier sent for the manager. Bowing from the waist, Gillygottle said: 'This is too much of an honour. Have a peppermint.'

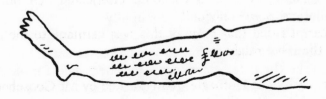

While the bank manager was talking to Frums Gillygottle, in came the eleven other red-bearded dwarfs.

'We do not come as cheques,' said Farjole Merrybody, 'we come to see fair play.'

'Your friend,' said the manager, 'has no account with this bank.'

'What is an account between friends?' asked Churm Rincewind.

'Money is money, cheque or no cheque,' said Molonay Tubilderborst.

'And a cheque is money in fancy dress,' said Scorpion de Rooftrouser.

'Gentlemen, please!' implored the manager.

'Shall it be said,' asked Guttergorm Guttergormton, 'that the left leg of Frums is less valuable than a bit of paper?'

'This cheque,' said the manager patiently, 'which you have inscribed on your left leg, says "pay cash". You must try to realise that we have no money of yours.'

'Why should you have?' riposted Frums Gillygottle, 'I don't chuck my money about indiscriminately.'

'Maybe,' suggested Amaninter Axling, 'we could all club together and start an account with the amount you give Frums; we could write out cheques for you on proper cheques if you gave us a book. That would prove our good faith, and nobody would be out of pocket.'

The manager sighed heavily.

Before the manager had recovered his equilibrium, Frums Gillygottle said: 'My ancestors, who came over with Mrs Sprok, have
used this bank for longer than you would care to remember if you
were born last Wednesday. All over Asia there is a saying, "A
Gillygottle's word is as good as a wink from a blind horse." You
ask why I use my leg as a cheque. Have you never heard of Fried?
It is a hate-love complex of childhood's days, when my aunt made
me eat gristle.'

Speechless, the manager nodded stupidly.

An indignant lady was trying to get to the counter to pay in a
cheque. 'Take these telegram forms, teacher,' said Farjole Merrybody, with a bow, 'they may help you to forget, as you sit by the
fire, listening to the fruit falling off the frees.'

The lady looked around for the manager, but he was hemmed
in by four of the dwarfs, who were singing 'lumpydumpy' to him.

Cleveland Zackhouse had got behind the counter and was
yelling, 'Anyone who buys a dozen stamps will receive a tiny
brass blow-lamp.'

Then the twelve made their exit, singing in chorus 'Red Beards
in the Sunset'.

*　　*　　*

Wordsworth on the trombone

My recent love song to a woman trombonist (trombonette?) brought
me a request for anything written by the great poets about this
instrument. Here are Wordsworth's well-known lines:

> Brass goddess of the brazen throat,
>   Hush thy dread voice, for here doth dwell
> An old man bearded like a goat,
>   Whose ears are sealed to music's swell.
> By some lone tarn he gathers weeds
>   And many a solitary stone,
> Nor counts among his simple needs
>   Such comradeship as thine, trombone.

Good news

Ho Sir, this is our lukky day. We was orl three perobubly born
under Siggaturius as yore hastronomer royul would say. We are

of sining a kontrak to hippere at a gnawthun niteklub. In uther wordz, we are striking the high spotz, going to places, and ritterning to the nylon lites and the limelite of pooblick hexerebishuns of our hart. Wot about reersuls, they said. We do not reerse, we said. Our iffez is spontinaneus, and our jestures is doktated by the wim of the momink and the intxericatin rothem of the plonk, now hup, now down. Wish us joi, ho yes, please. We remane rispeckfully,

Ashura, Kazbulah and Rizamughan

This is more than I can stand

The ugly word 'payola' has been used in connection with my occasional praise of the Snibbo products. Having consulted my solicitors, and commissioned a few foul oaths from them, I shall shortly take an action against the *Nibblestone and Piff Argus and Messenger*, which used these words: 'One would like to know what sums "Beachcomber" has received for his ceaseless and vulgar boosting of Snibbo Ltd.' Messrs Faffnage, Coalhouse, Bulp, Sniggering, Quacke, Furthermore, Sawback, Pillow, Morfle, Idge, Idge, and Idge, solicitors, have the matter in hand.

Restful interior

Tiny triangular concrete candles standing in massive glass egg-cups give her larder-cum-studio the Lapp look. In the wall holes are bored, and from each hole hangs a large yellow stalactite made of dried ox-tongue. The two-inch-high chairs are of crimson beechwood, with corrugated iron backs. In one corner, concealed by a green and blue rug hung from the Japanese ceiling, is a combined cocktail cabinet and television set overlaid with thin strips of jagged tin, painted mauve and brown. In this exotic paradise she writes her down-to-earth novels.

You never know

A newly published book poses the problem: What happens if a bee pushes a golfer's ball into the hole? If it comes to that, what does the referee do when a swarm of bees pushes a football through the goal?

PRODNOSE: An unlikely occurrence.

MYSELF: The unexpected often happens. Who could have foretold that thousands of ants, migrating from their hill, would push a croquet ball through a hoop at Frinton last summer?

PRODNOSE: What evidence have you?
MYSELF: I was playing for Frinton Rovers in that very game.

Bravo! Bravo!

Ho Sir,

   Our furst performince, our preemiair, as the smart sett korls it, was a smack hit. Our hact was hipplorded like madmen. The nitespot klyunteel falls over each hother for our hortygraffs, and a brewnet like a bath bell plonted a kiss on Ashura's hupturned feetyers. To see his bloshes was like dorn on a mounting rainge. 'Menny thankyous,' says Ashura. 'Yore wellcum,' larfs the bell. So you see seesaw hath not losst its hippeal to hartistick persuns. 'Howe do you held the plonk steddy on yore belli?' harsks a himpressario. 'Konsentrayshun,' says Kazbulah, strikin a hattitood. 'Rimmarkabul,' replies the himpressario, puffin his seegah like Vossoovias in hirrupshun.

We are, ho yes,
Ashura, Kazbulah and Rizamughan

Here is the poem by Ashura to the 'bath bell' who kissed him after the show:

> No roes is harf as butiful
>   As you was, my brewnet,
> When yore rubby lips
>   Broshed the mourning jew
> Off my feetyers.
>   The futmark of yore kiss
> Is hingravied on my brou
>   Up till my foonerall persesshun.
> Wot a gerzell you are, aren't you?
> (Kopprite in orl Kounties)

Something wrong somewhere

WANTED: 14 tons of boiled mackerel, all mod. con., near bus route, small garden, garage, for ex-officer willing to go anywhere, speaks French, would exchange plough or combine-harvester, up-to-date dredger for river work may be seen by appointment, miss you every day, Julia, 14 tons of boiled mackerel.   (*Advt.*)

Allow me to explain

The *Nibblestone and Piff Argus and Messenger*, undeterred by my threat of an action for libel, alleges that, apart from any sums of money I may have received from Snibbo, I accepted sundry gifts. They mention 124 tins of tooth-polish, a day trip to Boulogne, a macintosh, a pair of braces, a mustard-pot, a sieve, free tickets for a lecture on cement, and a lorry load of scrap. I would recommend this scurrilous rag to get its facts right. All the gifts mentioned (except the sieve, which I refused) were presents from a firm which had no official connection with Snibbo, until it was taken over by them shortly afterwards.

A love letter

Deer Lunnone Brewnet,

   To pervent idol tungs waging, I told Mrs Ashura that yore kiss was plutonic, and was a cymbal of yore love of seesaw art hinsted of me. So if we mete ergane, do not cast yore harms round me, howevver wiled you are of me. Grete me like ices, and I shull rase my hatt and smole in gintlemannish fashun. But, ar, my booty, our seekrit bilongs to us two, and my hart goeth pitta patta like a seesaw when I think of you. Farwell, beelovid.

Yore cavverleer,
Ashura of Thurralibad

Mayfair incident

The manager of the bar was on holiday. A note, purporting to be from him to the head barman, introduced a temporary extra barman. His approach to customers was odd. He would say, 'What is yours, sir? ... Ah ... So is mine.' The other barman, seeing the new employee drinking all the time, imagined that the customers were standing him drinks. This went on until an indiscreet customer shouted, 'Hello there, Foulenough! How's tricks?'

   'My name,' said the barman with dignity, 'is Farragut, and tricks are pretty good.'

   'If you're not Foulenough,' said the new customer, 'I'm the King of Peru.'

   'It is a pleasure to serve your Majesty,' said Foulenough angrily, pouring himself a stiff whisky before slipping out by a side door.

Mounted billiards

A game of billiards on horseback seems, at first sight, rather absurd, as though golfers were to play from traction-engines. At second or third sight, it remains puzzling, especially if the table is the usual size. To claim it as a 'test of skill' is no doubt true. It would be a test of skill to use a football and a ping-pong racket for a game of cricket. However—

PRODNOSE: What on earth is this leading up to?

MYSELF: To a blow on the jaw for you, if you interfere.

Kazbulah, too

... We wos always tolled that yore Inglish gurls wos kolled, well then wot about orl this? Furst Ashura and the brewnet, and now I, Kazbulah, has a flour throne at me by a blonbomshell, as I erd a spiktater korl her. Is there a gorjus reded waytin to try er wyalls at Rizamughan? Ixpeck no wodding bells chyming for us seesawers, even if we leaf behind brawken arts gillore when we shall shake the dirt of Inglund from off our foot, for we have wifes in Filthistan. But I will ware the bomshell's flour in my hatt like the nites in harmor. Ashura says press it in yore angelo-pershun dikshunnery. I say no, I will florish it in pooblick. The siaren must be sick of love for me ...

My dream

I do not often have amusing dreams, but two days ago I woke up laughing. I had dreamed that Mr Harold Macmillan was sitting in my drawing-room. He was telling me about a man who, for spite, put out his grandfather's bonfire. We both roared with laughter. I rose and did a few dance steps. 'Oh,' he said, 'so you know that dance.' I then took off my socks and put them in a box in the corner of the room. Then I woke up. Over to the psycho-psychiagogues. I have not invented a word of this.

A good answer

A man who produced a bottle from his pocket and began to drink from it was asked, very courteously, to leave a picture-gallery.

'What you are doing,' said an artist who had observed the breach of etiquette, 'is hardly in the best interests of art.'

'Perhaps not,' said the man, 'but it's in the best interests of drinking.'

What! No Italian trombone?

'Anything to declare?'

'Yes. A toy horse-collar, the key of a Belgian castle, thirty-two ball-bearings, a model of the River Meurthe in wax, a stick-on bath-tap cover, a grocer's doormat, a tin filled with grass, a pig-tail, a bronze lobster, four ferrets, a tightrope, a cotton snowball, three Dutch clogs, and a mechanical tuning-fork in satinwood.'

Moral: Customs could not stale his infinite variety.

Chess on ice

A correspondent who was intrigued by my recent reference to billiards on horseback says he is all for new developments in games. He should try chess on ice. Every piece on the board is fitted with tiny skates, and the whole art of the game is to give a push that will land the piece where it is intended to go. As for mounted billiards, great skill is needed in handling the cue as you lean from the saddle.

And now Rizamughan

(To the ravenaird nomph wot blewed a kiss at me.)

Orl I kan say is
   I wish we was in the moonlite
On a gongdoolia in Venniss.
   But Mrs Rizamughan was brort up
Old-fashund, and she wood nok off my blok.
   So you must soffer in sailens.
Fate is more krull than a pak of starving krokkodials.

One thing and another

A dairy was fined the other day for selling a bottle of milk with a field-mouse in it. The culprits should have pleaded that it was a gift-scheme, a mouse being given away with every bottle of milk. Any old sailor could have testified that it is easier to put a field-mouse in a bottle than the model of a ship, milk or no milk.

Here, there and everywhere

GEORGE and Henry Goscombe, twins who live near Stockport, are so unalike that nobody ever suspects that they are twins. One is a confectioner's assistant, the other a member of a lifeboat crew.

A THRUSH which flew into a kitchen in Lewes laid an egg in an egg-cup. 'Very handy,' said Mrs Fawkes, who was preparing breakfast for her godson. 'If only it had been a hen.'

POSING as a stamp-dealer, 43-year-old Rudolf Moat fell from a ladder in a public library onto a reader. Both were uninjured.

Understanding wives

The wives of the three Persian seesawists have written a joint letter to the proprietor of the night-club where their husbands are appearing:

... We the undersined resint the hinnienndos of that gurnalist to trete the hisperrited larks of our spousers so seeryusly. The blewing of kissis by pheemails of the hordiuns are not ennything but a bit of extrer ipplaus, like battaring the flaw with the fut. Seesaw is the honnly dippartemink of the hartisteric wurld that has morruls. Nun of us ever herd of a deevorst seesawer. We like our housebins to ern hadmershun, evin from seeside bath syeruns and blondeded teanaggers ...

Eat as though you meant it

A rebuke to those who take 'an over-demonstrative pleasure in food' will please every puritanical prig and milksop within miles. Give me the man who laughs and sings when his food is set before him, and praises it in blazing rhetoric, and to the devil with all stone-faced mumblers. Give me the swashbuckling eater, who uses his knife like a sword and his fork like a spear, grimaces ecstatically, rolls his eyes, and roars great oaths in his delight. And may eighty-three cartloads of demons run away with the wretch who gets more fun out of filling his tank with petrol than out of filling his body with food.

Rather cross purposes

'He's a vulgarian,' said the hostess, 'but I must introduce you to him.' She led her guest across the room and introduced him.

'I've never been to Bulgaria,' he said, having misunderstood his hostess.

'Me, too, neither,' was the reply.

'His English is shaky,' said the man to himself. 'But,' continued the man, 'I once went on a tour to Bucharest.'

'So near and yet not Sofia, ha, ha, ha,' said the vulgarian, jabbing the ice in his glass with his thumb. 'Now we've broken the ice. How's tricks?'

'I am not a conjuror,' was the haughty response.

The hostess then intervened to restore order.

The secret wedding

So closely was the secret kept
That nobody turned up except
The television camera corps,
Agents, reporters by the score,
Producers, managers, and stars,
Friends and relations in their cars,
Photographers in crowded vans,
And forty thousand screaming fans.

24

Mrs Wretch and the Circus

Wugwell Tries Again

The great Wugwell, proprietor of Wugwell's Circus, has never abandoned hope of luring Mrs Wretch, once Zaboula of Wugwell's, back
to the ring. Every year, as Christmas approaches, she and Colonel
Wretch live in terror of a visit from her old associates. Mrs Wretch
began in a humble capacity as the girl in tights and spangles who
balanced a bottle of port on the ape's head. She worked her way up,
and ended as the Equestrian Thunderbolt, who rode two horses (one
leg on each) through a fiery hoop. Her husband has never forgotten
the day when he entered his drawing-room to find Anselmo the
Snake-Man twining himself round chair-legs and hissing at Mrs
Wretch, who was cowering in a corner. She had just refused to
rejoin for a week.

Wugwell himself called at Wretch Manor yesterday. Colonel
Wretch winced at the mere sight of him and explained that
his wife's engagements and her whole mode of life made even
a temporary return of La Belle Zaboula to the circus impossible.
Wugwell said sadly, 'Zabby was the only one who could ever get
the seal to catch fish in its mouth in time to the music.'

The colonel grimaced like one whose mouth is full of vinegar.

Then, lowering his voice and speaking more confidentially, Wugwell said, 'We always thought, between you and me and the doorpost, that she'd marry Borinelli of the Three Flying Borinellis. He kissed her once behind a horse.'

A telephone call put the colonel out of his misery.

The next caller at the Manor was Moggo the clown. Mrs Wretch was unable to prevent him from bawling like a baby, and lying full-length on the floor. To the colonel he said, 'Ask your better half about the time she side-stepped when I squirted soda-water at her. The lion-tamer got it in the face.'

'Indeed,' said the colonel.

'If it'd been champagne, wild horses wouldn't have budged her an inch,' continued Moggo, with a coarse laugh. As Mrs Wretch was shepherding the visitor to the door, the vicar was announced.

Going down on all fours, and barking at him, Moggo shouted, 'Throw us a bone, bishop!'

'Dear me,' said the vicar, 'I fear I intrude.'

'That's all right,' said Moggo. 'If they let me in, it ought to be all right for you, your Reverence.'

Bortsch the lion-tamer, after offering Colonel Wretch an acid drop from a paper bag, said, 'We're badly in need of someone to put her head into the lion's mouth. I suppose your lady wouldn't oblige – just for evening performances?'

'Out of the question,' said the colonel with brutal abruptness.

'Oh, well,' said Bortsch, 'the girl we've got is such a little silly that she tried to put the lion's head in *her* mouth. She'd got the wrong idea.'

'Doubtless,' said the colonel.

'It's an art,' said Bortsch. 'My Leo won't let everyone do it, and I don't blame him. What lion wants all sorts of people shoving their heads into his mouth? Eh?'

'Quite,' said the colonel.

His mission a failure, Bortsch held out his bag of acid drops. 'You can have these,' he said with simple friendliness. 'Olive oil, soldier.'

The ringmaster, Augustine Kekewich, had a very superior air. He was announced as Mr Kekewich, and the unsuspecting colonel asked: 'Surely you were at Harrow with my younger brother?'

'We played in that township last year,' said the ringmaster. 'What name was your brother using? Was he the chap who raked the sand?'

Mrs Wretch then entered to find her husband tongue-tied.

'Ah, Zaboula,' said the ringmaster, 'I trust you have not forgotten your pristine equestrian skill. Can your boon-companion Kekky prevail upon you to adorn the ring as of yore, at this festive season? Or has a baser if more elevated condition of life corrupted you to a less unconventional mode of riding than was your wont?'

'Once and for all,' replied the chatelaine, 'I tell you all, I have done with the circus.'

'Our loss, dear lady,' said Kekewich, bowing himself out.

Upset by the visits of the circus people, Colonel Wretch said angrily, 'Before we know where we are we'll have elephants in the library, and you'll be asked to ride two horses at once round the drawing-room before jumping through a hoop.'

'Pray do not exaggerate,' replied Mrs Wretch. 'The past is dead.'

'How you could ever have demeaned yourself,' said the colonel, 'by getting mixed up in a circus is beyond me.'

'May I remind you,' replied his wife, 'of the story told of a certain young Oxford man named Wretch who arrived at a theatre during the second act of an Ibsen play and shouted "Bring on the chorus girls!" ' Silence fell.

What was the delight of Wugwell and of every member of his circus when, at an afternoon performance, they saw, sitting in the best seats, La Belle Zaboula herself! It was a kindly gesture. Less kindly was the gesture of the elephant, Fido. Blessed with the good memory of his tribe, Fido recognised the lady who had once eaten a bun intended for him. Ambling round the ring, Fido coiled his trunk round her, lifted her from her comfortable seat, and deposited her, amid wild applause, in the ninepennies. Not all the cajolings of ringmaster Kekewich could induce the lordly denizen of the jungle to convey the humiliated ex-equestrienne back to a better seat.

* * *

Lullaby

'Children are becoming too sophisticated for lullabies.'

(Morning paper)

But not grown-ups. There is an exquisite lullaby sung over Mr Transom by his niece:

> Sleep, Uncle, Sleep.
> See! The silver moon glows,
> And a pale ray illumines
> My Uncle Fred's nose.
> Hushabye, Uncle,
> Lie snug as a mouse,
> And your snore like a trumpet,
> Will shake the whole house.
> Rockabye, Uncle,
> Safe in your nest.
> Then – a snort like a bullock's,
> And Uncle's at rest.

206 yawns a day

A man who boasts of having yawned 206 times in twelve hours may be said to be leading a hand-to-mouth existence – that is, if he remembered his manners. But how on earth did the judges decide which was a genuine yawn and which was a contrived yawn? They look much the same to the layman, and even to the clergyman. Again, were they all full-throated yawns, or did he slip in a couple of dozen of those half – or quarter – yawns which never come to maturity? When it was all over he must have been too bored and tired even to yawn.

Dr Rhubarb's corner

J.L. WRITES: When my nephew got hiccoughs we put a key down his back. He laughed so much that his nose bled, so we told him to hold his breath and count 350. When he got to 14 he got cramp in his foot. What should we have done?

DR RHUBARB SAYS: You should have told him to put his foot into the wrong side of a glass of water. That would have cured all these ailments.

Nasal melon-pushing?

Evans the Hearse set up a new record yesterday by pushing a walnut with his nose for a distance of five miles in nine hours, fourteen minutes. Iron-Nostril Balzarotti retorted by pushing a large potato for three miles in eight hours, seven minutes. Said Evans: 'It is up to one of us to push a melon up Snowdon. The pea is becoming old hat.'

Foulenough to Vita Brevis

Sweet ringdove,
 Surely the approach of the festive season will defrost that Arctic heart of yours. Meet me tomorrow at 12.30 in the Mayfair bar which I call ours because you once let me hold your hand while ordering refills – a generous impulse which went to my head quicker than the martinis. If you have forgotten what I look like, so long ago seems our last meeting, you will recognise me by the flame in my eyes. And if they are bloodshot, attribute it to the winds of winter.

Vita Brevis to Foulenough

My pest,
 Your reference to the occasion when you held my hand in a Mayfair bar omits to mention that you were after my martini. It was greed rather than sentimentality on your part. As to your eyes being bloodshot, I can quite believe it. But is it the winter winds that make them bloodshot in mid-summer? I recall that when I rescued my hand and my drink from your clutch, you said, 'Don't spoil our beautiful friendship.' Stick to the drink, and leave me alone – and I mean your own drink.

Free-for-all

An untoward scene marred the production of the ballet *Elefante* yesterday. The famous *pas du tout* was being danced by the whole company when Serge Trouserin caught his foot in Tumbelova's dress and stumbled against Semolina. Tapioca tried to stop her falling and cannoned off the Japanese dancer, Sago, with the grace of a billiards ball on its way to a pocket. There were shouts from all over the theatre. 'Foul!' 'Send her off!' 'Where's the ref?' 'Good shot, ma'am!' 'Offside!'

The orchestra collapsed in helpless laughter, and the conductor cried, 'It's like a struggle in a No. 11 bus.'

The team on the stage sorted itself out with many an outlandish oath, while the more serious balletomanes tut-tutted. When the ballet recommenced it was noticed that the dancers went to work warily.

'It's not meant to be funny,' said a connoisseur disapprovingly, and in a loud voice, to a man who had stuffed his handkerchief into his mouth.

Interlude

'Mice suffer from the cold, like all other creatures.'

(News item)

I knew a lady who knitted warm woollen wainscots for her mice. She was the daughter of a retired admiral who lived in Market Harborough, where she won a women's chess competition. She married a librarian who lost an ear in a tram accident. She—

PRODNOSE: What on earth is all this about?

MYSELF: Patience! Await the *dénouement*, nincompoop. Well,
    she had two sons. One became a fire brigade chief, and the
    other went to Brazil. Both were left-handed, you see.

PRODNOSE: Is that all?

MYSELF: Isn't it enough to be going on with, idiot?

Printer's frolic

'The new market centre is to be built in tears.'   *(News item)*

Even the builders will turn away, sobbing, when they see what they are building.

Man-about-town

The self-raising hat, which has a mechanical gadget fixed to it, sounds very labour-saving. You pull a wire attached to your buttonhole and the hat lifts eurythmically to a lady. I myself avoid the fatigue of hat-raising by delegating the chore to my man Mason, who accompanies me everywhere, carrying my umbrella. When I see anyone I care to be seen talking to, Mason steps forward, raises my hat, and carefully replaces it. To the more important ladies he bows slightly on my behalf.

Advance publicity

... Speshul denownsment. In the Youlltide we three see-saw expurts will prissent a gnovvelti. Hour seesaw will be dikkerated with Chineez lanterns orl erlong the plonk, and Kazbulah with the plonk on his belli will sing Gud King Wenzleas and uther karills wile we go now hup now down, ho yes. The rothum will go to the hedds of the hordiuns like Persian brandy. Kum to the old reegul theerter at Pippsbury and sulve the seekrit of prepettial moshun, and a merri Youlltide to wunanawl. Wot a garler, wot phun and james ...

Old memories

I cried. It was not a mere blubbering but those deep-throated sobs which shake strong men in novels. A letter asked if I was the man of the same name who captained a Midland hockey team years ago. All the old faces, all the old hockey sticks floated before my eyes ... my winning goal against Burslem ... Lady Hallcraft handing me the cup, half-filled (the stingy harridan!) with inferior champagne ... the dinner at the Womersley Arms, where I was carried shoulder-high round the fig pudding. Ah, well! It is good to be remembered by the old crowd. Above the mantelpiece in my drawing-room, mounted on an oak board, are the trousers I wore against Market Harborough – faded now, but dearer to me than the Book Society honourable mention for unsplit infinitives.

Decorative rather than useful

The ingenuity of Christmas gifts has inspired Dr Strabismus (Whom God Preserve) of Utrecht. He has invented the perfect gift for anyone who knows what he doesn't want. It is described in an advertisement as an oblong wooden peg which props up a built-in sieve. The angle of the sieve makes it possible to sift things sideways, so that what falls through goes into a bucket clamped vertically to the wall.

Christmas at Rissole Mio

The usual notice will shortly be posted in the hall at Rissole Mio, close to the mistletoe. The notice says:

> This festive plant is intended to encourage seasonal expressions of good will, not to be made the excuse for the tendentious embrace which so often becomes horseplay. The tradition of the house is a chaste salute, which need mantle no female cheek with the blush of shame. The male boarders are requested to set an example of restrained gaiety. The female boarders will kindly refrain from senseless tittering, arch glances, and other provocations. Encounters under the mistletoe should be fortuitous, not the result of loitering in the passage or lying in ambush in a doorway.

Ideal gift

The very long-playing record of the famous *List of Huntingdonshire Cabmen*, made by a popular BBC performer, is a good present to give. The *List* is unabridged and unexpurgated, and contains every name from Adams, B.R., to Younghusband, F. The background music, from Bizet's *L'Arlésienne*, induces a mood of tranquillity and disarms criticism. As Aurora Punnet has written, 'One seems to see each cabman in the room, so vivid do the names and initials become.'

Suet and Mimsie Slopcorner

Charlie Suet had taken Mimsie Slopcorner to a lecture on the Balance of Payments. 'It's time they got married,' said Mr Slopcorner.

'Give them time,' his wife replied. 'Rome wasn't built in a day.'

'I haven't the figures by me for the time it took,' said the father, 'but I don't see what that's got to do with it. They've been keeping company for years.'

'Better a good, steady man,' she answered, 'than a flighty fellow mad on nightclubs. You wouldn't like her to be swept off her feet by a rascal.'

'Suet,' said Slopcorner, 'may be said to be gently pushing her off her feet at the rate of half an inch per annum.'

Silence fell.

Mimsie came in. 'Well?' said her father.

'We're engaged,' said Mimsie, blushing.

The mother embraced her. The father muttered: 'The impetuous Casanova!'

News of those little men

A student of intonsiology has asked what has become of the red-bearded dwarfs whose misadventures I once recorded. Their leader, Churm Rincewind, has, for reasons of his very own, changed his name to Ondelsnorge. Scorpion de Rooftrouser is wanted more than ever by the police. He scrawled above a Titian in the National Gallery: 'Rooftrouser Loves Samantha'. Frums Gillygottle still pushes cartons of frozen gravy into letterboxes in Clarges Street. Molonay Tubilderborst sells gherkins outside West End stage-doors. Guttergorm Guttergormton and the remaining seven are lying lower than usual.

. . . and Bapchild, S.D.

Dear Sir,

I may not be 'with it', but I cannot see the point of the *List of Huntingdonshire Cabmen*. I realise that no such publication exists, and, in that case, why pretend it does? What exactly is the joke in these names and initials? I am sure there is an explanation, otherwise you could not go on with such nonsense year after year.

'Puzzled Reader'

Aboard the houseboat

Said Mrs Withersedge: 'We're leaving this old skow all shipshape and Cookham fashion afore comin' ashore for Christmas. The boss is stowin' away 'is charts. We wouldn't 'arf be up a gumtree if 'e couldn't study which was the deep end of Sydney 'Arbour, or 'ow many fathoms there was in the Red Sea. My sister's little nipper can't see why me arms isn't tattooed with anchors an' things. But I can always spin 'im a yarn about 'ow we rounded the 'Orn in a trade wind and show 'im the 'ornpipe we danced that day.'

Odd lion out

'People think that wild animals, as opposed to domestic animals, have no feelings.'   (*Correspondence column*)

Dear Sir, Pray do not forget the cry which rang out across the arena: 'Oh, look! That poor lion hasn't got a Christian!'

Plain speaking from Narkover

Dr Smart-Allick said yesterday, 'Whatever plans the Government may have for Narkover, tradition will be too strong for the innovators. Narkover provides an education for life as it is lived today in all its beastliness. The principal object of an industrial community is the amassing of wealth, and the boys who leave Narkover have learned this lesson. Those who criticise what goes on here should realise that it is not the gambler or the swindler who is reduced to penury by taxation.'

Dr Rhubarb's corner

E.N.P. WRITES: Have you any suggestions for Christmas presents for cats? Our cat always wears a hat from a cracker, but that

hardly counts as a present.
What can we give Bobbity
that he will enjoy?
DR RHUBARB SAYS:
A mouse, madam.

Envoi

'You have an ox-wagon mentality,' said a friend to me. Never
was a truer word spoken. I prefer fresh air to polluted air, a quiet
countryside to a noisy one, and real food to sham food. I detest
cars, and would rather see and hear birds in the air than planes. I
like melodious music, intelligible poetry, pictures, and sculpture,
and architecture with a sense of proportion. I would rather see an
old-fashioned comedy than the latest rancid muck. Remembering
my ox-wagon boyhood I am convinced that a slower rhythm of
life is more conducive to happiness than an hysterical excitement,
which is mistaken for pleasure. For a Christmas present I would
rather have an ox than a helicopter, or even a hovercraft, or a
speed-boat.

Epitaph for a village

The postern-gate of childhood's paradise
        Is closed for ever. Here we used to play.
Here, in this hideous tomb a village lies,
        Butchered to make a motorist's holiday.

25

The Beachcomber
Christmas Compendium of Fun

Here is a game for Christmas parties. Lay two lines of matches horizontally on a table, with one vertical match at the side, thus:

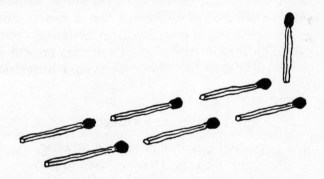

Then say quietly: 'A street in Tiflis by day.' Then light the vertical match and say, with more emotion in your voice: 'A street in Tiflis by night.' The game is called 'The Streets of Tiflis.'
OR
Pick a Brussels sprout to pieces carefully, and then put it back together again, using glue where necessary.
OR
Put some cheese in a mousetrap. Competitors approaching the trap on all fours try to snatch the cheese in their mouths without getting their noses caught in the trap.
OR
Much laughter can be caused by trying to draw a cork from a bottle of wine with a telescope.
OR

Scatter bits of fluff over the floor. Then see who can pick up twelve bits first, wearing boxing gloves.

OR

Blindfold half a dozen people. Walking backwards, they thrust alternate elbows backwards. The winner is the one who first catches his elbow a crack against a wall, door, or piece of furniture.

OR

See who can crack an egg with his nose, using it as a hammer.

OR

Try to get a felt hat into an empty hock bottle.

OR

Tie the legs of four men together, leaving one outside leg free. Do the same with four other men. Then start them on a race round the room. The two men with one free leg can hardly move, as they have to drag the others with them. Both teams will probably end up in a struggling heap on the floor.

OR

Fill a bath-mat with anthracite and roll it up to look like a football. The first person to kick it fifteen feet gets the bath-mat.

ALTERNATIVELY

Snibbo have put on the market an enormous plushy Christmas cracker, forty feet long, to be pulled by two twelve-a-side tug-of-war teams at big parties. It contains a small Thanatos Four runabout car, and a motto: *Get With Snibbo*. Price £720. Two for £1,480.

Gallery

Illustrated thriller

'Listen to me,' said Sir Charles.
'I am all ears,' replied Freddy.

Nocturne

H.J. Allwether in the padded clothes he
wears for eating boiled turbot.

A succulent dainty

Some of the neat plastic holes for the new
pre-processed cheese, made by Snibbo in
their factory at Vileness-on-the-Wold.

Do it yourself

The electric beetroot-scraper, which can
be plugged in.

Neat, but foolish

Triangular plastic hat worn by Mr E.N.
Spordle, who has a triangular bump on
his head. 'The bump fits into the hat,'
commented a passer-by.

A handy gadget

Indiarubber bulb with spikes for prodding
granules through sieves. The crooked
spike in the middle is for dislodging
anything left after the prodding is over.

Gracious living

An elliptical saucepan for boiling tautened elastic bands.

Food note

Part of the horseshoe found in the bun at the Kosikorna Tea-Den in Munching-Daubeny. The proprietress said: 'It was put in for luck.'

Do it yourself

The Bapchild triangular blowpipe, which operates sideways in all weathers, is used for welding embossed designs on zinc flower-vases.

Labour-saving

An amusing gadget for picking holes in charcoal. It folds up when not in use.

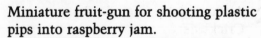

Gracious living

'Recumbent Nymph'. A photograph of the statue which it is proposed to place on the village green at Snoddisham-in-the-Vale.

Do it yourself

Miniature fruit-gun for shooting plastic pips into raspberry jam.

Superfunctional

A square sieve for sifting mulberries, or, alternatively, a working model for a new block of offices to replace the Haymarket Theatre.

The winning tomatoes

Reading from left to right: (*Back row*) Ruddy Ralph, Worthing Bon, Stalky, Long Tom, Big Head. (*Front row*) Babs, Royal Flush, Rosy Joe.

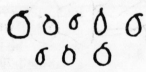

A useful *vade mecum*

The Garland-Thompson track-edge candel for cleaning paper-weights by steam-pressure.

Functional

Side view of a table with no legs, for eating off the floor.

Round the galleries

The empty goldfish bowl. A still-life by the Walsall aquarium keeper, Henry Froth.

A moving ceremony

The two bits of the match which was sawn in half at the opening of Nantwich Match Factory.

Round the galleries

Woman with a mouthful of mud, by Agnes Tupp (age 6).

Not worth opening

A gate without bars for letting things through.

Alone with Nature

A fractional part of the Thames at Cricklade.

Haute coiffure

'Duncan,' whispered Jonquil, 'I think that nuthatch has nested in my hair!'

Round the galleries

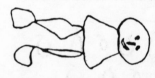

'Reclining Figure', by Ferdinand Frasch. Of this controversial masterpiece E.P. Rattle wrote: 'The weight and mass of the large feet suggest, in a subtle way, disillusionment and fatigue. One seems to sense

a cosmic *Weltschmerz* in the passivity
adumbrated by the positional inertia.'

Why not?

An apple with three stalks, grown by
Mrs Westcote in her Brondesbury garden.

Household amenities

The leather button which controls the
new electric shoe-horn.

What next?

Part of a mouse's tail seen through a
wooden triangle.

All in the day's work

Grated cheese photographed from low-
flying helicopter.

Do it yourself

Cut this out to mark the spot.

Making things easy

Deal box to hold one inch of water.

So it seems

A clip for shredded beetroot, I believe.

The Wiggliwhiff

The crooked cigarette for the sophisticated
smoker.

Plumber's niece weds Eskimo

Cut this out, send it to the Society for
the Prevention of Railway Cod, and win
a pet grass-snake.

Do it yourself, Mrs Fluff

A waterproof plummet for sounding the
depth of bathwater, and/or combing soap.

Nature hits back

Strange potato grown by Mr Alfred Baker at Shepperton.

'Lifelike,' says astronomer

The new Golpurtz photographic process was used to photograph these wrinkles on the forehead of a heifer near Barnstaple, from a distance of eight miles.

There they are!

Twins at a Bayswater window.

Do it yourself, Mrs Fluff

A clock without hands or figures. The correct time can be written on the clock-face at any moment, day or night, by checking with an ordinary clock or watch.

The new shape

The Egg Board's long egg from a hen fed on whelks.

Photographers at play

A worm turning, or, alternatively, a narrow horseshoe with a bit of something stuck to it. (Copyright in all countries except Chile.)

Round the galleries

Ball-bearings in a tree, by Odgo Molf.

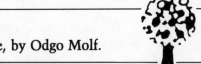

Crossword puzzle

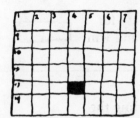

Down 1. Clergyman's hat. 9. By royal command. 10. What, again? 15. No wonder. 17. It was empty. 19. No fly could. *Across* 1. Worse luck. 2. Not so thick. 3. Only a badger. 4. Built to last. 5. Spanish walnuts. 6. No fur. 7. Coloured cloth.

by J.B. Morton

As Beachcomber

Mr Thake
Mr Thake Again
By The Way
Morton's Folly
The Adventures of Mr Thake
Mr Thake and the Ladies
Stuff and Nonsense
Gallimaufry
Sideways through Borneo
A Diet of Thistles
A Bonfire of Weeds
I Do Not Think So
Fool's Paradise
Captain Foulenough & Company
Here and Now
The Misadventures of Dr Strabismus
The Tibetan Venus
Merry-Go-Round

Collections

The Best of Beachcomber
The Bumper Beachcomber

History & Biography

The Bastille Falls
The Dauphin
Saint-Just
Brumaire
Camille Desmoulins
Marshal Ney
Sobieski
Hilaire Belloc: a Memoir
Ste Thérèse of Lisieux

Short Stories

Springtime

Politics

The New Ireland

Essays

Enchanter's Nightshade
Penny Royal
Old Man's Beard
Vagabond

Novels

The Barber of Putney
Skylighters
Drink Up, Gentlemen
The Cow Jumped Over the Moon
Hag's Harvest
The Gascon
Maladetta

Travel

Pyrenean

Verse

Gorgeous Poetry
Tally-Ho!
Who's Who in the Zoo
1933, and Still Going Wrong
The Dancing Cabman

Fairy Tales

The Death of the Dragon

Contributions to:

Parody Party
Press Gang
Did It Happen?
101 Ballades
The Funny Bone
Bridge Over The Rainbow
The Book of Fleet Street

Journals

Daily Express
Sunday Express
The Times
The London Mercury
Time & Tide
The Spectator
The Tablet
Lilliput